Substance

Substance: Its Nature and Existence is one of the first accessible introductions to the history and contemporary debates surrounding the idea of substance. An important and often complex issue, substance is at the heart of Western philosophy. Substances are distinguished from other kinds of entities such as properties, events, times, and places. This book investigates the very nature and existence of individual substances, including both living things and inanimate objects.

Taking as their starting point the major philosophers in the historical debate – Aristotle, Descartes, Spinoza, Locke, and Hume – Joshua Hoffman and Gary S. Rosenkrantz move on to a novel analysis of substance in terms of a kind of independence which insubstantial entities do not possess. The authors explore causal theories of the unity of the parts of inanimate objects and organisms; contemporary views about substance; the idea that the only existing physical substances are inanimate pieces of matter and living organisms, and that artifacts such as clocks, and natural formations like stars, do not really exist.

Substance: Its Nature and Existence provides students of philosophy and metaphysics with an introduction to and critical engagement with a key philosophical issue.

"The authors' clarity of presentation and lucidity of style enable them to discuss a wide range of difficult but important metaphysical questions in a way that is accessible to intermediate and advanced-level undergraduates. . . . At the same time they present and defend some highly original ontological claims which are sure to provoke widespread discussion amongst professional philosophers."

E. J. Lowe, University of Durham

Joshua Hoffman and **Gary S. Rosenkrantz** are Professors of Philosophy at the University of North Carolina at Greensboro. They recently co-authored *Substance Among Other Categories*.

The Problems of Philosophy

Founding editor: Ted Honderich

Editors: Tim Crane and Jonathan Wolff, *University College London*

This series addresses the central problems of philosophy. Each book gives a fresh account of a particular philosophical theme by offering two perspectives on the subject: the historical context and author's own distinctive and original contribution.

The books are written to be accessible to students of philosophy and related disciplines, while taking the debate to a new level.

DEMOCRACY
Ross Harrison

THE EXISTENCE OF THE
WORLD
Reinhardt Grossman

NAMING AND REFERENCE
R.J. Nelson

EXPLAINING EXPLANATION
David-Hillel Ruben

IF P, THEN Q
David H. Sanford

SCEPTICISM
Christopher Hookway

HUMAN CONSCIOUSNESS
Alastair Hannay

THE IMPLICATIONS OF
DETERMINISM
Roy Weatherford

THE INFINITE
A.W. Moore

KNOWLEDGE AND BELIEF
Frederic F. Schmitt

KNOWLEDGE OF THE
EXTERNAL WORLD
Bruce Aune

MORAL KNOWLEDGE
Alan Goldman

MIND–BODY IDENTITY
THEORIES
Cynthia Macdonald

THE NATURE OF ART
A.L. Cothey

PERSONAL IDENTITY
Harold W. Noonan

POLITICAL FREEDOM
George G. Brenkert

THE RATIONAL FOUNDATIONS
OF ETHICS
T.L.S. Sprigge

PRACTICAL REASONING
Robert Audi

RATIONALITY
Harold I. Brown

THOUGHT AND LANGUAGE
J.M. Moravcsik

THE WEAKNESS OF THE WILL
Justine Gosling

VAGUENESS
Timothy Williamson

PERCEPTION
Howard Robinson

THE NATURE OF GOD
Gerard Hughes

THE MIND AND ITS WORLD
Gregory McCulloch

UTILITARIANISM
Geoffrey Scarre

SUBSTANCE
Joshua Hoffman &
Gary S. Rosenkrantz

Substance

Its nature and existence

Joshua Hoffman and
Gary S. Rosenkrantz

Routledge
Taylor & Francis Group

LONDON AND NEW YORK

First published 1997
by Routledge
11 New Fetter Lane, London EC4P 4EE

Simultaneously published in the USA and Canada
by Routledge
29 West 35th Street, New York, NY 10001

Transferred to Digital Printing 2004

Routledge is an imprint of the Taylor & Francis Group

© 1997 Joshua Hoffman and Gary S. Rosenkrantz

Typeset in Times by
Ponting–Green Publishing Services, Chesham,
Buckinghamshire
Printed and bound in Great Britain by
Selwood Printing Ltd, West Sussex

British Library Cataloguing in Publication Data
A catalogue record for this book is available from the
British Library

Library of Congress Cataloging in Publication Data
Substance: Its nature and existence / Joshua Hoffman and
   Gary S. Rosenkrantz.
     p.   cm. – (The problems of philosophy)
     Includes bibliographical references
     1. Substance (Philosophy)   I. Hoffman, Joshua and
Rosenkrantz, Gary S. II. Title. III. Series: Problems of
philosophy (Routledge (Firm))
BD331.H573   1996
111'.1 – dc20   96–15069

ISBN   0–415–11250–8 (hbk)
ISBN   0–415–14032–3 (pbk)

For my wife, Ruth, and my sons, Noah and David
(J.H.)

For my wife, Sheree, and my daughters, Jessica and Dara
(G.R.)

Contents

Preface   ix

Introduction   1
  1 Substance and folk ontology   1
  2 Kinds of physical substance   3
  3 The concept of a spiritual substance   5
  4 Skepticism about substance   7

1 The concept of substance in history   9
  1 Two Aristotelian theories: substance as that which
    can undergo change and as that which is neither
    said-of nor in a subject   9
  2 Substratum and inherence theories of substance   17
  3 Independence theories of substance   20
  4 Cluster theories of substance   26

2 An independence theory of substance   43
  1 Some difficulties for an independence theory of
    substance   43
  2 Ontological categories   46
  3 Substance   50
  4 Properties and tropes   53
  5 Places, times, and limits   55
  6 Events   60
  7 Privation   63
  8 Collections   69
  9 Other categories   69

3 On the unity of the parts of mereological compounds   73
  1 Kinds of compound physical things and their unity 73
  2 Two senses of "substance"   74

3 Skepticism about the commonsense view of compound
      objects   77
4 Preliminary data for analyses of unity   79
5 An analysis of the unity of a mereological compound   80

4 **On the unity of the parts of organisms**   91
1 The concept of organic life   91
2 Organisms and Aristotelian functions   93
3 What is the causal relation that unites the parts of an
      organism?   99
4 Aristotle's account of unity   100
5 Evolution, natural selection, and natural function   102
6 The emergence of life and natural function   105
7 An account of natural function   115
8 The degree of naturalness of an individual's life-
      processes   118
9 Vital parts and joint natural functions   121
10 Regulation and functional subordination   126
11 A preliminary analysis of unity   128
12 A final analysis of unity   133
13 Functional connectedness among basic biotic parts   135
14 Nonbasic biotic parts   142
15 Problem cases   145

5 **What kinds of physical substances are there?**   150
1 Atoms, mereological compounds, and ordinary
      physical objects   150
2 The problem of increase   154
3 Another conundrum: does mereological increase
      imply that a thing is a proper part of itself?   160
4 The problem of the ship of Theseus   163
5 The scientific argument against the reality of artifacts
      and typical natural formations   165
6 The explosion of reality: a population explosion for
      living things?   177
7 Is there a principle of composition for physical
      things?   179

Appendix: Organisms and natural kinds   188
Notes   192
Index   215

Preface

In this book we investigate the nature and existence of individual substances, including both living things and inanimate objects. A belief in the existence of such things is an integral part of our everyday world-view. The great philosophers of the past, of course, were profoundly interested in the concept of an individual substance. Aristotle, for instance, believed that individual substances were the basic or primary existents, as did Descartes, Spinoza, Leibniz, Locke, and Berkeley. Kant went so far as to maintain that human beings cannot conceive of a reality devoid of substances. All of these philosophers (and many others) spent much time and effort trying to clarify the concept of an individual substance.

In Chapter 1, we critically survey the main historical attempts to provide an analysis of the concept of an individual substance. These attempts include those of Aristotle, Descartes, Spinoza, Locke, and Hume.

In Chapter 2, we draw upon these historical attempts, in particular those of Aristotle and Descartes, to provide what we hope is an adequate analysis of the concept of an individual substance. The main idea behind our analysis of substance is a traditional one: it is that a substance satisfies an *independence condition* which could not be satisfied by an insubstantial entity. Our new analysis of substance in terms of independence incorporates the insight of Aristotle that the independence of substance is to be understood in terms of the relation of the category of Substance to the other categories, and the insight of Descartes and Spinoza that there can be a substance that is independent of any other substance.

Chapters 3 and 4 include an examination of important historical views about the nature of the causal relation which unites parts that compose a compound piece of matter, and historical theories of the causal relation which unites parts that compose an organism. We focus on the idea that these unifying causal relations are the relations of being bonded together and being functionally interconnected, respectively. Chapters 3 and 4 then attempt to provide satisfactory principles of unity for the parts of compound pieces of matter and organisms by drawing upon the aforementioned historical views together with discoveries in physics and biology.

Chapter 5 critically examines the views of a number of contemporary philosophers about what sorts of physical things exist, and uses ideas from Chapters 3 and 4 to defend the thesis that there are three different classes of physical things: fundamental particles, compound pieces of matter, and organisms. Arguments are given which imply the unreality of artifacts and typical examples of what we shall call inanimate natural formations. Finally, there is an appendix which discusses the status of various kinds of organisms in biology.

Several acknowledgements are in order. We should like to express our appreciation to Jenny Raabe for her editorial assistance, and for her valuable insights about ways in which we could improve this book. Thanks are also due to the University of North Carolina at Greensboro, for subsidizing Jenny Raabe's work for us under the auspices of their Undergraduate Research Assistant Program, and for supporting Gary Rosenkrantz's work on this project with a Research Council leave during the Fall of 1994. We have benefited greatly, as well, both from the criticisms and suggestions for revisions made by an anonymous referee who reviewed the first draft of this book and from those made by Tim Crane, the editor of the Problems of Philosophy series. We should also like to express our gratitude to Jonathan Lowe for his encouragement and stimulating comments. Finally, we should like to thank Fred Feldman, John King, Bruce Kirchoff, and Robert O'Hara for their helpful discussions.

We have incorporated parts of the following co-authored or singly authored articles of ours: "The Independence Criterion of Substance," *Philosophy and Phenomenological Research* 51 (1991), pp. 835–853; "Concrete/Abstract," in *Companion to Metaphysics*, edited by Jaegwon Kim and Ernest Sosa (Oxford: Basil Blackwell, 1995), pp. 90–92; "Boscovich, Roger Joseph," and "Mereology," in *The Cambridge Dictionary of Philosophy*, edited by Robert Audi (Cambridge: Cambridge University Press, 1995), pp. 84 and 483 respectively. We should like to express our appreciation to the editors of *Philosophy and Phenomenological Research*, Basil Blackwell, and Cambridge University Press for permitting us to include this material.

Introduction

1 SUBSTANCE AND FOLK ONTOLOGY

Our culture possesses a single ordinary, commonsense, or "folk" conceptual scheme which has certain ontological presuppositions. Foremost among these presuppositions is the idea that there are enduring things, or individual substances: continuants such as human persons, rocks, flowers, and houses. The idea that there are such substantial beings is at the core of this commonsense or folk ontology. Other kinds of beings which common sense appears to recognize are events, places, times, properties, and collections, as well as surfaces, edges, shadows, and holes. In common parlance, entities of these other kinds are insubstantial. At least since the time of Aristotle, philosophers have tried to organize and relate entities of the kinds which belong to the commonsense or folk ontology, kinds which Aristotle called categories.

In one of its ordinary senses, the term "thing" just *means* individual substance. It might be objected that "thing" means entity, and that "thing" has no ordinary sense in which it means individual substance. It is true that in one of its senses "thing" means entity. Yet it is also clear that there is a narrower sense of "thing," according to which it would be correct to say, for example, that prudence is not a *thing*, but a quality of a thing.

To this it might be replied that what this example shows is that in this sense, "thing" means concrete entity, and not individual substance. But evidently, there is an even narrower sense of "thing," according to which it would be correct to say, for instance, that a chameleon's turning color, although concrete, is not a *thing*, but a *change* in a thing, and that a surface or hole, although concrete, is not a *thing*, but a *limit* or *absence* of a thing. There is no plausible alternative to the idea that in the latter cases "thing" means individual substance.

Accordingly, it is not possible for a thing or an object in this ordinary sense either to occur (as an event does) or to be exemplified (as some properties are). To suppose otherwise is to commit what Ryle called a category mistake. This is the source of the apparent incoherence of saying, for example, that Socrates occurs or is exemplified by something. Likewise, it is a category mistake to identify a thing or substance with an absence, such as a hole, or a limit, such as a surface. A hole is an absence, and a surface is a limit, *of* a thing, and, hence, each of these is *not* a thing or individual substance. Nor is it possible for a material substance to be identical with a place: for one, a material substance can move, but a place cannot. Furthermore, it is not possible for an enduring individual substance to be identical with an interval of time, since the latter has times as parts, but the former cannot.

Intuitively, individual substances have the following fundamental properties.

(1) It is necessary for each individual substance to have features; each is characterizable in various ways, for instance, as being square or being happy.

(2) Since any substance *has* certain features, these features are unified by their all being features *of* a particular substance.

(3) No feature can be a *part* of a substance. Intuitively, the arms of a chair *are* parts of the chair, but the shape and size of the chair are *not* parts of the chair.

(4) Any individual substance can exist at more than one time. Furthermore, it is possible for some individual substance to persist through changes in its *intrinsic* features. For example, there could be a rubber block that is cubical at t_1 and slightly oblong when it is stretched at t_2, and there could be a person who is pleased at t_1 and displeased at t_2, and so forth. In addition, it is possible for some individual thing to persist through a change in its *relational* features, for example, a feature such as being four feet from a door, or being seated at a table.

(5) Individual substances can have both *accidental* and *essential* features. An accidental feature of a substance is a feature of it that it can exist without. For instance, suppose that Jones is now happy and seated at a table. It is possible for Jones to have lacked these features now. Thus, being happy now and being seated at a table now are accidental features of Jones. On the other hand, being extended

is an essential feature of a certain table: the table in question could not exist without that feature.

(6) Typically, individual substances can be created and destroyed. Thus, it is possible for there to be substances whose existence is contingent.

(7) Ordinarily, the length of time for which a substance exists is accidental. For instance, it is possible for there to have been a person who died in 1961, but who could have lived until 1996.

(8) It is possible for there to be two individual substances which are indistinguishable with respect to their qualitative intrinsic features.

The modalities (the possibilities and necessities) employed in (1)–(8) are metaphysical ones. Some introductory remarks about these modalities are in order. A *de dicto* metaphysical modality applies to a *dictum* or proposition, for example, necessarily, if something is a cube, then it has six faces; it is impossible that a triangular circle exists; and it is contingent that horses exist, i.e., it is possibly true that horses exist, and possibly not true that horses exist. A *de re* metaphysical modality applies to a *res* or thing, for example, Bill Clinton is essentially (necessarily) a living thing, and accidently (contingently) a Democrat (since although a Democrat he is possibly not one).

We follow the customary practice of understanding such modal attributions in terms of possible worlds.[1] A necessary proposition is true in all possible worlds, an impossible proposition is false in all possible worlds, a possible proposition is true in some possible world, and a contingent proposition is true in some possible world and false in some possible world. On the other hand, an entity, e, which has an attribute, P, has P essentially just in case e has P in every possible world in which e exists; and an entity, e, which has an attribute, P, has P accidentally just provided that e lacks P in some possible world in which e exists. Finally, an entity, e, has necessary existence if and only if e exists in all possible worlds; and an entity, e, has contingent existence if and only if e exists in the actual world and e fails to exist in some possible world.

2 KINDS OF PHYSICAL SUBSTANCE

According to folk ontology, a substantial entity such as a piece of wood, a house, a mountain, or a tree is a *physical* thing. Indeed, this ontology appears to imply that physicalism of some kind is correct, and hence that human persons are physical things of some sort as well.

Intuitively, physical objects have the following six necessary characteristics. First, a physical object can exist unperceived, or at least, does not exist in virtue of its being perceived.[2] Second, a physical object occupies or is in space. Third, a physical object in its entirety is not located in two places at once. Fourth, a physical object possibly moves. Fifth, if a physical object is perceivable at all, then it has sensible features, is publicly observable, and is perceivable by more than one sensory modality. Sixth, parts which compose a compound physical object have a unity in virtue of their instantiating an appropriate unifying causal relation. Thus, a physical object can be created or destroyed by assembly or disassembly (except in the case of fundamental particles, which cannot be physically divided).

One important type of physical object is a *material* object or piece of matter. Intuitively, a physical object of this type has three additional necessary features.

First, material objects have a three-dimensional interior and exterior. Thus, a cubical solid, which is a material object, has three spatial dimensions, while a *face* of a cubical solid has only two spatial dimensions, and is therefore not a material object. Moreover, the *surface* of a spherical solid (though three-dimensional) does *not* have a three-dimensional interior and exterior, and is therefore not a material object, unlike a spherical solid.

Second, a *part* of a material object is either a material object or a portion of matter. The *detachable* parts of a material object are material objects, while any *nondetachable* parts of a material substance are at least portions of matter (but may not be substances themselves).

Third, it is impossible for two material objects to coincide exhaustively in space. Nevertheless, some philosophers would distinguish between a statue, for example, and the statue-shaped piece of bronze which constitutes it, or, in other words, between a statue which can gain or lose a part, and a spatially coincident piece of matter which has its parts essentially. If these philosophers are correct in recognizing physical objects of both of the aforementioned sorts, then there are two things of the same kind, viz., two physical objects, which are spatially coincident. However, we employ a "robust" notion of materiality whereby a material object is a piece of matter having its parts essentially. Hence, what our third intuitive characteristic implies is that no two *pieces of matter* can exhaustively coincide in space. If there are such physical objects as statues which are distinct from those physical objects which are pieces of matter, then objects of the former kind are what we shall call nonmaterial physical objects. This classification includes any physical object which does not have its parts essentially, or is such that two things of the kind of nonmaterial substance in question can exhaustively coincide in space, or does not have a three-dimensional interior and exterior.

For example, organisms are nonmaterial physical objects because they do not have their parts essentially. The possibility of a second kind of nonmaterial physical object is implied by the theory that there are fundamental particles exhibiting a phenomenon known as transparency: under certain circumstances two fundamental particles of this sort can "pass through" one another, occupying for a moment the very same place.

Another possible example is provided by Boscovichian point-particles, or *puncta*, which are zero-dimensional physical things. Boscovich, in advocating *puncta*, held that they are indistinguishable in their intrinsic qualitative properties, and sought to explain all physical phenomena in terms of their attractions and repulsions.[3] Boscovich's theory has proved to be empirically inadequate to account for phenomena such as light. A philosophical problem for Boscovich's *puncta* arises out of their zero-dimensionality. It seems that any power must have a basis in an object's intrinsic properties, and *puncta* appear to lack such support for their powers. However, it is extensional properties which *puncta* lack, and Boscovich could reply that the categorial property of being an unextended spatial substance provides the required basis for its dispositions.

3 THE CONCEPT OF A SPIRITUAL SUBSTANCE

As we have noted, folk ontology seems to imply that human persons are substantial beings of a physical sort. But are human persons really identical with physical things, or do human souls exist?

As we understand the concept of a soul, a soul is a nonphysical entity.[4] More specifically, a soul is an unlocated substance which is capable of consciousness.[5]

Souls conceivably exist; for as Descartes argued, a thinking thing could rationally doubt the existence of a physical world, while remaining certain of its own existence. Yet, it has been charged that souls are unintelligible.

A first argument protests that the nature of a soul cannot be explained unless a soul is described *negatively*, i.e., as *unlocated*. We reply that there are intelligible entities whose nature cannot be explained unless they are described negatively: e.g., to explain the nature of a photon, a photon must be described as having zero rest mass.

A second argument complains that souls lack a principle of individuation. Bodies, it is claimed, are individuated by their occupying different places at a time; but souls do not occupy places. We respond that places *themselves* do not occupy places. Consequently, places are no better off than souls in the relevant respect, and the argument under discussion collapses; as does the related argument that souls, not occupying places, lack a criterion of persistence.

This might elicit the response that while bodies are separated from one another at a time by their spatial apartness, nothing would separate unlocated souls from one another at a time. We answer that if bodies are separated by their spatial apartness, then souls would be separated by their epistemic apartness, i.e., their incapacity to be directly aware of one another's mental states.

Since there seems to be no reason to deny the intelligibility of souls, we affirm their logical possibility.[6] Nevertheless, given the modern scientific picture of the nature of human beings and their place in the natural world, there seems to be no need to posit the existence of human souls. Since this scientific picture is extremely plausible, it appears unlikely that there are human souls. In other words, it is plausible that some sort of physicalism or naturalism is the best explanation of our experience. This physicalistic or naturalistic picture of the world implies that human persons are physical things of a certain kind, namely, organic living things.

While the foregoing line of reasoning may be convincing, it fails to provide an altogether *decisive* argument for the conclusion that human souls do not exist. That is, it fails to rule out entirely the possibility that there are human souls. Our reasons for this assessment are as follows. First, souls are logically possible. Second, it is a mystery how mental qualities of a human person, such as pain, pleasure, and consciousness, derive from the fundamental properties of physical objects, for instance, shape, size, mass, motion, order and arrangement of parts, and so on. Thus, it *might* be the case that these mental qualities inhere in a soul. As Leibniz observed:

Perception and that which depends upon it *are inexplicable by mechanical causes*, that is, by figures and motions. And supposing that there were a machine so constructed as to think, feel and have perception, we could conceive of it as enlarged and yet preserving the same proportions, so that we might enter it as into a mill. And this granted, we should only find on visiting it, pieces which push one against another, but never anything by which to explain a perception. This must be sought for, therefore, in the simple substance and not in the composite or in the machine.[7]

It might be argued that we cannot *know* that there are no human souls until we have solved the mystery of how mental qualities such as pain, pleasure, and consciousness derive from the fundamental properties of physical objects. Nevertheless, since it seems improbable that there are human souls, we are prepared to adopt the idea that human persons are organic living things as a reasonable working hypothesis.

4 SKEPTICISM ABOUT SUBSTANCE

Any ontologist must begin as a point of reference with a consideration of folk ontology, even if in the end he or she revises it in some way. If entities of a certain kind belong to folk ontology, then there is a *prima facie* presumption in favor of their reality. Since living and nonliving things or individual substances are a part of folk ontology, there is a presumption in favor of their existence. Belief in the existence of such entities is justified so long as this presumption is not undermined. Thus, those who deny their existence assume the burden of proof.

It is sometimes alleged that theoretical physics, for example, the wave–particle duality posited by quantum mechanics, or the existence of the four-dimensional space-time continuum posited by relativistic physics, entails that a belief in substance is mistaken. It is argued that physics implies an ontology of space-time and events or particularized qualities. A natural response to the foregoing allegation is that if it is true, then so much the worse for theoretical physics. After all, theoretical physics is justified only to the extent that it explains the observed data upon which it is based. But there being *any* such data whatsoever presupposes that there are substantial beings, namely, human observers. Surely, a theory which undermines the justification of *all* of the data upon which it is based is unjustified. Moreover, only certain interpretations of quantum mechanics, for example, the Copenhagen interpretation, are alleged to have the entailment in question. At least one important alternative interpretation, that of David Bohm, does not have this entailment.[8] Finally, relativistic physics, at least, does not seem to be incompatible with a belief in substance, since it appears that there could be a four-dimensional material substance which occupies a part of space-time.

An historically important philosophical argument against the existence of substantial beings claims that we do not possess a meaningful concept of substance.[9] This claim has been inferred from the following two premises: (i) someone has a meaningful concept of substance only if he is directly aware of a substance, and (ii) nobody is directly aware of a substance. But even if the first premise is granted, the second appears to be indefensible. For each one of us seems to be directly aware of at least one substance, namely, oneself.

It has also been claimed that we do not possess a meaningful concept of substance on the ground that there is no adequate analysis or definition of the concept of substance. Let us proceed, then, to our examination of the main historical attempts to analyze or define the concept of an individual substance.

Chapter 1

The concept of substance in history

From Aristotle to Kant and beyond, the concept of an individual substance has played a deservedly prominent role in the attempts of metaphysicians to characterize reality and to think reflectively about the terms of such a characterization. Any attempt to provide an analysis of substance should be informed by a critical awareness of the efforts of these great philosophers of the past to characterize the ordinary concept of an individual substance, and the analysis of this concept which we shall defend in Chapter 2 is indeed grounded in one of the traditional approaches to characterizing it. In this chapter, we shall survey and assess several historically important attempts to analyze the ordinary concept of an individual substance.

1 TWO ARISTOTELIAN THEORIES: SUBSTANCE AS THAT WHICH CAN UNDERGO CHANGE AND AS THAT WHICH IS NEITHER SAID-OF NOR IN A SUBJECT

The first historically important attempts to analyze substance are due to Aristotle. The notion of substance plays a self-consciously central role in his whole metaphysics.[1] According to the first of Aristotle's characterizations of substance which we shall consider, a substance is that which can persist through change. A relevant quotation is the following:

> It seems most distinctive of substance that what is numerically one and the same is able to receive contraries. In no other case could one bring forward anything, numerically one, which is able to receive contraries.[2]

The idea that a substance is that which can persist through change is an attractive one, since it seems to provide the basis for a distinction between substances and entities such as times, places, and (abstract) properties. Nevertheless, there are problems.

The first difficulty facing this view, a difficulty which is raised by Aristotle himself, is that entities *other* than substances can undergo change. Aristotle gives the example of a belief which is at one time true and at another false.[3] Since a belief or a proposition is not a substance, but can undergo a change, that is, in truth-value, Aristotle's analysis appears not to provide a logically sufficient condition of being a substance. Aristotle attempts to answer this objection by noting that:

> In the case of substances it is by themselves changing that they are able to receive contraries . . . statements and beliefs, on the other hand, themselves remain completely unchangeable in every way.[4]

Aristotle's reply presupposes a distinction between intrinsic and relational change, and he says that we have an instance of the former when something is "changing by itself." Thus, while his example suggests an argument that nonsubstances such as beliefs or propositions can undergo change, his reply is that such entities, unlike substances, can undergo only relational changes. This reply to the example of changing beliefs suggests that his actual analysis of substance is in terms of intrinsic change, rather than in terms of change *per se*. In that case, if he is entitled to the distinction between intrinsic and relational change, then Aristotle's reply to his own example of the changing belief is cogent.

Nevertheless, it might be argued that the distinction between intrinsic and relational change is itself unclear,[5] and that therefore, without an analysis of *it*, Aristotle cannot use the distinction to reply effectively to the objection in question. Since Aristotle does not provide such an analysis, the claim that his account of substance in terms of intrinsic change calls for an analysis of the intrinsic/relational change distinction is pertinent to the assessment of Aristotle's analysis of substance in terms of intrinsic change. As a preliminary to such an assessment, let us explore the question of whether an analysis of intrinsic change is possible.

Following Aristotle, let us say that for something to change is for it to instantiate contrary or contradictory properties at different times.[6] Given this, it seems natural to say that if a thing undergoes an intrinsic change, then it instantiates contrary or contradictory *intrinsic properties* at different times, and if it undergoes relational change, then it instantiates contrary or contradictory *relational properties* at different times. Some examples of intrinsic properties are being spherical, being two feet thick, and being in pain, and examples of relational properties are being five feet from Socrates, being thought of by Plato, and being shorter than Aristotle. Thus, it appears that if there is any lack of clarity in the distinction between intrinsic and relational change, this is because the distinction between intrinsic and relational properties is obscure. Can this distinction be elucidated?

A first attempt to do so might be to say that P is an intrinsic property if and only if necessarily, for any x, if P is a property acquired or lost by x, then x is a substance. A relational property could then be defined as a nonintrinsic property. This attempt is obviously viciously circular in the context of trying to define substance. Furthermore, there seem to be relational properties that are *essential* to anything which instantiates them, that is, could neither be acquired nor lost. For example, being diverse from Zeno and being such that $7 + 5 = 12$ are essential to anything which instantiates them. If either of these examples is correct, then when one substitutes for P the property, being diverse from Zeno, or the property, being such that $7 + 5 = 12$, the antecedent of the definiens is necessarily false. In that case, the definiens is vacuously satisfied, and the definition falsely implies that the relational property, being diverse from Zeno, is an intrinsic property of Anaxagoras, and that the relational property, being such that $7 + 5 = 12$, is an intrinsic property of Protagoras. Hence, the foregoing definition of an intrinsic property does not provide a logically sufficient condition of being an intrinsic property. This counterexample cannot be avoided by permitting substitutions only of accidental properties, since Aristotle himself recognizes the existence of essential intrinsic properties.

A second attempt might be to try to analyze an intrinsic property as (roughly) a property that is possibly exemplified when one and only one entity exists. A relational property could then be defined as a property that is not intrinsic. The intuitive idea here is that it is possible for there to be one and only one thing, and for this thing to exemplify rectangularity (an intrinsic property), while it is not possible for there to be one and only one thing, and for this thing to exemplify being five feet (apart) from Socrates (a relational property).

This second attempt, at least in the version stated, fails to distinguish intrinsic from relational properties correctly. For it is not possible for *any* property to be exemplified when one and only one entity exists. Consider the previous example, where it is supposed that there is one and only one thing, and it is rectangular. Necessarily, if rectangularity is exemplified, then there exists not only a thing which is rectangular, but also rectangularity, being a shape (which rectangularity must exemplify), parts of a rectangular thing, and, arguably, times, places, a surface of a rectangular thing, and so forth. Other possible versions along the lines of this second attempt to define an intrinsic property are not likely to avoid the kind of difficulties raised here.

Given the failure of various attempts to elucidate the intrinsic/relational distinction, its cogency might be defended by arguing that this distinction is primitive. For the sake of argument, let us grant this suggestion. Nevertheless, Aristotle's definition of substance as that which can undergo intrinsic change is subject to refutation by counterexample.

First, consider the case of a hurricane that has different intensities at different times. It is not unnatural to say of the hurricane that it changes its intensity over time. Thus, this seems to be a case of a nonsubstance, that is, an event, which undergoes an intrinsic change. If so, then Aristotle's definition does not provide a sufficient condition for something's being a substance.

However, this purported counterexample implies that events, which are changes, can themselves undergo change, which seems somewhat peculiar. Perhaps the peculiarity is brought out by the following considerations. It appears to be a distinctive feature of an event that if it occurs in its entirety at a time of length l, then it occurs in its entirety at a time of length l in every possible world in which it exists. Moreover, it is a plausible principle that if any contingent entity, e, which is not necessarily eternal, begins to undergo an intrinsic change at a moment, m, then it is possible for e to have gone out of existence at m instead. These two propositions together imply that contingent events which are not necessarily eternal (such as our hurricane) cannot after all undergo genuine intrinsic change.

The premise that an event's temporal length is essential to it can be supported by appealing to the following two propositions: (i) it is necessary for a temporally extended event to have temporal parts; and (ii) an event's temporal parts are essential to it. Of these, (ii) is somewhat controversial. An alternative to (ii) is (iii): if an entity has temporal parts, then it cannot undergo intrinsic *change*. Rather, it has parts (temporal ones) which have different properties. Either (ii) or (iii), conjoined with (i), yields the desired conclusion that events cannot undergo intrinsic change.[7] Hence, the example of the hurricane which is supposed to undergo intrinsic change is not actually a plausible counterexample to Aristotle's definition of substance as that which can undergo intrinsic change.

A second kind of counterexample should prove to be more convincing. Consider the surface of a rubber ball, a surface which undergoes a change in shape whenever the rubber ball does. This appears to be a case of a nonsubstance, namely, a surface, undergoing an intrinsic change. And there seems to be no effective reply along the lines of the preceding discussion to this counterexample. Thus, it seems that the capacity to undergo intrinsic change is not a logically sufficient condition of being a substance.

To our counterexample of the surface of the rubber ball, Aristotle might have replied that surfaces do not really exist, not even in the attenuated sense in which entities in the ten categories other than Primary Substance exist (such as places, qualities, times, etc.). This rejection of the reality of surfaces may or may not be correct. Aristotle's list of categories is certainly somewhat arbitrary and redundant, and it is a matter of controversy whether entities such as surfaces exist.[8] What seems indisputable is that a criterion of substance which does not presuppose a particular ontology of entities other than substance is preferable to one which does. So at the very least, Aristotle's definition of substance in terms of intrinsic change is not as *ontologically neutral* as it ideally should be.

There is another respect in which the Aristotelian definition of substance in terms of intrinsic change is implicitly not ontologically neutral. It is incompatible with even the *possibility* of Democritean atoms, necessarily indivisible particles which have volume and which are incapable of undergoing intrinsic change. Democritean atoms are material substances, so if atoms of this kind are even possible, then the capacity to undergo intrinsic change is *not* a logically necessary condition of being a substance.

As the foregoing discussion demonstrates, Aristotle's attempt to analyze the ordinary concept of substance in terms of the possibility of undergoing change (or intrinsic change) is not entirely successful. It presupposes the unanalyzed intrinsic/relational property distinction, and, more seriously, it presupposes a rather arbitrary ontology which excludes the very possibility of entities such as Democritean atoms and surfaces.

The second of Aristotle's definitions of individual or "primary" substance which we shall consider appears in chapter 5 of his *Categories*. There he says:

> A *substance* – that which is called a substance most strictly, primarily, and most of all – is that which is neither said of a subject nor in a subject, for example, the individual man or the individual horse.[9]

In chapter 4 of the same work, Aristotle provides a list of the ten categories of being (apart from Individual Substance). The list is as follows: (Secondary) Substance; Quantity; Quality or Qualification; Relative or Relation; Place; Time; Being-In-A-Position; Having; Doing; Being Affected.[10] Earlier, Aristotle tries to explain what he means by something's being said-of a subject and by something's being in a subject.[11]

An evaluation of Aristotle's explanations of the said-of and in relations is complicated by the fact that there is scholarly controversy over how to interpret those relations. Because we prefer to avoid having to choose among these interpretations, we shall present each of the major interpretations and argue that this second of Aristotle's accounts of substance is unsuccessful no matter which interpretation is chosen.

The first major interpretation is that of John Ackrill (among others), who says that the text implies the following definitions of the said-of and in relations, respectively:[12]

> (D1) A is said-of B = df. A is a species or genus of B.

> (D2) A is $in_a B$ = df. (a) A is $in_b B$, and (b) A is not a part of B, and (c) A is incapable of existing apart from B.

The "in" which occurs in the definiens of (D2) cannot on pain of circularity be the same "in" that occurs in the definiendum. Ackrill offers the following plausible account of the former, which we label "in_b":

> (D3) A is $in_b B$ = df. one could naturally say in ordinary language either that A is in B, or that A is of B, or that A belongs to B, or that B has A (or that . . .).[13]

The "in" which occurs in the definiens of (D3) is just the "in" of ordinary language, as opposed to the technical terms defined by (D2) and (D3).

According to Ackrill, Aristotle employs the notion defined in (D1) to distinguish species and genera (which Aristotle terms secondary substances) from individuals, and employs the notion defined in (D2) to distinguish substances (primary or secondary) from nonsubstances (or accidents). Since Aristotle's ontology in the *Categories* includes only individual substances, secondary substances, and accidents, for Aristotle only individual or primary substances are neither said-of nor in$_a$ a subject. In his view, species and genera in the category of Substance (for example, man, animal) are said-of a subject (for example, Socrates is a man), but are not in$_a$ any subject (since mankind can exist apart from Socrates). These are the so-called secondary substances, and are essences according to Aristotle. Individuals in categories other than Substance, that is, individual characteristics or tropes,[14] are in$_a$ a subject but are not said-of any subject (for instance, *this* courage is in Socrates). Finally, species and genera in categories other than Substance (accidental general characteristics) are both said-of a subject (for example, the knowledge of grammar is knowledge) and in$_a$ a subject (for example, knowledge is in minds; minds have knowledge).

Montgomery Furth defends an alternative interpretation of Aristotle.[15] According to Furth's interpretation, a characteristic which is *in* a subject is not an individual characteristic or trope, but is rather a sort of universal: an accidental property of one or more individuals, and a property which is a lowest species of one of the categories other than Substance.[16] Furth's understanding of Aristotle's said-of relation is substantially the same as that of Ackrill.

The question remains of whether this second of Aristotle's analyses is correct, on either of the two major interpretations just discussed. To this question we now turn.

To begin with, consider the property of being a horned horse. Since it is false that the class of horned horses has a member, this class does not subsume any other class. Nor is it true that the property of being a horned horse is exemplified. Hence, this property is not said of anything. Furthermore, in the relevant Aristotelian sense, the property of being a horned horse is not "in" anything. On Ackrill's reading, this is because one could *not* naturally say in ordinary language (where A = being a horned horse) either that A is in x, or that A is of x, or that A belongs to x, or that x has A (or that . . .), for any x. On Furth's reading, this is because there is not a lowest species of being a horned horse, since a lowest species must be exemplified. Consequently, it appears that on either reading, Aristotle's analysis implies that the property of being a horned horse is neither in nor said-of anything, and therefore is a primary substance. Because this is absurd, it seems that Aristotle's analysis does not provide a sufficient condition of being a primary substance.

Since Aristotle would have said that every property must be exemplified, he would have answered this objection by asserting that there is no such property as being a horned horse. Because Aristotle would have to have made this reply to avoid this objection, his analysis presupposes a certain ontology of properties, a highly controversial one, according to which there can be no unexemplified properties. Once again, it is preferable to have an analysis of individual substance that is neutral with respect to such controversies.

In addition, on Ackrill's interpretation, Aristotle's analysis of substance is subject to a more serious objection. Consider an individual substance such as a dog, d. Obviously, Aristotle's view that d cannot be said of anything is correct. On the other hand, d cannot exist apart from space, is not a part of space, and one *could* say in ordinary language that d is in space. Consequently, it certainly seems that d *is* in$_a$ something, namely, space. If so, then Aristotle's definition implies wrongly that d is *not* an individual substance. In that case, his definition (as understood by Ackrill) does not provide a necessary condition of being an individual substance.

In defense of Aristotle it might be replied that in the ordinary sense of "in" employed in (D3), d is *not* in space. We see no justification for this contention. For such a reply to be at all persuasive, it would have to be backed by an analysis of the relevant ordinary sense of "in," and that analysis would have to rule out our case, but let in all the desired ones. An analysis of this kind is conspicuously lacking in Aristotle's account, and it is difficult to see how one could be forthcoming. Therefore, our second counterexample to Aristotle's definition of individual substance (on Ackrill's interpretation) reveals a serious defect: that Aristotle has resorted to inessential linguistic criteria where straightforwardly ontological ones are needed.

Thus, Aristotle's attempt to analyze individual substance in terms of the said-of and in$_a$ relations, like his analysis in terms of change, suffers from a lack of ontological neutrality and is arguably subject to fatal counterexamples.

2 SUBSTRATUM AND INHERENCE THEORIES OF SUBSTANCE

Philosophers such as Descartes and Locke have, according to some interpretations, subscribed to another important theory of substance, namely, that a substance is a substratum in which properties subsist or inhere.[17] According to such a substratum theory, a substance is a propertyless or bare particular which gives unity to the properties which inhere in it.

There is some reason to think that both Locke and Descartes subscribed to some version of the substratum theory. For example, Locke wrote that:

> Not imagining how these simple ideas can subsist by themselves, we accustom ourselves to suppose some *substratum* wherein they do subsist and from which they do result, which therefore we call *substance*.[18]

And Descartes wrote:

> *Substance*. This term applies to every thing in which whatever we perceive immediately resides, as in a subject, or to every thing by means of which whatever we perceive exists. . . . The only idea we have of a substance itself, in the strict sense, is that it is the thing in which whatever we perceive . . . exists, either formally or eminently.[19]

At another point Descartes also said that:

> We do not have immediate knowledge of substances, as I have noted elsewhere. We know them only by perceiving certain forms or attributes which must inhere in something if they are to exist; and we call the thing in which they inhere a "substance."[20]

There is a controversy among scholars concerning whether or not either Descartes or Locke actually subscribed to the substratum theory. Some have taken the quotations of Descartes cited here merely to be expressing the point that one cannot apprehend or conceive of a substance except in terms of its properties or attributes.[21] If so, then neither the substratum theory nor any other theory of substance is implied by such remarks. In Locke's case, some have taken the quoted passage (and similar passages) to be part of an *attack* on rather than a defense of the substratum theory.[22]

There are two important versions of the substratum theory which we shall examine here. The first (which we call ST1) maintains that an individual substance is to be identified with the substratum itself. The second version (which we call ST2) holds that an individual substance is a complex or collection of a substratum together with the features[23] which subsist or inhere in that substratum. ST2 has the advantage over ST1 of endorsing the commonsense belief that dogs, trees, and rocks *are* individual substances.

An important first objection to both a theory which identifies a substance with a substratum and to the alternative theory which takes a substance to be a complex of a substratum and features is that the idea of a substratum is incoherent and self-contradictory. A substratum, according to the usual definition, exemplifies no properties. Because it is a necessary truth that *any* entity exemplifies properties, any theory which implies that there could be a substratum, a property-less entity, is incoherent. Nor can anyone grasp or apprehend or conceive of anything which fails to exemplify any property.[24] The substratum theory is self-contradictory because the substratum theorist himself must attribute various properties to the substratum. Among these are the property of being such that properties can subsist or inhere in it, the property of being concrete, the property of being a substance, and (absurdly) the property of lacking all properties! Finally, another serious challenge to the consistency or coherence of the theory is that it asserts *both* that properties subsist or inhere in the substratum *and* that the substratum fails to exemplify any property. Yet it appears to be necessarily true that if a property P inheres in x, then x exemplifies P. Thus, if by subsisting or inhering in a substratum the substratum theorist means just that a property is *exemplified* by the substratum, then he contradicts himself in also asserting that the substratum is "bare." On the other hand, if by subsisting or inhering in a substratum the substratum theorist does *not* after all mean that a property is exemplified by the substratum, then it is not clear what, if anything, is meant by subsisting or inhering in a substratum. In ordinary language, a substance or thing literally *has* certain properties, that is, exemplifies them (in technical language). But according to the substratum theorist, a property's inhering or subsisting in a thing does not imply that the thing literally has that property. Hence, the substratum theorist owes us an explanation of what he means by saying that properties inhere in a substratum, an explanation which he fails to provide, yet without which the relation between properties and substratum is left utterly mysterious.

Both ST1 and ST2 conflict with intuitive data concerning the nature of individual substances. Any successful theory of substance must be adequate to these intuitive data. ST1 conflicts with the following data for a theory of individual substance: (1) no individual substance can be propertyless or featureless; (2) it is possible for some individual substance to persist through an intrinsic change; (3) it is possible for some individual substance to persist through a relational change; and (4) it is possible for some individual substance to have both an essential intrinsic feature and an accidental intrinsic or relational feature. ST1 is incompatible with (1) through (4) because according to the substratum theory, a substratum/substance has no properties or relations at all. Since ST1 conflicts with *so many* of the intuitive data for a theory of substance, and since, as we have already seen, it appears to involve contradictions, we conclude that ST1 is highly implausible.

ST2, the theory that a substance is a *complex* of a substratum and properties, also conflicts with certain intuitive data concerning substances. First, it conflicts with the datum that no substance has a property or relation as a *part*. Since ST2 asserts that a substance is a concrete collection or complex of a substratum and properties (and relations), and since what any concrete collection collects are parts of that collection, ST2 implies that a substance has the collected properties (and relations) in question as parts.

Second, it conflicts with the datum that it is possible for some substance to persist through intrinsic change. Since ST2 states that a substance is a collection of a substratum and properties (and relations), and since the parts of any collection are *essential* to that collection, ST2 implies that the collected properties (and relations) in question are essential to a given substance. Furthermore, the parts which constitute a substance, according to ST2, are either an entity (the substratum) which has no intrinsic features, or else items (the collected properties and relations) which have all of their intrinsic features essentially. Hence, it certainly appears that according to ST2, a substance has all of its intrinsic features essentially, from which it follows that a substance *cannot* persist through intrinsic change.

A final criticism pertains to ST2. It is that while, according to ST2, a substance has certain intrinsic and relational features, as measured against intuitive beliefs about the features of a substance, it has the wrong ones. ST2 implies that a cat does not have the property of being furry, does not have the property of being a quadruped, does not have the property of being carnivorous, and does not have the property of being a cat! Instead, a cat is a complex or collection which includes a substratum in which being furry, being four-legged, being carnivorous, and being a cat subsist or inhere. The cat does have certain properties, but intuitively, they are the wrong ones: the property of being a collection, the property of having a substratum as a part, the property of having certain properties as parts, and so forth.[25]

For all of the reasons we have provided in the foregoing discussion, substratum theories do not give adequate accounts of substance. Thus, we turn next to a brief examination of what we call the inherence theory of substance.

The inherence theory defines an individual substance as that in which properties inhere. This is to be distinguished from the substratum theory in that the former does not imply, as does a substratum theory, that the subject of inherence could exist without any properties. This difference between the two theories is not always clearly drawn. An example of the inherence theory seems to be provided by Descartes in the following quotation:

> *Substance.* This term applies to every thing in which whatever we perceive immediately resides, as in a subject, or to every thing by means of which whatever we perceive exists.[26]

What this definition of substance seems to say is that a substance is that in which properties "reside" (inhere). But the definition suffers from being too general, that is, it does not provide a logically sufficient condition of being a substance. The definition implies (correctly) that if there are substances, then there are properties. Because *every* entity must have properties which "reside" in it, the definition also implies that if there are substances, then there are properties in which properties "reside" or inhere. For example, the property of being rectangular has the property of being a property, and so forth. Hence, the inherence theory implies that if a substance exists, then a property is a substance! This result suggests that what the inherence theory provides a definition of is not a substance, but a subject of predication, which, of course, *every* entity is. Thus, what the inherence theory defines is being an entity and not being a substance.

[handwritten margin note: not what we perceive. However, we do perceive sound, weather etc.]

3 INDEPENDENCE THEORIES OF SUBSTANCE

Another important type of theory about substance, examples of which are found in Aristotle, Descartes, and Spinoza, is that a substance is that which is uniquely independent of all other entities.

We have already encountered Aristotle's attempt to formulate an independence theory of substance: it is the definition of substance as that which is neither said-of nor in a subject. And as we indicated earlier, this theory does not capture any sense in which a substance is an independent entity.

Thus we turn to Descartes. Here is one of his statements of his independence theory of individual substance:

> The answer is that the notion of *substance* is just this – that it can exist all by itself, that is without the aid of any other substance.[27]

This analysis of individual substance seems to suffer from the fatal flaw of vicious conceptual circularity, since the notion of substance appears in the definiens of that analysis. However, Descartes also provided the following definition:

> By *substance*, we can understand nothing other than a thing which exists in such a way as to depend on no other thing for its existence.[28]

If, in this second definition, "thing" means entity, then circularity has been avoided. According to Descartes, God is the only entity that satisfies this second definition of an individual substance. But, Descartes also says:

> But as for corporeal substance and mind (or created thinking substance), these can be understood to fall under this common concept: things that need only the concurrence of God in order to exist.[29]

From these citations and the text surrounding them, it appears that Descartes has something like the following overall account of individual substance in mind.

(D4) x is a basic substance = df. it is possible for x to exist without any other entity existing.

In Descartes's view, God is the only basic substance. Hence, according to Descartes:

(D5) x is a nonbasic substance = df. it is possible for x to exist without any other entity existing, except God.

(D6) x is a substance = df. x is either a basic substance or a nonbasic substance.

There appear to be a number of difficulties with this Cartesian account of substance. First, since (D5) and (D6) imply that if there is an individual substance, then God exists, Descartes's theory of substance suffers from an exceptionally extreme form of lack of ontological neutrality. Surely, it would be better for a theory of substance not to be committed to the existence of God.

Second, since Descartes holds the traditional view that God has certain essential properties, for example, omnipotence, omniscience, and omnibenevolence, it appears that God could not exist unless some other entities exist, that is, his essential properties. If so, then (D4) mistakenly implies that God is not, after all, a *basic* substance. In that instance, (D4) does not provide a necessary condition for being a basic substance. And from this it follows that (D6) is incorrect. Descartes might have tried to avoid this difficulty by appealing to the doctrine of divine simplicity, according to which all of God's properties are identical with one another *and with God*. However, this doctrine is of questionable coherence.[30]

In any event, there are also apparent counterexamples to Descartes's (D5). For example, consider a typical nonbasic substance, say, an iron sphere (call this iron sphere s). It is extremely plausible that necessarily, if s exists, then some other entities exist as well, that is, parts of s.

Furthermore, it seems that s cannot exist without there being certain nonsubstantial entities, for example, certain places, times, properties, and surfaces.[31] Consequently, it is *not* possible for s to exist without any other entity existing except God. Thus, (D5), Descartes's definition of a nonbasic individual substance, mistakenly implies that s is not a nonbasic substance. Consequently, (D5) does not provide a necessary condition of something's being a nonbasic substance. For a similar reason, (D6) is inadequate.

Descartes's theory of substance is subject to an important alternative reading, one framed in terms of *causal* independence instead of purely logical or metaphysical independence.[32] When read in this way, Descartes's theory of substance can be stated in terms of the following three definitions:

(D7) x is a basic substance = df. it is possible for x to exist without being caused to exist by any other entity.

(D8) x is a nonbasic substance = df. it is possible for x to exist without being caused to exist by any other entity, except God.

(D9) x is a substance = df. x is either a basic substance or a nonbasic substance.

However, this alternative independence theory of individual substance is also subject to several serious criticisms.

First, since (D8) implies that if there is a nonbasic substance, then God exists, (D8) and (D9) suffer from the same extreme form of lack of ontological neutrality as (D5) and (D6). Second, the theory is framed in terms of causal independence, but only some categories of beings *can* be caused to exist. Those entities which *cannot* be caused to exist, but which are *not* substances, will nevertheless satisfy (D7). For example, if there are properties or sets which are uncaused necessary beings, then they will satisfy (D7). In this case, (D7) implies that such properties and sets are basic substances, while they are obviously not. Therefore, if some nonsubstances are uncaused, then (D7) does not provide a sufficient condition for being a basic substance.

Descartes might have replied to this second objection that properties, sets, and so forth *are*, in fact, all causally dependent on God. There are two versions of this sort of reply. According to the first, properties are *directly* causally dependent upon God, and according to the second, properties are *indirectly* causally dependent upon God. A property, P, is directly causally dependent upon God if and only if God causes the existence of P, but does not do so by causing the existence of something other than P which causes the existence of P. A property, P, is indirectly causally dependent upon God just provided that God causes the existence of P, but does so by causing the existence of something other than P which causes the existence of P.

But if properties are directly causally dependent on God, then while they fail to satisfy (D7), they instead satisfy (D8), and then (D8) falsely implies that such properties are nonbasic substances. Thus, if this is Descartes's answer, then (D8) does not provide a sufficient condition for being a nonbasic substance.

Alternatively, because Descartes seems to accept the Aristotelian view that every first-order property[33] must inhere in an individual,[34] he might have replied instead that *all* properties must be caused to exist by God, insofar as the individuals in which they inhere must be caused by God. And if such properties are causally dependent upon those individuals, then they must be *indirectly* causally dependent upon God. God directly or indirectly causes all individuals other than himself, and in virtue of the fact that a first-order property cannot exist unless there is an individual in which it inheres, properties are causally dependent for their existence upon individuals. Thus, God indirectly causes a property to exist *by* causing an individual to exist, which in turn causes the property to exist. If Descartes could have defended this claim about properties, then he could have disputed the idea that properties satisfy either (D7) or (D8).

However, the following line of reasoning implies that properties do *not* have this sort of causal dependence upon the individuals in which they inhere. Even if one grants Aristotle's claim that a first-order property must inhere in an individual, it does not follow that properties are *asymmetrically* dependent upon such individuals.[35] Do such properties causally depend upon individuals in virtue of their necessarily inhering in them? They do so if and only if individuals causally depend upon their properties in virtue of their necessarily having properties. Thus, if properties are causally dependent upon God, then either nonbasic substances must causally depend upon their *properties* in addition to God, or else Descartes has *not* provided a reason to think that properties causally depend upon their *instances* in addition to God. Therefore, on the hypothesis that properties causally depend upon God, Descartes is faced with the dilemma that either nonbasic substances themselves do not satisfy (D8), or else he has given no reason to deny that properties satisfy (D8), and hence no reason why properties do not turn out to be nonbasic substances. Since we do not see any other way for Descartes to defend the adequacy of (D7), (D8), and (D9), we conclude that either (D8) does not provide a necessary condition for being a nonbasic substance, or (D8) does not provide a sufficient condition for being a nonbasic substance, respectively.

A final point concerning Descartes's theory needs to be made. Some philosophers have argued that the actual causal origins of certain substances are essential to those substances. For example, Saul Kripke and others have maintained that any human being is a physical substance which is essentially caused to exist by a certain sperm–egg pair.[36] If this is correct, then a human being cannot exist without being caused to exist by something *other* than God, and then that human being will fail to satisfy (D8). In that case, (D8) would not provide a logically necessary condition for being a nonbasic substance. Descartes thought that human beings have nonphysical souls, and therefore are not physical substances. Nevertheless, if he was wrong about this,[37] and if Kripke is right about human beings having their origins essentially, then (D8) is false. In fact, (D8) is false even if, while no *actual* human being has its origins essentially, it is *possible* for there to be a human being who is a physical substance and essentially came from a certain sperm–egg pair.

A final version of the independence theory of substance is that of Spinoza. His famous definition of substance is as follows:

> By substance I mean that which is in itself and is conceived through itself; that is, that the conception of which does not require the conception of another thing from which it has to be formed.[38]

The interpretation of this definition is, once again, a matter of dispute. It is clear, however, that Spinoza believed that for something to be an individual substance, it had to possess a very strong sort of independence. It had to be both causally and conceptually independent of any entity of the same sort. Thus, Spinoza's substance cannot be caused to exist; nor can it be sustained by any entity. Moreover, Spinoza maintains that a substance cannot share its nature with any other entity, since if it did, one could not conceive of one without conceiving of the other. On the basis partly of the premise that a substance cannot share its nature with any other entity, Spinoza reaches the remarkable conclusion that there is but one substance, namely, the entire universe, and that the nature of the universe is, in part, to be extended and conscious.

All of this follows from Spinoza's definition of substance, a definition which stands by itself, for Spinoza makes no effort to defend it. But a definition of substance should be adequate to the intuitive data regarding substances. And one of the most powerful of these data is the belief that each one of us has regarding *oneself*, namely, that one is an individual substance. It is also part of the commonsense ontology that there is a plurality of substances, including other people, animals, plants, and inanimate material objects. Spinoza gives no good reason to reject these data, so his definition of substance is unmotivated and merely stipulative. And while we don't want to reject the idea that substance is *somehow* to be understood in terms of independence, we do think that Spinoza's definition of substance attributes to a substance the wrong sort of independence, a sort which it does not possess.

Some philosophers have seen a resemblance between Spinoza's ontology and that of contemporary physics, in that both (it is thought) reject finite physical substances. If there *is* this resemblance, then for that reason we have similar objections to these two ontologies. See our earlier discussion of the challenge to substance thought to be posed by contemporary physics.[39]

4 CLUSTER THEORIES OF SUBSTANCE

The final historical account of substance which we shall discuss is known as the cluster theory of substance. It is also frequently referred to as the bundle theory of substance. There are two fundamentally different sorts of cluster theories about substance. The eliminative cluster theory holds that there are no substances. Instead, there are clusters or bundles of nonsubstances, which clusters or bundles are not to be identified with substances. This view usually maintains that what are *thought* to be substances are really clusters of insubstantial entities. At times David Hume seems to be a proponent of this view. For example, he writes as follows:

> As our idea of any body, a peach, for instance, is only that of a particular taste, odor, figure, size, consistency, etc., so our idea of any mind is only that of particular perceptions without the notion of anything we call substance, either simple or compound.[40]

Hume here seems to be the sort of eliminationist who thinks that there is no intelligible concept of substance, but it is possible to be an eliminationist and also hold that the concept of substance is a coherent one. Because we are surveying accounts of *substance*, and because an eliminationist cluster theory does not offer such an account, we shall not discuss this sort of theory further here.

A second sort of cluster theory is reductionist rather than eliminationist: it *identifies* substances with clusters of nonsubstances of a certain sort. For instance, despite his eliminationist inclinations, Hume sometimes speaks as though substances exist and can be identified with collections of particular qualities or impressions:

> We have therefore no idea of substance, distinct from that of a collection of particular qualities, nor have we any other meaning when we either talk or reason concerning it. The idea of a substance ... is nothing but a collection of simple ideas that are united by the imagination and have a particular name assigned them by which we are able to recall, either to ourselves or to others, that collection.[41]

Another apparent example is provided by Berkeley:

And as several of these [ideas] are observed to accompany each other, they come to be marked by one name, and so to be reputed as one thing. Thus, for example, a certain colour, taste, smell, figure and consistency having been observed to go together, are accounted one distinct thing, signified by the name *apple*; other collections of ideas constitute a stone, a tree, a book.[42]

Such a theory attempts to provide an analysis or definition of the concept of an individual substance as ordinarily understood by maintaining that necessarily, for any x, x is a substance if and only if x is a collection of nonsubstances of an appropriate sort. Thus, the basic idea of this theory is that the substantiality of a substance is just the collecting of those nonsubstances in a certain way. Since we are interested in attempts to analyze the ordinary concept of substance, it is this second, reductionist, sort of cluster theory which concerns us. And while we are not sure that any cluster theorist has both clearly distinguished the eliminative and noneliminative versions of the theory, and subscribed to the latter version, this is not of great concern to us, for someone *could* do so. What matters is whether such a theory is correct.

Ontological parsimony is often the motivation for the attempt to identify substances with some other sort of entities. Since substances cannot be identified with properties, events, tropes, or similar items, apparently the only alternative for those who seek to reduce substance to or identify substance with an entity of another kind or ontological category is to reduce a substance to or identify a substance with a *cluster* of nonsubstances.

There are different versions of the cluster theory, depending on the *sort* of clustering relation that is utilized, and the *sort* of nonsubstances that are clustered. One sort of nonsubstance is a sharable quality or universal such as redness or triangularity. A nonsubstance of this kind is an *abstract* entity. A theory which identifies a substance with a cluster of abstract entities is subject to the following decisive criticism. Any cluster of *abstracta* is itself an abstract entity. But a substance is a concrete entity.[43] Hence, a cluster theory of this kind is guilty of a categorial confusion of an abstract entity with a concrete one.[44]

One sort of clustering relation results in what logicians call a set. The standard view is that sets are abstract entities. Although some sets have only concrete elements, others have only abstract elements. Moreover, the null set is totally empty – without any elements at all!

It is apparent that sets which have only abstract elements, as well as the null set, are insubstantial entities. Such an entity is a paradigm case of an abstract entity. Since the category, Set, is an ontological division, and since the concrete/abstract distinction seems to be the most fundamental of all ontological divisions, it is extremely plausible that if some sets are abstract entities, then all of them are, including those which have only concrete elements. It seems to follow that any theory which identifies a substance with a *set* of nonsubstances is also guilty of a categorial confusion of the aforementioned kind.

really?

In the light of the foregoing arguments, it appears that the cluster theory is viable only if it analyzes or defines a substance as a concrete cluster of insubstantial concrete entities of some kind. The most likely candidate is a collection, that is to say, a mereological sum of concrete entities.[45] A collection in this sense is a concrete entity: it must be composed of concrete parts. In contrast to sets, which may have a single element, no collection can have but one proper part. But for any two *concreta*, x and y, there is a third thing, z, which is the collection of x and y, and which has no proper parts which are not parts of either x or y (or both). Moreover, no collection can fail to have a noncollection as a part, and some formal collection or mereological theories designate noncollections which have no proper parts, "atoms." Finally, as we conceive of collections, no collection can have as proper parts two collections which have a common part which is itself a collection. Thus, a collection which has a finite number of atomic parts must have a finite number of parts overall.

We shall call an account of substance which analyzes or defines a substance as a concrete cluster of insubstantial concrete entities of some sort a collectionist theory of substance. Examples of insubstantial concrete entities which might be thought to compose collections of this kind are impressions of sensation or reflection (in Hume's sense), ideas (in the sense of Descartes, Locke, and Berkeley), and events.

The collectionist sees the collection as functioning as a kind of substitute for a substratum, a substitute in which the items collected allegedly inhere, in the sense that they are qualities of the substance which is identified with the collection. Since events cannot inhere in anything (they are too substance-like for this), it is implausible to suppose that a substance is a collection of events. Thus, we shall not single out event-collectionism for any special consideration. Nevertheless, a number of our criticisms of other forms of collectionism will apply as well to the claim that substances can be identified with collections of events.

Another example of a concrete insubstantial entity is what has been called a trope, a nonsharable concrete feature such as the particular curiosity of Aristotle, or *that* particular triangularity. Accordingly, the contemporary theory which identifies a substance with a collection of tropes is also a collectionist theory of substance.[46]

Hume doubted, and Berkeley denied, the existence of unperceived concrete entities. More specifically, they doubted or denied the existence of mind-independent physical things. Although Hume and Berkeley were skeptical about, or rejected, the existence of unperceived impressions and ideas, many contemporary trope theorists accept the existence of mind-independent physical things and unperceived tropes. Nonetheless, Berkeley's ideas, Hume's impressions, and tropes are entities of similar kinds: concrete, yet attribute-like.

The version of collectionism inspired by Berkeley and Hume that identifies substances with collections of concrete insubstantial entities that cannot exist unperceived may be called phenomenalistic collectionism. Of course, this version of collectionism is incompatible with the folk ontological belief in mind-independent physical things. Since we are prepared to assume that this belief is justified, it is trope-collectionism, and not phenomenalistic collectionism, that is the focus of our attention. Nevertheless, the critique we shall provide of trope-collectionism can be easily adapted to apply to phenomenalistic collectionism as well.

In what follows, we shall develop three criticisms of trope-collectionism. Not only will the first criticism apply to the theory that substances are collections of tropes, but parallel criticisms will apply to the theory that substances are collections of properties, impressions, ideas, events, or the like. The second and third criticisms will apply to the theory that substances are collections of tropes, and parallel criticisms will apply to the theory that substances are collections (or sets) of properties, and to theories which identify substances with collections (or sets) of other *concreta*, such as impressions, ideas, or events. That is, the latter criticisms will apply to sets as well as collections, whereas the first kind of criticism applies to collections but not to sets. Although we intend the second and third kinds of criticisms to apply to both collections and sets, henceforth we shall refer only to collections and their parts with the understanding that parallel remarks apply to sets and their elements. Likewise, although we shall refer only to tropes as parts of collections (and implicitly as elements of sets), we shall do so with the understanding that parallel observations apply to properties, impressions, ideas, and events.

A first objection to the collectionist theory is based on the intuitive datum that no feature of a substance is a *part* of that substance. For example, intuitively, the right and left halves of a material object, *o*, *are* parts of *o*, but the shape and size of *o* are *not* parts of *o*. But, according to the collectionist, *o* is a collection of tropes, one of which is the shape of *o*, and since the items which a collection collects are parts of the collection, the shape of *o* is, according to the collectionist, a part of *o*. Thus, the collectionist theory conflicts with a datum for an adequate analysis of substance. The implication that the shape of *o* is a part of *o* also conflicts with another datum for a theory of substance: that the parts of a material substance are either material substances or portions of matter. That collectionism has implications which conflict with these data is an indication of a category mistake in the identification of substances with collections. A collection can have *any* kind of concrete entity as a part, but a material substance can only have a material substance or portion of matter as a part.[47]

In the foregoing argument, we appealed to certain data concerning the intuitive concept of an individual substance. An analysis of substance should, *prima facie*, be compatible with such data. Since such data are only *prima facie* regulative of any analysis of substance, there are circumstances in which some of the data (but not all of them) can be overturned. More specifically, in the context of conceptual analysis, a *prima facie* datum can be overturned only if there is good reason to think that it is incompatible with either another *prima facie* datum or a conjunction of other such data. It is, of course, illegitimate to defend the view that the shape of a physical object is a part of that physical object simply by rejecting the intuitive datum that a feature of a thing is not a part of that thing. That is, this defense is illegitimate *because* it does not involve a demonstration that the datum in question is incompatible with other data for being a substance. After all, the point of a philosophical analysis of substance is to explicate the *intuitive* concept of substance. Nor does it appear likely that any defense of the proposition that a substance has properties as parts *could* be made. For it does not seem likely that it could be shown that the datum "a substance cannot have properties as parts" is incompatible with other data for being a substance. In any case, the burden of proof is on one who would reject this datum.[48] Two other main difficulties, of which we now give a preliminary sketch, confront the collectionist.

First, there is the unity of qualities problem. Consider the collection of the orangeness of a carrot, the savor of a piece of licorice, the sound of a bell ringing, the shape of a banana, the odor of a clove of garlic, and so forth. Alternatively, consider a collection of diverse psychological qualities of different persons. For instance, consider the collection of S_1's belief that snow is white, S_2's feeling of joy, S_3's sensation of purple, S_4's fondness for cats, S_5's feeling of curiosity, and so on, where S_1, S_2, S_3, S_4, S_5, etc. are different persons. Collections of this kind are obviously *not* substances, but it is not clear that a collectionist theory can avoid implying that they are. The items collected in these two examples may be interpreted in terms of either tropes, properties, impressions, ideas, or events. It is clear that on any of these interpretations, there is a perfectly good collection of items, but such a collection is not an individual substance. Notice that since a collectionist theory of substance should distinguish a nonsubstantial collection from a substance in any *possible* case, it appears that it ought to do this in the case *both* of material objects and nonphysical souls.

Second, there is the problem of excessive essentialism. It seems that there could be individual substances that have accidental qualities and endure through changes in some of their intrinsic qualities. However, since it is extremely plausible that a collection has *all* of its parts essentially,[49] it is hard to see how a collectionist can satisfactorily account for the full range of such accidental qualities and changes.

The challenge for the collectionist is to provide a satisfactory account of the distinction between those collections which are substances and those which are not. This requires that there be a unifying relation which holds only among the parts of those collections that are substances. One part of this challenge is to specify a relation which overcomes the unity of qualities problem, and the second part is to specify a relation which overcomes the problem of excessive essentialism. We shall next discuss attempts to specify a relation among the parts of a collection which solve the unity of qualities problem for a collectionist account.

What might such an attempt look like? It must not presuppose the existence of any noncollectionist substances, whether material or spiritual, or else it fails of its purpose. There are five possibilities: (Pi) The parts of the collection are unified by their being in the same place at the same time, that is, by their completely coinciding in space. (Pii) The parts of the collection are unified by their each standing in some causal connection to the others. Perhaps it is supposed that this causal connection is analogous to the causal connection in a human body between the heart, the lungs, the kidneys, the brain, the liver, the blood, etc. If any of these organs ceases to function then this would cause all of the other organs to cease to function. (Piii) There is a logically or metaphysically necessary connection among the parts of the collection. (Piv) The parts of the collection are unified by some combination of the foregoing criteria. (Pv) There is some other unifying relation among the parts of the collection.

There are a number of problems confronting (Pi). First, (Pi) presupposes that a substance is located in space, and so is incompatible with the very possibility of a nonphysical soul. (Pi) explains the unity of a substance in terms of the spatial coincidence of its qualities. Since a nonphysical soul is not in space, the unity of its qualities cannot be so explained. Thus, (Pi) implies the impossibility of souls. Since souls seem possible, (Pi) appears not to provide a logically necessary condition for a collection of tropes being a substance.

Second, it is possible that there is an item such as a lightning flash, or the like, which is an event and not a substance. But an entity of this kind can possess spatially coincident tropes of shape, size, charge, and so forth. Hence, spatial coincidence of tropes is not a logically sufficient condition for those tropes belonging to a substantial collection. How is the difference between a collection of tropes which belong to an event and a collection of tropes which belong to a substance to be explained?

A third problem for (Pi) arises from this seeming possibility: there could be two completely penetrable, spatially extended substances, that is, nonmaterial physical substances, having the same shape and size that can interpenetrate, so that the two can occupy the same place at the same time.[50] Two such objects can also separate and occupy different places at the same time. At the time when the two substances are in the same place, there is no one substance in that place which has all of the tropes that each of the two objects has, as (Pi) requires. Hence, spatial coincidence is not a logically sufficient condition for the substantial unity of a collection of tropes.

(Pii) attempts to characterize the concept of a substance in terms of a relation of causal dependence holding between the parts of a collection of tropes. This approach holds out the hope of avoiding some of the difficulties which beset (Pi). For example, (Pi) could not allow for immaterial substances or for penetrable nonmaterial physical substances, but it isn't as obvious that (Pii) could not do so.

What would the causal relation among the parts or elements of a collection be? There are two proposals for causal criteria that need to be considered. The first is given by the following definition:

(D10) a, b, c, . . . are the tropes which are parts of a substantial collection ⇔ in *every* nomically possible situation, if any one of them goes out of existence, then its going out of existence causes all of the other tropes which are parts of the collection to go out of existence.

The second proposed criterion can be stated as follows:

(D11) a, b, c, . . . are the tropes which are parts of a substantial collection ⇔ in *some* nomically possible situation, if one of them goes out of existence, then its going out of existence causes all of the other tropes which are parts of the collection to go out of existence.

The attempt to characterize the unity of a substantial collection of tropes in terms of their causal relations stated by (D10) is subject to the following decisive objection. Every substance possesses some particular quality essentially, for example, its particular quality of being a substance. Hence, (D10) rules out the possibility of a substance's undergoing a change in an intrinsic quality, since on (D10), if any particular intrinsic quality of a substance, x, goes out of existence, then all of the intrinsic qualities of x go out of existence, including those essential to x, which implies that x ceases to exist. Thus, (D10) is incompatible with the following intuitive datum for a theory of the intuitive notion of substance: it is possible for a substance to undergo a change in one of its intrinsic features (without the substance going out of existence), that is, it is possible for it to lose one of its intrinsic features without losing all of them. For instance, an object's particular color is not physically necessary for its particular shape, and vice versa; an object's particular shape is not physically necessary for its particular volume; and an object's particular volume is not physically necessary for its particular shape. In addition, a cubical piece of rubber having a volume of eight cubic centimeters can either be stretched into a noncubical rectangular solid (eight by one by one centimeters) having a volume of eight cubic centimeters, or be compressed into a cube of a smaller volume, respectively.

Thus, a substance can change one of its particular intrinsic features without changing all of them, contrary to what (D1) implies. We call this problem the problem of excessive nomic essentialism, for (D10) states so strong a unifying condition for the parts of a collection of tropes that the tropes cannot be "pulled apart" at all.

(D11) avoids the objections to (D10), since (D11) requires only that in *some* circumstances the going out of existence of some particular feature of a substance causes all of the other particular features of that substance to go out of existence. This is compatible with the possibility, in other circumstances, of the persistence of a substance through change. Thus, the defender of (D11) would assert that any case in which a substance is annihilated is a case in which the going out of existence of one particular feature, for example, an essential trope of a material object such as its being extended, causes the going out of existence of all of its other particular features. It seems that (D11) provides a logically necessary condition of a collection's being a substance. But the trouble arises when we ask whether (D11) provides a logically *sufficient* condition of a collection's being a substance. Consider the following example. Two fragile china cups are beside one another. Thus, there is a collection, c, whose parts are the particular features of the two cups. In some nomically possible situation, a bull causes the first cup to crash into the neighboring one, thereby destroying both of them. The going out of existence of the particular being-at-rest of the first cup causes the going out of existence of all of the features of both cups, that is, all of the features collected by c. Consequently, c qualifies as a substance on (D11), but c is not a substance. Hence, (D11) does not provide a logically sufficient condition for being a substance.

According to strategy (Piii), one can define a substantial collection in terms of *metaphysically* necessary connections holding among the tropes belonging to the collection, for example:

(D12) a, b, c, ... are the tropes which are parts of a substantial collection ⇔ in any possible situation, if any one of them exists, then its existing metaphysically necessitates the existence of all the others.

However, (D12) is subject to all of the same counterexamples as (D10). Therefore, it is unnecessary to discuss (D12) any further.

Strategy (Piv) attempts to analyze the concept of a substantial collection of tropes by combining earlier approaches. One such attempt combines spatial coincidence with causal interdependence:

> (D13) a, b, c, ... are tropes which are parts of a substantial collection $\Leftrightarrow$ (i) a, b, c, ... are spatially coincident, and (ii) a, b, c, ... are such that in *every* nomically possible situation, if *any* one of them goes out of existence, then its going out of existence causes all of the other tropes which are parts of the collection to go out of existence.

Far from being an improvement on (D10) or the spatial coincidence criterion, (D13) is subject to some of the defects of both. It is refuted by the possibility of souls, since souls, being nonspatial, are substances which do not satisfy (i) of (D13), and by the possibility of intrinsic qualitative change in substances, because (ii) of (D13) incorrectly rules out this possibility, as we have argued. But perhaps another combination would fare better:

> (D14) a, b, c, ... are tropes which are parts of a substantial collection $\Leftrightarrow$ (i) a, b, c, ... are spatially coincident, and (ii) a, b, c, ... are such that in *some* nomically possible situation, if *some* one of them goes out of existence, then its going out of existence causes all of the other tropes which are parts of the collection to go out of existence.

As in the case of (D13), the possibility of souls argues against (D14), since a soul is a substance which fails to satisfy (i) of (D14). Thus, (D14) does not provide a logically necessary condition for being a substance. Moreover, there could be an *event* all of whose particular features are spatially coincident and satisfy (ii) of (D14). For example, possibly, a piece of copper's being spherical is an event (call it e). Since e is the event of a piece of copper's having a certain shape, e itself has that same shape, viz., being spherical. Thus, the particular sphericity of the piece of metal is exactly similar to the particular sphericity of e, and is spatially coincident with it, though presumably diverse from it. Consider the collection, c, of tropes which belong to e. Because an event is insubstantial, c is a nonsubstantial collection. But there is some nomically possible situation in which if one of e's tropes goes out of existence, for instance, its particular sphericity, then its going out of existence causes e to go out of existence, and hence, causes all of the other tropes which are parts of c to go out of existence. It follows that c is a nonsubstantial collection that satisfies (D14). Hence, (D14) does not provide a logically sufficient condition for substancehood.

A final approach to solving the problem of unity for the collectionist theory falls under (Pv), that the unity of a substantial collection is provided by some hitherto as yet unnoticed relation. What might this nonspatial, noncausal, nonlogical relation be? One sort of answer is given by the contemporary metaphysicians Bertrand Russell and Hector Neri-Castañeda.[51] According to each of them, there is an *undefined* relation which does the job, a relation which Russell calls "compresence," and a relation which Castañeda calls "consubstantiation." Such an undefined relation is supposed to account for the synchronic unity of the parts or elements of substantial collections or sets.[52] Adopting this relation as undefined is unsatisfactory, since it would seem that without an account of this relation we have no notion of what this relation is. For instance (Castañeda):

> We take physical objects to be very special systems of guises intimately related to one another by just one very special relation that cannot receive a better name than *consubstantiation*.[53]

Of course, it won't do to say that, for example, green and triangular are consubstantiated just when an object is green and triangular, inasmuch as this presupposes the ordinary concept of individual substance, and an account of this ordinary concept cannot appeal to this ordinary concept. Nor will it do to say the following (Russell):

> Two events are "compresent" when they are related in the way in which two simultaneous parts of one experience are related. At any given moment, I am seeing certain things, hearing others, touching others, remembering others, and expecting yet others. All these percepts, recollections, and expectations are happening to me now; I shall say that they are mutually "compresent."[54]

In this passage, Russell explicitly appeals to the *self* as that to which various mental particulars are related. But a reduction of substances to collections cannot rely on a unifying relation which has no intuitive content other than a relation of mutual inherence in a substance. Thus, it would seem that neither Russell nor Castañeda has provided a unifying relation for substantial collections.[55]

Finally, there seems to be an argument which reduces *all* forms of collectionism to absurdity. Consider a sphere, s. Necessarily, if, $S*$, a particular sphericity, is part of s, then a particular hemisphericity, H, is a spatial part of $S*$. Necessarily, parthood is transitive. Hence, H is part of s. Thus, H is part of any collection with which s is identical. But collectionism says that an object's features are those which are parts of the collection with which that object is identical. Therefore, absurdly, H is a feature of s, that is, s is simultaneously *both* a sphere and a hemisphere! (This criticism, unlike earlier difficulties pertaining to the unity of qualities, does not seem to apply to set-theoretical versions of the cluster theory, since the elements of a set are not parts of it; but remember that set-theoretical versions of the cluster theory commit the category mistake of identifying a concrete entity with an abstract one.)

We turn now to the problem for collectionism of excessive essentialism. Even if the problem of the unity of qualities could be solved, the collectionist would face this second problem. To begin with, it is an intuitive datum that it is possible for some individual substance to undergo a change in its intrinsic qualitative properties while remaining numerically one and the same. For instance, suppose that Plato at time t_1 is attentive and is identical with a collection of tropes, c, one of whose parts is that trope which is a particular attentiveness, and all of whose parts exist at t_1. Plato can change from being attentive at t_1 to being inattentive at a later time, t_2. But it would seem that if Plato were identical with c, then he could not undergo such a change. This is because it is extremely plausible that the parts of a collection are essential to it. Since c contains Plato's particular attentiveness as a part at t_1, and does not contain his particular inattentiveness at t_1, c cannot exist at time t_2 while containing the latter property nor exist at time t_2 while failing to contain the former property. Yet, at t_2, Plato does have a particular inattentiveness. Hence, Plato is not identical with c.

It might be thought that a cluster theorist who identifies a substance with a set of abstract properties is better off with respect to the problem of excessive essentialism vis-à-vis change. On the view we have in mind, a changing object is to be identified with a special kind of set of abstract entities. For each time that the object exists, and for each of the properties belonging to that object at that time, there is a corresponding temporally indexed or dated property which is an element of the set in question. A particular substance is identified with such a set, and the properties of the substance at a given time are determined by those properties in the set which are indexed to the time in question. Thus, the set with which Plato is identified contains being attentive at t_1 and being inattentive at t_2. It might seem at first that this view can accommodate Plato's changing from being attentive to being inattentive, inasmuch as this view seems to imply that Plato is attentive at t_1 and inattentive at t_2. However, because the elements of a set are essential to it, such a view implies that *any* temporally indexed feature had by an object is an essential feature of that object. For example, if Plato is attentive at time t, then the property of being attentive at t is essential to Plato. But, surely, it is an intuitive datum that attentiveness is an accidental property of Plato. In other words, it is an intuitive datum that possibly, Plato exists at t and is not attentive at t. It follows that an individual substance cannot be reduced to or identified with a set of properties of the sort indicated.[56]

Another attempt to avoid the problem of excessive essentialism identifies a changing object, o, with a temporal sequence, s, of collections of tropes such that for any time, t, at which o exists, s has as a part the collection of o's tropes at t. Strictly speaking, this is not a collectionist theory of substance, for it does not identify a substance with a collection, but rather with a *temporal sequence*.[57] Nevertheless, such a sequentialist theory of substance is a natural extension of collectionism, and so is appropriately dealt with here. An example of sequentialism is provided by Bertrand Russell:

> A piece of matter, which we took to be a single persistent entity, is really a *string of entities*, like the apparently persistent objects in a cinema. And there is no reason why we should not say the same of a mind: the *persistent ego* seems as fictitious as the *permanent atom*. Both are only strings of events having certain interesting relations to each other.[58]

Our first two criticisms of sequentialism are based on the intuition that the parts of a temporal sequence are essential to it: if a temporal sequence, s_1, in a possible world $W1$, and a temporal sequence, s_2, in a possible world $W2$, have different parts in $W1$ and $W2$, respectively, then s_1 does not count as the same sequence as s_2. This intuition supports two different criticisms of sequentialism. The first is that sequentialism does not allow for genuine intrinsic qualitative change in a substance.

If Plato is such a sequence, then he doesn't really *change* from being attentive to being inattentive (although this might appear to be the case). The argument for this conclusion is as follows. Recall our principle that if a contingent entity which is not necessarily eternal undergoes change, then it could have gone out of existence instead of changing.[59] Plato is a contingent entity who is not necessarily eternal and who undergoes change, for example, from being attentive to being inattentive. Thus, when Plato is attentive, he could subsequently have gone out of existence instead of having become inattentive. Suppose Plato was attentive at t_1 and became inattentive at t_2. Then he could have gone out of existence at t_2 instead of having become inattentive. But if Plato is a sequence of collections of tropes, then those collections are essential parts of the sequence. And since the collections essentially include those tropes which are their parts, it follows that each such trope is an essential part of the sequence (or at least essentially belongs to the sequence). From these propositions, we can infer that if Plato is a sequence of collections, then it is essential to Plato that his particular attentiveness (the attentiveness we stipulated as having belonged to him at t_1) be followed by his particular inattentiveness (the inattentiveness we stipulated as having belonged to him at t_2). This, however, is not compatible with our earlier principle, which implies that Plato could have gone out of existence after being attentive instead of having become inattentive. Thus, it follows from the principle in question that if Plato is a sequence of collections of tropes, then he did not, despite appearances, actually undergo any change from t_1 to t_2. Instead, one might say that Plato is a static, temporally expansive entity which is qualitatively heterogeneous across its temporal expanse from t_1 to t_2.

A second criticism of sequentialism is an implication of some of the premises for the first criticism: that the collections which are parts of a temporal sequence are essential to that sequence, and that the tropes which are the parts of each collection are essential to that collection. The implication is that if Plato is a sequence of the sort indicated, then his qualitative life history is essential to him. All of the features of Plato at the first moment of his existence are essential to him, as are all of the features he has at each subsequent stage of his existence. Thus, the implication is that Plato could not have been any different qualitatively from the way he actually was – an implication at odds with the intuitive data for the ordinary concept of substance.

In order to avoid the two criticisms of sequentialism just discussed, the sequentialist might reject our assumption that the parts of a sequence are essential to it. We find the assumption in question extremely plausible, and would insist on its correctness. Nevertheless, it is worth examining the proposal which such a sequentialist might put forward based on the rejection of our essentialist assumption, and we shall find that even this new proposal suffers from a form of excessive essentialism.

The proposal is that a temporal sequence of particulars is individuated by its first stage and, given that first stage, could have any number of different later stages. For example, if a, b, c, d, and e are the first five stages of sequence S, respectively, S could have had different stages e, f, g, and h, as its second through fifth stages instead of b, c, d, and e, respectively. Alternatively, S could have gone out of existence after its first stage (or after its second, etc.) instead of having persisted beyond it. We concede that if a sequence of particulars with identity conditions of this kind were possible, then it would avoid the two criticisms of sequentialism voiced earlier. On the other hand, a third criticism applies to this sort of sequentialism. On the view in question, the initial stage of a sequence is essential to it. The initial stage is a collection of tropes whose parts are essential to it. Thus, by identifying a substance with such a sequence, this view implies that for any feature, f, which a substance initially has, the property of initially having f is essential to that substance. For example, if a human being, H, comes into existence in New York City, this view implies that in every possible world in which H exists, H is initially in New York City. Or, if H has a certain mass when it first comes into existence, this view implies that H initially has this mass in every possible world in which H exists. These implications are at odds with the intuitive data for the ordinary concept of a substance: surely, H could have been born outside the limits of New York City, and just as surely, H's initial mass could have been slightly different.

Sequentialism of any kind also suffers from a diachronic analogue to the synchronic unity of qualities problem. How does the sequentialist insure that a later stage of a sequence is a stage of the same substance as an earlier stage? What is to prevent the unwanted infiltration into the sequence of stages from other (for example, exactly similar) substances? Suppose two substances, x and y, coexist throughout their histories, are exactly similar at every stage, and undergo changes. x is identified with a sequence of collections of tropes, a, b, c, d, and y is identified with a sequence of distinct collections of tropes, *e*, *f*, *g*, *h*. Sequentialism seems to imply falsely that there is also a substantial sequence consisting of the stages *a*, *f*, *c*, *h*.

One possible solution to the unity problem just posed which properly rules out the existence of such a substance requires that the stages of any substantial sequence be united by a relation of spatiotemporal continuity. But we have argued elsewhere that spatio-temporal continuity is neither logically necessary nor logically sufficient for the persistence of a material substance (or any of its parts).[60] Furthermore, for obvious reasons spatiotemporal continuity cannot be logically necessary or sufficient for the stages of a substantial sequence to be united if that sequence is to be identified with a nonphysical soul. Thus, we do not regard this strategy for solving the problem of diachronic unity to be a promising one. Nor do we think that a causal criterion of unity over time offers much hope of solving this problem. As shown in our earlier discussion of causal criteria, such criteria for unity at a time are unable to provide a logically sufficient condition for that sort of unity. We believe that parallel problems emerge for unity over time (because of possible relations of causal dependence holding between the stages of different substances).[61] Finally, there is the Castañeda-like view that a primitive relation of "transubstantiation" unites the stages of a substantial sequence. According to Castañeda:

> In such a view, the clustering of consubstantiated clusters along a spacetime vector must be viewed as another contingent genuine relation: the transubstantiation of consubstantiation clusters.[62]

We regard such a view as unsatisfactory: for parallel reasons, the unanalyzable terms "transubstantiation" and "consubstantiation" are vacuous.

In conclusion, theories which identify substances with or reduce substances to either sets or collections of properties, tropes, impressions, ideas, events, or the like, or sequences of such collections, face at least two apparently intractable problems: that of the unity of qualities and that of excessive essentialism. Having rebutted these theories, we shall defend a nonreductionist theory of substance, a theory which implies that a substance *cannot* be identified with or reduced to a set or collection of properties, tropes, and so forth. Although we have criticized historical attempts to analyze the notion of substance, in the next chapter we shall argue that the independence criterion of Descartes and others, and Aristotle's scheme of categories, contain elements and insights which can be employed in constructing an adequate theory of substance. According to the theory we shall defend, a substance is an entity which uniquely satisfies certain independence conditions.

Chapter 2

An independence theory of substance

1 SOME DIFFICULTIES FOR AN INDEPENDENCE THEORY OF SUBSTANCE

As we have seen, an important view in the history of metaphysics is that an individual substance is something which could exist all by itself or which in some sense is "independent." In this chapter, we develop a new analysis of the notion of an individual substance in terms of independence and defend its adequacy.

Our goal is to construct a satisfactory philosophical analysis of this ordinary notion of thinghood. In setting forth our analysis we shall presuppose our earlier arguments that a *thing* in this ordinary sense, that is, an individual substance, is not reducible to or identifiable with an entity of another kind or ontological category, for example, a set or collection of properties, ideas, impressions, or events.

There are many disputes among philosophers about what kinds or categories of entities could actually exist. Since such disputes are difficult to resolve, it is advantageous, epistemically speaking, to provide an analysis of substance which is ontologically neutral. Accordingly, we aim to provide an analysis of substance which is ontologically neutral, in the sense that it is compatible with the existence of entities belonging to any intelligible categories, given some plausible view about the natures, existence conditions, and interrelationships of entities belonging to those categories. The epistemic advantage of this procedure is that we can set forth and defend an analysis of substance without having to argue (questionably) that entities belonging to certain categories could not exist. As we shall see, such an ontologically neutral analysis of substance provides an adequate criterion by which objects of discourse that would be insubstantial entities if they were to exist – for example, places, times, events, afterimages, shadows, surfaces, and properties – can be distinguished from genuine substances.

However, entities of innumerable ontological categories might be said to be possible, many of which are of questionable intelligibility. In the light of this, it does not seem reasonable to expect a single chapter to provide both an analysis of substance and a complete argument that this analysis is ontologically neutral with respect to *any* entity which might be said to be possible. Thus, in this chapter we shall only try to show that our analysis of substance is neutral with respect to a broad range of apparently intelligible ontologies discussed by philosophers.

In Chapter 1 we discussed the views of several prominent figures in the history of philosophy who have defended an independence theory of individual substance, including Aristotle and Descartes. As indicated in our earlier treatment of Descartes, however, there is a difficulty facing attempts to analyze the notion of substance in terms of an independence condition. This difficulty is that if there is a substance, then there must be other entities too. There are a number of different sorts of examples of this difficulty.

First, suppose that there is a substance, for instance, a rock (call this rock r). It can be argued that if r exists, then there must exist many other beings as well. These other beings include some substances, for example, entities which are parts of r, and some nonsubstances, for instance, r's surface, properties of r (notice that if a property, F, is either an essential characteristic of r or a necessary being, then r's existence entails F's existence), places and times, occurrences involving r (such as r's having a certain shape at a particular time), and propositions about r. Moreover, theists would add God (a substance) to this list.

Second, consider the class, ψ, of all kinds of torus-shaped physical objects, examples of such objects being certain life-preservers and inner-tubes. Arguably, the existence of at least some of the members of ψ implies the existence of a nonsubstance, namely, a hole.

Third, it has been argued that every human must have originated from other earlier things, namely, a sperm and egg.[1]

Fourth, wives are substances, as are both widows and wives-to-be. However, if a wife (widow, wife-to-be) exists, then this entails that another substance exists (did exist, will exist), namely, a husband.

Each one of these four examples suggests that the independence of a substance from other entities is not a logically *necessary* condition of substancehood. Our analysis of substance in terms of independence will be compatible with examples of these kinds.

On the other hand, a Humean might argue that independence is not a logically *sufficient* condition of substancehood. To see this, assume for the sake of argument a neo-Humean ontology in which the only entities are instantaneous concrete events (similar to Hume's impressions), none of which is necessarily connected in any manner to another. Obviously, such an event is not a substance, but on Humean assumptions it is possible for one such entity to exist all by itself.

Hume gives a radical version of an argument of this kind, asserting that:

> If . . . anyone should [say] that the definition of a substance is *something which may exist by itself*; and that this definition ought to satisfy us . . . I shou'd observe, that this definition agrees to every thing, that can possibly be conceiv'd.[2]

Of course, this statement is incorrect, as was shown by the preceding discussion.

Furthermore, there could not be just one temporally extended event, since such an event would, of necessity, have parts which are themselves events. Moreover, Hume's assumption that there could be just one *instantaneous event* implies that there are *times*, since events are essentially temporal. Time is either absolute or relational.[3] Relational time consists in temporal relations of before, after, and simultaneous with, which hold either between the parts of an intrinsically temporally extended entity, or between two or more temporally located entities. Thus, the existence of just a single instantaneous (i.e., temporally unextended) event cannot give rise to relational time. It is necessary, therefore, that if there is such an event, then time is absolute. And this implies that there are (absolute) times. We conclude that a Humean counterexample to the sufficiency of a naive independence criterion of substance is unsuccessful: there could not be a single instantaneous event and nothing else.

On the basis of the foregoing argument, we can now make this observation: the claim that it is possible for there to be just one instantaneous event and absolute time is much more plausible than the claim that it is possible for there to be just one instantaneous event and nothing else. We shall construct our analysis of substance so that it is compatible with the former claim. As it turns out, that analysis will also be compatible with the latter claim.

A substance is an entity of a certain sort or ontological category. A crucial element of our analysis is that this category of Substance is one whose instances meet certain independence conditions *qua* being instances of that category, a category which is of a certain level of generality. This level of generality needs to be elucidated, since every entity falls under many different kinds or categories of varying levels of generality or specificity. Hence, in developing our analysis, we need to specify the level of generality of the ontological categories in question. This is accomplished in the next section.

As we noted earlier in this section, the instantiations of properties such as being a wife and being a torus have certain bothersome existential entailments for a naive independence criterion of substance. These existential entailments created difficulties by suggesting that independence is not a logically necessary condition of being a substance. Because the category of Substance is at a certain level of generality, and because the instantiation of *this* category does *not* have bothersome existential entailments, these problems can be solved by stating an independence theory of substance in terms of a category variable that ranges only over ontological categories at the level of generality of the category of Substance. Moreover, Substance subsumes more specific properties like Wife and Torus, thereby guaranteeing that the latter properties are not categories at the level of generality in question. This is the strategy which we shall adopt in formulating our analysis of substance in terms of independence. Our way of avoiding the difficulties created by lower-level kinds of substantial entities shows that it is not *qua* substance that there being a wife or a torus creates difficulties for an analysis of substance, but *qua* wife or torus.

2 ONTOLOGICAL CATEGORIES

No comprehensive understanding of the world is possible without ontological commitments, commitments as to what kinds or categories of entities exist. Although the intuitive concept of a genuine ontological kind or category may be hard to analyze, this notion must be employed both in the study of ontology in general, and in the framing of a particular ontology.

Not all kinds, in the broadest sense of the term, are ontological categories. That is, not all kinds divide up the world in ontologically important ways. Examples of kinds which are not ontological categories are: being a green thing, being a triangular thing, being a widow, and (the disjunctive kind of) being a substance or an edge.

Paradigm cases of ontological categories include Property, Substance, Event, Time, Place, and Collection. Such categories are among the more general or fundamental kinds of beings. A system of classification which includes such categories and which is applicable to all possible kinds of beings helps clarify the nature of reality. Since our primary focus is on the category of Substance, our first task is to place this category within such a system of classification.

We begin with the observation that a substance is a concrete entity or *concretum*. The distinction between *abstracta* and *concreta* appears to be indispensable to ontology: for instance, the dispute between realists and antirealists over the existence of universals presupposes this distinction. In this debate, the realist affirms the existence of abstract universals, whereas the antirealist maintains that only *concreta* or particulars exist. We assume (plausibly, we think) that this very general division between *concreta* and *abstracta* is exhaustive and exclusive: necessarily, every entity either belongs to the ontological category of the concrete or belongs to the ontological category of the abstract, and there could not be an entity belonging to both of these categories. To illustrate the concrete/abstract distinction, we give the following examples of ontological categories which are species of *abstracta* and *concreta*, respectively, together with putative instances of these ontological categories. Species of *abstracta* include Property (for example, greenness, triangularity), Relation (for example, betweenness, diversity), Proposition (for example, that cows are vertebrates, that some vertebrates are dragons), Set (for example, the null set, the set of Thales, Anaximander, and Anaximenes), and Number (for example, the number 6, the number 7). Species of *concreta* include Substance (for example, material objects and spirits), Event (for example, hurricanes and blizzards), Time (for example, instants and durations), Place (for example, points and extended regions of space), Limit (for example, surfaces and edges), Privation (for example, holes and shadows), Trope (for example, the particular curiosity of Aristotle, *that* particular greenness), and Collection (for example, the mereological sum of Mars and Saturn, the mereological sum of Mars, Saturn, and Neptune).

As we have indicated, ontological categories are of various levels of generality, and are related to one another as species and genus. Thus, these categories constitute a system of classification which reflects these logical relations. In what follows we characterize this system.

To begin with, there is an intuitive notion of a hierarchy of levels of generality among ontological categories. We depict this hierarchy in Figure 1.

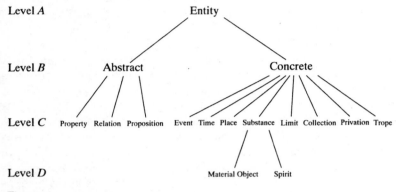

Figure 1

At the highest level (level A) is the category of being an entity which everything instantiates and which is therefore a kind of limiting case. At the next lower level (level B) are the categories of Concreteness and Abstractness. At the next lower level (level C) are the categories which are the various species of *concreta* and *abstracta*. At a level of generality lower than C (call it level D) are those ontological categories which are the various types of the categories at level C. For instance, at level D we find types of Substance, for example, Material Object, or Spirit; types of Event, for instance, Material Event, or Spiritual Event; types of Limit, for example, Surface, or Line, or Instant; and types of Privation, for instance, Shadow, or Hole. More specific kinds are at lower levels of generality. The following list enumerates some typical or core categories that would appear to be at level C.

List L: Property, Relation, Proposition, Event, Time, Place, Limit, Collection, Privation, and Trope.

Intuitively speaking, to say that an ontological category is at level C implies that it is of the same degree of generality as the categories on L. Examples of categories which would seem to be at level C yet which are not on L are Substance and Set.[4] As we shall see, the notion of an ontological category's being at level C can be used to explicate the intuitive distinction between the concrete and the abstract.

A preliminary account of the concrete/abstract distinction which has some plausibility goes as follows. A *concretum* is an entity which enters into spatial or temporal relations, and an *abstractum* is an entity which does not enter into such relations. This preliminary account does not employ the notion of an ontological category's being at level C.

One objection to this account is that there could be a *concretum* that does not enter into spatial or temporal relations, namely, God. However, it is debatable whether such a notion of God is intelligible. Thus, this first objection does not seem to be decisive.

But the preliminary account has a more serious shortcoming. It is that this account implies, incorrectly, that an *abstractum* does not enter into temporal relations. Consider, for example, an *abstractum* such as the property of being attentive. This property does enter into temporal relations, since it is instantiated by Plato at one time and not at another. Of course, attentiveness does not undergo intrinsic change, whereas Plato does. But an entity can enter into temporal relations without undergoing intrinsic change: for instance, a sphere which does not undergo intrinsic change and around which other spheres revolve enters into temporal relations.

We believe that we can improve upon the preliminary account of the concrete/abstract distinction stated earlier. To begin, we presuppose that there is a generic concept of parthood, a concept we take as a primitive. Entities of different kinds may have different kinds of parts, for example, spatial parts (for example, the right and left halves of a material object), temporal parts (for example, the first and second halves of a day), and logical parts (for example, the conjuncts of a conjunctive property).[5] But in the generic sense of "part" that we employ throughout this book, entities of different kinds have parts in the very same sense.

By using the notions of parthood and of a category's being at level C, we analyze the concrete/abstract distinction in the following manner. An entity, x, is concrete if and only if x is an instance of a level C category which could be instantiated by some entity, y, which has spatial or temporal parts; and an entity, z, is abstract if and only if z is not concrete.[6]

This account of the concrete/abstract distinction gives the correct verdict in the two foregoing problem cases. First, God is an instance of a level C category, namely, Substance, which could have some [other] instance with spatial parts, for instance, a cat. Thus, our account of the concrete/abstract distinction has the desired consequence that God is a *concretum*. Our account also has the desirable implication that attentiveness, which is an instance of the level *C* category, Property, is an *abstractum*. This is because there could not be a property which has spatial or temporal *parts*, even if there could be a property which enters into temporal relations.

3 SUBSTANCE

We shall argue that the concept of substance can be analyzed in terms of independence conditions derivative upon an entity's instantiating a level *C* ontological category. A preliminary attempt goes as follows.

(D1) *x* is a substance = df. *x* is an instance of a level *C* category, *C1*, such that: *C1* could have a single instance throughout an interval of time.

By an interval of time we mean a nonminimal time. And by *C1*'s having a single instance throughout such an interval, *i*, we mean that something instantiates *C1* throughout *i*, and there is no other instance of *C1* in *i*.

An entity which could be the sole instance of a level *C* category throughout an interval of time may be said to be independent-within-its-kind. (D1) tells us that among all level *C* categories, the category of substance is *unique* in possessing the potential to have an instance which is independent-within-its-kind. Although (D1) implies that there could be a particular substance that is independent of all other substances, it does not logically imply that *every* substance is independent of all other substances. In particular, (D1) is logically compatible with there being a compound substance that is dependent upon its substantial parts. Thus, according to (D1), an entity, *x* (regardless of whether *x* is simple or compound), is a substance in virtue of *x*'s instantiating a level *C* category which could have a single instance throughout an interval of time. (D1) uniquely characterizes a substance in terms of an independence condition pertaining to the instantiability of level *C* categories.

(D1) is compatible with either of two assumptions. On the first, and more plausible assumption, all individual substances have contingent existence: each such substance could fail to exist. On the second assumption, there is a single necessarily existing substance,

n, such as the God of traditional theism, a substance which could not fail to exist. On either of these assumptions, it is possible for there to be a substance, s, which exists throughout some interval of time, t, without any other substance existing within t. On the first assumption, there could exist throughout t but a single contingent substance. On the second assumption, if n exists in time, then there could exist throughout t but a single necessary substance; and if n exists outside of time, then there could exist throughout t but a single contingent substance.

We are skeptical of the traditional theological claim that God is essentially atemporal and question the intelligibility of there being both something which is in time and some substance which is outside of time. Nevertheless, as we have indicated, we allow for this possibility.[7]

According to Spinoza, necessarily, there is one and only one substance. Thus, (D1) is compatible with Spinoza's ontology of substance, but our analysis, unlike his theory of substance, is compatible with a plurality of substances. This difference illustrates one aspect of the ontological neutrality of our approach.

Another aspect of this ontological neutrality is that our claim that the category of Substance satisfies (D1) is compatible with the claim that every human being must have originated from other *earlier* things, i.e., a sperm and egg.

However, it might be objected to (D1) that if there is an individual substance, then there must be other substances, namely, the parts of the individual substance in question. But it is only true that a *compound* substance must be composed of other substances. It is possible for there to be a *simple* substance that has no other substance as a part, for instance, a voluminous material atom, a Boscovichian point-particle, or a soul.

It is apparent that a soul or point-particle has no other substance as a part; since they are *concreta* which lack spatial extension, they have no parts at all. On the other hand, atoms are voluminous and (hence) spatially extended. Thus, their not having a substance as a part requires some explanation. First, by an atom we mean a material substance which has volume and which is necessarily indivisible. Second, because an atom is voluminous, it has parts. Thus, what we maintain is that the parts of an atom are not substances. Unlike ordinary compound material objects, which depend upon their parts, but whose parts do not depend upon them, an atom is such that it depends upon its parts and its parts depend upon it. That is, neither can exist without the other. This fact about atoms is an implication of their metaphysical indivisibility, which entails the impossibility of the parts of an atom existing apart from the atom. Thus, assuming that there could be a contingently existing atom, a, and assuming that p is a proper part of a, p cannot exist independently of all other contingent substances which are neither proper parts of p nor earlier substances that played a role in the production of p: for p cannot exist independently of a, and a is a contingent substance other than p of the sorts specified. Intuitively, if an entity, e, cannot exist independently of all other contingent substances of the specified sorts, then e is not a substance.[8] Hence, it is plausible that the parts of an atom are not substances. For this reason, we think that the possibility of there being a single atom and no other substance which is not a part of that atom is, in fact, the possibility of there being a single substance. Hence, if it is objected to (D1) that the existence of *any* individual substance entails the existence of substantial parts of that individual substance, then that objection is unsound.

But if the proper parts of an atom are not substances, then what are they? They are not times, places, events, privations, abstract entities, or tropes. Indeed, they are not instances of any level C category so far admitted. It would seem that these entities are in fact instances of a level C category of being a concrete proper part. This category seems to intersect with all of the other level C categories of *concreta* so far mentioned, but is not equivalent to any of them. In fact, this category is not equivalent to any conjunction of the intersections of Concrete Proper Part with the other aforementioned level C categories, for, as we have seen, the proper parts of atoms are not instances of any of those other categories. A further question is this: does the category of being a concrete proper part satisfy the analysans of (D1)? It does not. Clearly, there cannot be just one concrete proper part: by definition, the existence of a concrete proper part of something implies the existence of at least one other concrete proper part. Since the category of being a concrete proper part does not satisfy the analysans of (D1), (D1) implies, correctly, that a concrete proper part, *qua* concrete proper part, is not a substance. This is compatible, as we have indicated, with there being *some* concrete proper parts which are substances, viz., the detachable parts of substances.

In the light of the foregoing arguments, it seems that, possibly, during an interval of time, t, there exists, in space (as opposed to space-time), an indivisible physical substance and no other substance, for example, just one spatially extended material atom, or just one point-particle. Such a physical substance lacks substantial proper parts and cannot undergo mereological alteration. It is extremely plausible to suppose that a simple substance would be essentially simple. Thus, we give no credence to the notion that if there is a simple physical substance, s_1, then this entails that there is *another* simple physical substance, s_2, which is constituted by s_1, spatially coincident with s_1, and possibly *nonsimple*. Moreover, we shall argue later against the reality of emergent nonmaterial physical objects such as s_2. An argument of this kind also implies that no such entailment holds.

We conclude that the category of Substance could have a single instance throughout an interval of time. We shall now proceed to argue that none of the following categories could have a single instance throughout an interval of time: Property, Trope, Relation, Proposition, Set, Place, Time, Limit, Event, and Collection.

4 PROPERTIES AND TROPES

We shall establish that the category of Property does not satisfy (D1) by showing that there could not be just one property. To do this we need to discuss two important views about the existence conditions of properties and other *abstracta*. According to the first view, there are infinite totalities of properties and other *abstracta* which are isomorphic to the infinite totalities of numbers and sets posited by mathematics and set theory, respectively. This view is neutral on the question of whether there are unexemplified properties. According to the second view, for example, as held by D. M. Armstrong, the existence condition of a genuine property is that it is exemplified and needed for the purpose of causal explanation.[9] The second view entails a much more parsimonious ontology of properties than the first, more platonistic view. We shall argue that on either the more platonistic theory of the existence conditions of properties, or the causal theory of their existence conditions, properties fail to satisfy (D1).

On the more platonistic theory, because of the many logical entailments of any property, it is easy to show that there could not be just one property. For example, necessarily, if there is the property of being crimson, then there are other properties, for instance, the property of being red, the property of being colored, and so forth. Moreover, necessarily, if there is the property of being red, then there is another (higher-order) property, for example, the property of being a property, and so on.[10] An argument of the same kind applies to any property whatsoever and implies that there could not be just one property. Parallel arguments apply to other categories of *abstracta*, such as Relation, Proposition, and Set, and lead to the conclusion that there cannot be an entity of such a sort which is the only entity of that sort. In particular, if there is a relation, $R1$, then there must be another relation, $R2$, such that $R1$'s instantiation necessitates $R2$'s instantiation; if there is a proposition, $P1$, then there must be another proposition, $P2$, such that either $P1$ necessitates $P2$ or $P1$ necessitates the negation of $P2$; and if there is a set, then there must be at least two sets, namely, the null set and the null set's singleton. It follows that none of these categories of *abstracta* satisfy the analysans of (D1). Moreover, as far as we can tell, there is no other level C category which satisfies the analysans of (D1) and which could be instantiated by an abstract entity of any of these kinds. Thus, (D1) implies, as it ought to, that neither a property, nor a relation, nor a proposition, nor a set is a substance.

On the causal theory of the existence conditions of properties, the existence of any property, P, entails that an instance of P, i, figures in some causal relationship, so that i figures in a causal relatum R. Supposing that R figures in some causal relationship, there must be another property, P^*, an instance of which, i^*, figures in a causal relatum, S, which is either a cause of R or an effect of R. Evidently, every causal relationship must involve a cause and an effect which differ in their attributes. Hence, on the causal theory of properties, there could not be just one property.

Let us turn our attention to tropes, which are concrete entities. To show that a trope does not satisfy (D1) we need to show that there could not be just one trope. It is relevant that there are two views about the existence conditions for tropes which parallel the two views about the existence conditions of properties described earlier. The first, more generous view, maintains that there is an infinite totality of tropes which is isomorphic to the infinite totalities of numbers and sets posited by mathematics and set theory, respectively. The second, more stingy view, holds that necessarily, a trope exists just in case it is needed for the purpose of causal explanation. We shall argue that on either the more generous theory of the existence conditions of tropes, or the causal theory of their existence, tropes do not satisfy (D1).

On the more generous theory, because of the many necessary

connections between tropes, it is easy to demonstrate that there could not be just one trope. For example, necessarily, if there is a particular crimsonness (say, the particular crimsonness of *that* rose), then there are other tropes, for instance, a particular redness, a particular coloredness, and so forth. Moreover, necessarily, if there is a particular crimsonness (of *that* rose), then there is another (higher-order) trope, for example, a particular tropehood (of the particular crimsonness of *that* rose), and so on.[11]

On the causal theory of the existence of tropes, an argument parallel to the one just given with respect to properties on a causal theory of the existence conditions of properties implies that there could not be just one trope.

Since if there is a trope, *T1*, then there must be another trope, *T2*, the category of being a trope does not satisfy (D1). Furthermore, it would seem that there is no other level *C* category which satisfies the analysans of (D1) and which could be instantiated by a trope. Thus, (D1) has the welcome consequence that a trope is not a substance.

An overall assessment of the status of (D1) vis-à-vis properties and tropes is now in order. We have distinguished more platonistic or generous views of properties and tropes from causal views of them. On the latter views, empirical science alone provides a rationale for the existence of properties or tropes; whereas on the former views, *a priori* sciences such as logic and mathematics provide such a rationale. It is highly plausible that if there are either properties or tropes, then either the more generous view of properties or tropes, or the causal view of properties or tropes, is correct. Since (D1) gives the correct verdict on the status of properties and tropes on either the more generous view of properties or tropes, or the causal view of properties or tropes, namely, that properties and tropes are not substances, it is highly plausible that (D1) gives the correct verdict on the status of entities of these kinds.

5 PLACES, TIMES, AND LIMITS

In what follows, we argue that since there could not be just one place, time, or limit, the categories of Place, Time, and Limit do not satisfy (D1).

We begin by explaining some preliminary concepts. To say that space or time is dense is to say that there are discrete places or times, and that between any two discrete places or times, there is another place or time; and to say that a subregion, R, of space or time is dense is to say that there are point-positions or instants which bound R, and that between any two discrete places or times which belong to R, there is another place or time. A dense space or time (or a dense subregion of space or time) may also be said to be continuous in the sense that the densely ordered series of places or times in question can be put into one-to-one correspondence with the real numbers. On the other hand, space and time are radically discontinuous if and only if there are minimal places and times which have no places and times between them, and for every minimal place or time, m, there is a spatial or temporal direction, d, such that there is another minimal place or time, m', which is *next* to m in direction d.

On the assumption that, necessarily, if space and time exist, then there are dense continua of places and times, it is obvious that there could not be just one place or just one time. Nevertheless, even granting the possibility of radically discontinuous space and time, (D1) has the desirable implication that places and times are insubstantial entities. There are two arguments in favor of this conclusion.

To set up the first argument, let us ask the following question. If it is possible that space and time are radically discontinuous, then could there be but *one* minimum place or time?[12] Necessarily, if space exists, then it is either relational or absolute; and likewise for time. If space and time are relational, which seems to be the majority view these days, then given one minimum place or time, there must be other places or times. This is true for the following reasons. First of all, necessarily, there is relational space only if there are at least two (noncoincident) spatial entities which are spatially related to one another; and necessarily, there is relational time only if there are at least two (nonsimultaneous) occurrences which are temporally related to one another.[13] However, there being at least two such spatial entities entails that there are at least two places, and there being at least two such occurrences entails that there are at least two times. It follows that it is impossible for there to be a relational space or time which consists of just a single minimum place or time. And more generally, we conclude that there cannot be a relational space or time consisting of only one place or time.

On the other hand, suppose that space and time are absolute. In this case, could there be just one minimal place or time? An absolute minimal place or time, existing without any other place or time existing, strikes us as a most peculiar entity. Thus, we don't give much credence to the possibility of there being just one absolute minimal place or time. We remind the reader that our goal in this chapter was to "provide an analysis of substance which is onto-logically neutral, in the sense that it is compatible with the existence of entities belonging to any intelligible categories, given some *plausible* [new italic] view about the natures, existence conditions, and interrelationships of entities belonging to those categories." Elsewhere we have argued that the view that there could be radically discontinuous space or time is not a plausible view about the natures, existence conditions, and interrelationships of spaces or times.[14] Even less plausible in these respects is the claim that there could be a single minimal absolute place or time.

In any case, we have a second, more decisive, argument which demonstrates that there cannot be just one place, or just one time, and which is compatible with space and time being radically discontinuous. It goes as follows.

The notions of time and change are logically interrelated, as are the notions of space and motion. Specifically, each of the following four propositions is a necessary truth: (i) for any c, if c is a change, then c occurs in time; (ii) if time exists, then time allows for the occurrence of change within it – in other words, if time exists, then time has an intrinsic structure which is compatible with the occurrence of change; (iii) for any x, if x moves, then x's motion occurs in space; (iv) if space exists, then space allows something to move within it – in other words, if space exists, then space has an intrinsic structure which is compatible with the occurrence of motion.

However, necessarily, space allows something to move within it only if there are at least *two* places. This is because necessarily, an entity, x, moves only if there is a temporal interval, t, and two places, p_1 and p_2, such that: x (or a proper part of x) occupies p_1 at the start of t, and x (or a proper part of x) occupies p_2 at the end of t.

Notice that necessarily, if an object, x, moves in a linear fashion, then x moves from one place to another. On the other hand, it is possible for an object, x, to move without x moving from one place to another. For instance, this would occur if x is a sphere which rotates on its own axis. However, in any such case, there must be a *proper part* of x which moves from one place to another, for example, a hemisphere of x. Thus, necessarily, if an object, x, moves and x does not have a proper part, i.e., x is a moving point-particle, then x moves from one place to another.

On a proper understanding of what is meant by an atomic or

minimal place, the following principle should be affirmed: necessarily, no minimal place is only *partially* occupied by an entity. Thus, there cannot be rotational motion in a single, minimum, extended place. For if there were such a motion, then, as noted already, a proper part of the rotating object would first occupy only part of the place in question, and then only another part of the place. To put this point in another fashion, the existence of minimal places implies that motions have a minimal size equal to the size of a minimal place. Rotational motion within a single minimal extended place involves angular motions whose sizes are smaller than the size of that minimal place.

Since it is necessary both that space permits motion, and that motion requires more than one place, it is impossible for there to be just one place.

It might be thought that the "Big Bang" theory in cosmology implies the possibility of a single, unextended place. In particular, one might think that the primal "singularity," which exploded in the "Big Bang," was both a zero-dimensional entity and the same size as the entire physical world. Fortunately, it does not seem necessary to understand the "Big Bang" theory in this way. The primal "singularity" might either be minuscule, but extended, or be a zero-dimensional particle occupying an extended absolute space. In any case, a single, unextended place threatens to be a counterexample to (D1) only if such a place can persist. But the "Big Bang" theory provides no reason to think that this is possible, for it seems that if the start of the "Big Bang" were the beginning of extended space, then it would also be the beginning of extended time.

With respect to Time, we observe that necessarily, Time allows for the occurrence of change within it only if there are at least *two* times. This is because, necessarily, change occurs only if there are two times t_1 and t_2 such that either something exists at t_1 which does not exist at t_2, or something exists at t_2 which does not exist at t_1, or something has a certain feature at t_1, but lacks that feature at t_2, or something lacks a certain feature at t_1, but has that feature at t_2. Because it is necessary both that time permits change, and that change requires more than one time, it is impossible for there to be just one time.

It might be objected that the Boethian doctrine that God perceives everything in an eternal "now" implies the possibility of there being a single, unextended, time. But what this Boethian doctrine says (even according to its proponents) is that God is an *atemporal* being.

Thus, if this doctrine is intelligible, then it seems not to imply the possibility of a single, unextended, time, but rather the possibility of some nontemporal mode of being.

Next, we argue that it is impossible for there to be just one limit. The first step is to argue that the existence of a limit is incompatible with the radical discontinuity of space and time. We establish this as follows. A limit, for instance, a surface, a point-limit, or a beginning, is a boundary of an extended entity which has at least one more dimension than the limit in question. But, necessarily, if space and time are radically discontinuous, then there are no such boundaries: there are minimal spatial and temporal entities without any spatial or temporal entities between them, and these minimal spatial and temporal entities do not bound any spatial or temporal entities.

If the minimal temporal or spatial entities are unextended, then, obviously, these entities do not have boundaries. And even if they are extended, it follows (paradoxically) that they do not have boundaries. Suppose that the extended minimal entities in question are spaces or times. Paradoxically, such extended places or times are not bounded, since if they were bounded, there would be places or times, namely, the boundaries in question, which are smaller than the extended places and times with which we began.[15] Alternatively, suppose that the minimal entities in question are extended substances or events. In that case, given the assumption that space and time are radically discontinuous, there are extended minimal places or times which the minimal substances or events occupy. Now suppose that a minimal substance or event has a spatial or temporal boundary, respectively. It follows on this assumption that there is a minimal place or time. This minimal place or time corresponds to the boundary of the minimal extended substance or event, and this minimal place or time is the boundary of the extended minimal place or time which is occupied by the substance or event in question. This contradicts the conclusion of our earlier argument that minimal extended places and times cannot have boundaries. Consequently, there being a limit is incompatible with space and time being radically discontinuous.

We are now in a position to argue that there cannot be just one limit. The foregoing line of reasoning implies that if there is a place or a time which is a limit, then space and time are not radically discontinuous. If space and time are not radically discontinuous, then there are subregions of space and time which are dense continua of places and times.[16] It follows that if there is a place or time which is a limit, then there are infinitely many other such limits. For example, if there is an instant (a time which is a limit), then there must be infinitely many other instants; and if there is a point-position (a place which is a limit), then there must be infinitely many other point-positions. Of course, there could be a limit which is *not* a time or place, for example, a surface, edge, corner, beginning of a process, or ending of a process. But the existence of such limits presupposes that there are other limits which *are* places or times and which are occupied by the former limits. It follows that there could not be just one limit.

There is a second argument which implies that there cannot be just one limit. The first premise is that necessarily, if L is a limit of dimension, n, then there is an extended entity, e, of dimension $n + 1$, such that L is a limit of e. For example, if there is a zero-dimensional corner, there must be a one-dimensional edge whose end point it is; if there is a one-dimensional edge, there must be a two-dimensional surface whose edge it is; and if there is a two-dimensional surface, then there must be a three-dimensional object whose surface it is.[17] The second premise is that necessarily, whatever is extended has extended proper parts. Therefore, necessarily, if there is a limit, L, then there is an extended entity, e, of which L is a limit, and e has infinitely many extended proper parts, for instance, halves, quarters, eighths, and so on, which have boundaries with adjacent extended proper parts of e. Since these boundaries are limits, the existence of L entails that there are infinitely many limits. Hence, there could not be just one limit.

The arguments of this section have shown that Place, Time, and Limit are all such that they cannot have just one instance. Therefore, the categories of Place, Time, and Limit do not satisfy the analysans of (D1). In addition, as far as we can tell, there is no other level C category which could have a single instance throughout an interval of time and which could be instantiated by a place, a time, or a limit. Thus, (D1) has the happy consequence that neither a place, nor a time, nor a limit is a substance.

6 EVENTS

We shall now argue that the category of (concrete) Event does not satisfy the analysans of (D1). We consider two possibilities: either that there could only be events that are of some minimal temporal length, for example, instantaneous events, or that there could be both such events and ones that occur at a temporal interval (i.e., at a nonminimal time). If events could only be of some minimal temporal length, then the level C category of Event does not satisfy the analysans of (D1), because of its requirement that a level C category could have an instance which exists *throughout an interval of time.*

We remind the reader that our analysis of substance is not stated in terms of a notion of what might be termed bare independence, but rather in terms of an enriched notion of independence, viz., independence through an interval of time. (And recall that by an interval or period of time we mean a nonminimal time.) Because of this feature, and because an insubstantial entity of an instantaneous sort, for example, an instantaneous event, cannot, by definition, exist throughout an interval of time, (D1) implies that any such entity is not a substance, even if there being such an entity does not entail that there is any other entity. Therefore, (D1) has the desirable consequence that such events of a minimal temporal length would not be substances.

On the other hand, suppose that there could be events which occur at a temporal interval as well as events of some minimal temporal length. If there is a temporally extended event, e, occurring at a temporal interval, t, then there must also be an event other than e occurring at a time, t^*, which is a part of t. Such an event will be a temporal part of e. Consequently, there could not be an event, e, occurring throughout an interval, t, unless there were *other* events in t.

Thus, whether there could only be events of some minimal temporal length or whether both such events and events which occur at a temporal interval are possible, the category of Event does not satisfy the analysans of (D1). It seems impossible for there to be an event that instantiates a level C category which satisfies (D1)'s analysans. We conclude that an event fails to satisfy the analysans of (D1). Hence, (D1) has the welcome consequence that an event is not a substance.

The following observations show that there are contrasts between the categories of Event and Substance vis-à-vis the analysans of (D1) which are indicative of a fundamental difference between these categories of *concreta.* As we have seen, the occurrence of a temporally extended event, e, at an interval of time, t, entails that e has as a temporal part another temporally extended event which occurs at an interval of time, t^*, such that t^* is a proper part of t.

Recall that because of this entailment, the category of Event does not satisfy the analysans of (D1). On this basis, we concluded that (D1) implies that an event is not a substance.

The contrast between the existential entailments of the occurrence of a temporally extended event and of the existence of an enduring substance vis-à-vis the analysans of (D1) can now be brought out as follows. That a substance, s_1, endures over an interval of time, t, does *not* entail that either s_1 has a temporal part which endures through an interval of time, t^*, which is a proper part of t, or that s_1 has a temporal part which exists at an instant, i, which falls within t. In particular, s_1's enduring through t does not entail that there is another, shorter-lived, nonmomentary, substance, s_2, which is a temporal part of s_1 and which endures through t^*. For example, it is possible for there to be an atom, s_1, and a period of time, t, of one hour through which s_1 persists, while there is no other atom which is a temporal part of s_1 and which only lasts for the first half of t. Notice that (D1) requires that it is possible for s_1 to endure through t while there is no such shorter-lived substance, s_2. This is because according to (D1), a substance is an instance of a level C category such that possibly, this category has a single instance over an interval of time.

We wish to point out that our commitment via (D1) is only to the *possibility* of an enduring substance which does not have substantial temporal parts. Thus, (D1) is compatible with its being *possible* for an enduring substance to have substantial temporal parts, just so long as it is not *necessary* for a substance to have such parts. Some philosophers who prefer an ontology of space-time to one of space and time seem to think that physical substances do in fact have such temporal parts.[18] Again, we can allow for this possibility, just so long as the claim is not that four-dimensionality is *necessary* for the existence of an enduring substance.

Of course, (D1) is compatible with its being *impossible* for there to be an enduring substance which is in space-time. Some philosophers assert this impossibility, for example, Chisholm, Broad, Prior, Geach, and Simons. In particular, Simons wonders whether the notion of an enduring physical object in space-time is capable of an intelligible formulation on the grounds that all attempts thus far to explicate this notion implicitly appeal to an ontology of three-dimensional continuants, while space-time is supposed to preclude the existence of such continuants.[19]

7 PRIVATION

A category of insubstantial entity which has not yet been considered is Privation. But it can be argued that the category of Privation is at level C and could have a single instance throughout an interval of time. Thus, it is arguable that (D1) incorrectly implies that a privation is a substance. If that were the case, then (D1) would not provide a logically sufficient condition for substancehood.

For example, consider the possibility of there being nothing but two temporally separated flashes and a period of darkness, d, between them. The analysans of (D1) requires of a substance that it be an instance of a category which can have but a single instance throughout an interval of time. In our imagined situation, d seems to be the only privation throughout the interval of time in question. Thus, it might appear possible for there to be a single privation throughout an interval of time. Since it can be argued that the category of Privation is at level C, it is also arguable that the category of Privation satisfies the analysans of (D1).

Our first response to the latter argument is to modify (D1) by adding a second clause:

(D2) x is a substance = df. x instantiates a level C category, $C1$, such that: (i) $C1$ could have a single instance throughout an interval of time, and (ii) $C1$'s instantiation does not entail the instantiation of *another* level C category which could have a single instance throughout an interval of time.

By *another* level C category we mean a *nonequivalent* level C category. And by a category F-ness and a category G-ness being equivalent we mean that necessarily, for any x, x is F if and only if x is G.[20] For example, Event and Occurrence are equivalent categories.[21]

Condition (ii) of (D2) implies that an entity, x, is a substance only if x's instantiation of a level C category is *independent* of the instantiation of another level C category which could have a single instance throughout an interval of time. We maintain that the category of Substance satisfies clause (ii) of (D2). Our argument is as follows.

It may be supposed that if there is a substance, then this entails that there are in addition entities of one or more of the following other kinds: properties, or times, or concrete occurrences, or propositions, or places, or limits. However, as argued earlier, the level C

categories that these other entities instantiate do not satisfy clause (i) of (D2). On the other hand, although the category of Privation apparently *does* satisfy this clause, there being a substance obviously does *not* entail that there is a privation. So, our contention is that any level C category the instantiation of which is entailed by the instantiation of the category of Substance either does not satisfy clause (i) of (D2), or else is equivalent to the level C category of Substance. It follows that the category of Substance satisfies clause (ii) of (D2), a clause requiring the possibility of a level C category being instantiated without there existing an entity of another level C category that satisfies clause (i) of (D2).

As we have seen, the category of Substance satisfies clause (i) of (D2). Thus, if the instantiation by an entity, x, of a level C category, $C1$, other than Substance, entails the instantiation of the category of Substance, then $C1$ fails to meet clause (ii) of (D2). And if there is no other level C category which satisfies clauses (i) and (ii) of (D2) and which x instantiates, then (D2) implies that x is not a substance.

Condition (ii) of (D2) is an Aristotelian independence require-ment. An Aristotelian would argue that the instantiation of *any* level C category other than Substance entails the instantiation of the category of Substance. He would argue that necessarily, there is a property only if there is a substance which exemplifies a first-order property; necessarily, there is a limit only if there is a *concretum* of a certain kind which is limited, and there being a *concretum* of that kind entails the existence of a substance; and that insubstantial entities of other categories, for example, tropes, events, times, places, privations, and collections, depend upon substances in sim-ilar ways. Such an Aristotelian argument implies that every level C category instantiated by a nonsubstance fails to satisfy clause (ii) of (D2), and hence that any nonsubstance fails to satisfy (D2). Although an argument of this kind lends further support to our analysis of substance, and has some attractions, we do not need or want to appeal to it. Nevertheless, it can be argued that at least *some* categories of concrete entities other than Substance could not be instantiated unless the category of Substance were instantiated, for instance, being an event, being a trope, and being a privation. Thus, arguably, entities of these categories are not substances because of the failure of these categories to satisfy clause (ii) of (D2).

Let us assess the plausibility of such an argument with respect to privations. Does the existence of a privation entail the existence of a substance? If the answer is yes, then the category of Privation will not satisfy clause (ii) of (D2). On the other hand, if there could be events (or tropes) without substances, as event (or trope) ontologists believe, then it seems that there *could* be a privation without a substance. For example, there could be a period of darkness which exists between two temporally separated flashes. For the following reasons, we hesitate to insist that events, tropes, and privations depend upon substances. First, some philosophers have held event or trope ontologies, according to which there are events but no substances,[22] or tropes without substances. Other philosophers, such as Aristotle, have argued that one cannot conceive of a change without a subject of change. However, we hold that our conceptions of ontological categories are suggested to us by our experiences. Since some of our experiences of events (for example, our seeing a lightning bolt) are not experiences of a substance or any other subject undergoing change, the existence of such events seems to be conceivable. For this second reason we do not assert that it is impossible for there to be events without substances. Of course, one might hold that a lightning bolt does in fact involve substances undergoing change, viz., charged particles in motion. However, it is the *possibility* of there being events without substances which is at issue here. Finally, if there could be events without substances, then there could be privations without substances, as argued earlier.

On the other hand, if there could not be an event or trope without a substance, then it seems that there could not be a privation without a substance. Thus, whether privations satisfy clause (ii) of (D2) turns on further metaphysical questions of these kinds. Since we prefer to remain neutral about the answers to these questions, we need to amend (D2). Although clause (ii) of (D2) may not be sufficient to solve the problem about privations, this clause will be retained because it helps to deal with other categories discussed later. Accordingly, we amend (D2) by adding a third clause, thereby arriving at our final proposal.

(D3) x is a substance = df. x instantiates a level C category, $C1$, such that: (i) $C1$ could have a single instance throughout an interval of time, and (ii) $C1$'s instantiation does not entail the instantiation of another level C category which could have a single instance throughout an interval of time, and (iii) it is impossible for $C1$ to have an instance which has as a part an entity which instantiates another level C category, other than Concrete Proper Part, and other than Abstract Proper Part.

Three comments about clause (iii) of (D3) are in order.

First, note that if *both* concrete and abstract proper parts are possible, then a putative *ontological category* of being a proper part would seem to be both below level *B* and not a species of either being concrete or being abstract, something which is impossible. Thus, being a proper part is a *category* only if either just concrete proper parts are possible or just abstract proper parts are possible. But neither of these alternatives is evidently the case. It is for this reason that in clause (iii) of (D3) we speak instead of the categories of being a concrete proper part and being an abstract proper part.[23]

Second, notice that if Concrete Proper Part and Abstract Proper Part were counted as level *C* categories, then apparently there could be a substance which has an entity of another level *C* category as a part. The portion of clause (iii) of (D3) which excepts the categories of Concrete and Abstract Proper Parts takes care of this possible difficulty. Henceforth, this complication can be ignored.

Third, observe that clause (iii) of (D3) expresses an independence condition. In particular, this clause implies that an entity, *x*, is a substance only if *x* is an instance of a level *C* category whose instantiation by an item is *independent* of any *other* level *C* category's being instantiated by a *part* of that item.

We are now ready to argue that the category of Privation does *not* satisfy clause (iii) of (D3), a clause which requires that it be impossible for an entity of a level *C* category to have as a part an item which instantiates another level *C* category. We shall argue that it *is* possible for there to be a privation which has as a part an item that is not a privation.

To begin with, a privation is a concrete entity which is an absence of a concrete entity or entities. Intuitively, a privation is either wholly extended between parts of a bounding concrete entity or wholly extended between bounding concrete entities. For example, the hole in a doughnut is an absence of the sort of cake of which the doughnut is made. This hole is wholly extended between *parts* of the doughnut. Another example is Franconia Notch. This notch is wholly extended between the peaks of the Franconia and Kinsman mountain ranges, for the notch does not extend above the tops of those peaks.

It would seem that if a privation such as a hole (in a doughnut) exists, then it has as a part each one of the extended places inside that hole. For instance, the hole has a certain volume of space as its right half, and another volume of space as its left half.

To this it might be objected that a hole does not have *places* as parts, but other privations. For example, it might be argued that a round hole, h, has around its perimeter numerous concavities which face inward toward its axis, and that each of these concavities is a part of h. This may be correct. But consider a circular place, c, whose axis is the same as that of h, whose radius is half the length of the radius of h, and whose perimeter is everywhere equidistant from the perimeter of h. c is a part of h, but there is no entity which is coincident with c, and which is a privation on our definition, since there is no bounded absence which is coincident with c. Thus, while some of the parts of h may be privations, at least some of the other parts of h must be places and not privations.

Notice that our view that a hole in a doughnut has places as parts implies, first, that when the doughnut moves, the hole moves, but, second, that when the hole moves, it must lose some or all of these places as parts. To this it may be objected that when a thing moves all of its parts can move with it. Our reply is twofold. First, it is true that if by a "thing" is meant a *substantial being*, then when a thing moves all of its parts can move with it. But, of course, a hole is *not* a thing in this sense, but rather a privation, an insubstantial being. Second, although we are willing to concede the existence of holes for the purposes of our analysis, it must be admitted that holes are peculiar entities which are ontologically suspect. As we see it, the fact that holes must alter some of their parts whenever they move is one aspect of their oddness.

It also appears possible for a privation to have *times* as parts. For example, it seems that if there is a period of darkness which is temporally extended between two temporally separated flashes, then that period of darkness has as a part each one of the temporal intervals between the flashes, that is, the periods of time through which the darkness in question endures. Since every such subinterval of the period of darkness is not bounded by flashes, and since, intuitively, a period of darkness (or any other privation) must be bounded by light at each end (or by something of a relevant sort), there is no period of darkness which is coincident with any such interval, and, we may assume, no other privation which is coincident with some such subinterval. Hence, every period of darkness has parts which are not privations.

These two examples illustrate the fact that it is possible for some privations to have places or times as parts. But we may assume that the categories of Place and Time are at level C and other than Privation. It follows that the category of Privation fails to satisfy clause (iii) of (D3). Additionally, as far as we can see, there is no other level C category which satisfies the analysans of (D3) and which could be instantiated by a privation. Hence, (D3) has the desired consequence that a privation is not a substance.

We shall now argue that the category of Substance, unlike the category of Privation, does satisfy clause (iii) of (D3). To begin with, clause (iii) of (D3) requires that it be impossible for an entity which is an instance of a level C category, $C1$, to have a part that instantiates another level C category. So, let $C1$ = Substance. Is it possible for a substance to have a part that instantiates another level C category of the sort in question? For example, is it possible for a material thing or a nonphysical soul to have as a part either an event, a property, a time, a place, a privation, a limit, or a proposition? Certainly not, since a part of a material substance could only be a material substance or a portion of matter, and since a nonphysical soul is a simple thing. And in general, a part of a physical substance could only be a physical substance or a portion of physical stuff. Hence, it appears to be impossible for a substance to have a part that instantiates another level C category of the sort under discussion. Thus, the category of Substance seems to satisfy clause (iii) of (D3).

These claims about the parts of a physical substance can be supported by the following line of reasoning. A substance can have an entity of another (level C) kind as a part only if a substance is reducible to or identifiable with an entity of that kind or a collection of such. Based on our argument that a substance is *not* reducible to or identifiable with an entity of another kind or ontological category, we conclude that a substance cannot have as a part an entity of another (level C) kind.[24]

It might be objected that a physical object can be said to have a privation or a limit as a part, for example, an organism's bodily orifices are integral parts of it, or the boundary of a handball court is a part of it. We answer that in these examples "part" is being used in a metaphorical sense. The meanings of these sentences are captured in the following translations: an organism's bodily orifices have important functions; and the boundary of a handball court is on the court. These translations do not imply that an organism has an orifice, or that a court has a boundary, as a part. Moreover, since orifices are ontologically suspect, and an organism is not, it is doubtful that an organism can have an orifice as a part. Also notice that when it is said that a handball lands on the court's boundary, this does not imply that it lands *only* on the boundary, since the court's boundary is one-dimensional and a handball is of higher dimensionality. Lastly, it seems to be necessarily true that for any physical object, x, and any proper part, y, of x, the existence of y does not entail that there is a nonbasic physical object of which y is a proper part. Yet, if an orifice is a proper part of an organism, or a boundary of a court, then the existence of this orifice or boundary entails that there is a nonbasic physical object of which that orifice or boundary is a proper part. Thus, an orifice seems not to be a part of an organism, and a boundary seems not to be a proper part of a court. In sum, we find it plausible, *a priori*, that a limit or a privation is not a part of a substance.

8 COLLECTIONS

Next, let us consider the category of being a (concrete) collection. We shall argue that this category fails to satisfy clause (iii) of (D3). This clause of (D3) requires that it be impossible for an entity of a level C category to have as a part an item which instantiates another level C category. However, a member of a collection is a part of that collection, and it is clearly possible for some collections to have as members items which instantiate a level C category other than the category of Collection, for example, items such as substances, events, and places. Hence, the category of Collection does not satisfy clause (iii) of (D3). Moreover, as far as we can tell, there is no other level C category which satisfies the analysans of (D3) and which could be instantiated by a collection. Therefore, (D3) has the intuitively plausible consequence that a collection is not a substance.

In addition, if a collection, c_1, exists throughout a nonminimal time, t, then c_1 must have at least two parts, x and y, both of which exist throughout t. In that case, there must exist a shorter time, t^*, which is a subtime of t and which is part of another collection, c_2, for example, a shorter-lived collection either composed of t^* and x, or composed of t^* and y. Hence, it seems that if a collection, c_1, exists throughout an interval of time, t, then there must be another collection, c_2, that exists in t. Thus, it can be argued plausibly that the category of Collection also fails to satisfy clause (i) of (D3).

9 OTHER CATEGORIES

Schemes such as Aristotle's provide a fixed list of categories of being. It is tempting to argue along Aristotelian lines that L contains every level C category except for Substance. Nevertheless, we allow that there might be level C categories not on L in addition to Substance. Someone might suggest as examples of such categories Sense-Datum, Nation, and Sentence-Type. However, it would seem that each of *these* examples is a species of a category at level C. For instance, it can be persuasively argued that Sense-Datum is a species of Event, Nation is a species of Collection, and Sentence-Type is a species of Property. If so, then the categories of Sense-Datum, Nation, and Sentence-Type are *not* at level C, and these categories are too specific to be values of the category variable in (D3).

On the other hand, assume for the sake of argument that these categories *are* at level C. We contend that on this assumption these categories fail to satisfy (D3). For example, if there is a nation, then it is possible for a nation to have a city as a part. Moreover, if being a nation is at level C, then being a city is also at level C. Finally, being a nation is other than being a city. It follows that since a nation could have as a part an instance of another level C category, being a nation does not satisfy clause (iii) of (D3).

Furthermore, as we stated earlier, we presuppose that an individual substance is not reducible to or identifiable with an entity of another ontological category. Given this presupposition, and assuming that the categories of Nation and Sense-Datum are at level C, it is extremely plausible that the instantiation of either one of these two categories entails that the category of Substance is instantiated, i.e., that there is a piece of territory or a person, or that there is a sensing organism or creature, respectively. For reasons explained earlier, this entailment, together with the fact that the categories of Nation and Sense-Datum are other than the category of Substance, implies that the categories of Nation and Sense-Datum do not satisfy clause (ii) of (D3). Hence, we infer that these categories do not satisfy this clause. On the other hand, being a sentence-type fails to satisfy clause (i) of (D3). This is because there cannot be just one sentence-type.

Thus, if the categories of Nation, Sense-Datum, and Sentence-Type are at level C, then none of these categories satisfies the analysans of (D3). Furthermore, it appears that if the categories of Nation, Sense-Datum, or Sentence-Type are at level C, then there is no other level C category which satisfies the analysans of (D3) and which could be coinstantiated with one of the former categories. Therefore, (D3) has the welcome implication that neither a nation, nor a sense-datum, nor a sentence-type could be a substance.

Another possible example of a level C category is the category of being a space-time. The concept of space-time does not, of course, belong to the ordinary conceptual scheme, but arises from philosophicoscientific theorizing. Since our system of categories is open to suggestions from such sources, our analysis of substance should be adequate to them as well. This category is distinct from the categories of Place and Time, since places have only spatial dimensions, and times have only temporal dimensions, but space-times have both spatial and temporal dimensions. On the other hand, intuitively, space-time is like space and time in being both insubstantial and concrete. The insubstantiality of a space-time can be argued for as follows.

(i)   Necessarily, if a space-time is a substance, then it is a physical substance.
(ii) Necessarily, if there is a physical substance, then it could move.[25]
(iii) Necessarily, if there is a space-time, then it could not move.

Therefore,

(iv) Necessarily, a space-time is not a substance.

This conclusion can also be supported by means of the following related argument.

(a) Necessarily, if a space-time is a substance, then it is a physical substance.
(b) Necessarily, if there is a physical substance, then it *occupies* (or is *in*) either a place or a space-time.
(c) Necessarily, if there is a space-time, then it does not *occupy* (or is not *in*) either a place or a space-time.

Therefore,

(d) Necessarily, a space-time is not a substance.

In defense of (c), notice that although it can be said that every space-time is either a proper or improper *part* of some space-time, and that every space-time stands in spatiotemporal relations to other space-times, for example, spatiotemporal distance relations, this is *not* to say that a space-time *occupies* or is *in* a space-time. Similarly, although it can be said that a space-time is *identical with* a space-time, this is *not* to say that a space-time *occupies* or is *in* a space-time. It is an entity such as a physical object, event, or trope, and not a space-time, that could occupy a space-time.

Fortunately, though, the category of Space-Time fails to satisfy clause (i) of (D3). Arguments parallel to those which show that the categories of Place and Time fail to satisfy this clause show that the category of Space-Time cannot have just one instance over an interval of time. Accordingly, arguments parallel to those which show that (D3) implies that a place or a time is not a substance show that (D3) implies that a space-time is not a substance. This is a desirable outcome.

Arguments parallel to the foregoing ones seem to apply to any other possible level C category, for example, to categories of *concreta* such as being a reflection, being a rainbow, or being a storm, and to categories of *abstracta* like being a set, being a number, or being a fact. In other words, either such a category is a species of a category at level C (for example, Set and Number are species of Property, Fact is a species of Proposition, and Reflection, Rainbow, and Storm are species of Event), or else such a category is at level C but there is no level C category which could be coinstantiated with it and which satisfies the analysans of (D3) (for example, the categories of Set, Number, and Fact do not satisfy clause (i) of (D3), and if the categories of Reflection, Rainbow, and Storm are at level C, then these categories do not satisfy clause (ii) of (D3)). Thus, it seems that there is no counterexample to the sufficiency of (D3) in which a nonsubstance instantiates a level C category not on L.

If our analysis, (D3), of the concept of an individual substance is correct, then this concept can be analyzed in terms of a conjunction of three independence conditions. Unlike some previous accounts, (D3) does not claim that other kinds of entities depend on substance, but not vice versa. Thus, (D3) does not assert that substances possess a *two-term* asymmetric independence of all other sorts of entities. Instead, (D3) asserts a more complex asymmetric independence of substance.[26]

Chapter 3

On the unity of the parts of mereological compounds

1 KINDS OF COMPOUND PHYSICAL THINGS AND THEIR UNITY

A compound physical substance or thing is one which has parts, parts which can be separated or detached from the object in question. One kind of compound physical object which belongs in any comprehensive physical ontology is a mereological compound, or compound piece of matter. Necessarily, at any time at which a mereological compound exists it has its parts essentially. In other words, a mereological compound cannot undergo mereological change: it cannot gain or lose a part. We can distinguish three other kinds of compound physical objects. First, an artifact is a physical object such as a house, a knife, a chain, or a thermometer. Second, an organic living thing is a physical object such as a fish, a cat, or a tree. Finally, an inanimate natural formation is a physical object such as a glacier, a crystal, a mountain, or a lake. Because an artifact, an organic living thing, or an inanimate natural formation can undergo mereological change, and because a mereological compound cannot, a mereological compound is to be distinguished from a physical object of any of these three kinds.[1]

According to a key commonsense intuition, there is a relation that unites parts which compose a compound physical object. An implication of this intuition is that a compound physical object can be created or destroyed by assembly or disassembly. On the other hand, basic material objects *cannot* be created or destroyed by assembly or disassembly. Consider a voluminous Democritean atom that has a left half and a right half. Although such a basic particle has parts, it is indivisible. The unity of a particle of this sort is a limiting case of the unity of the parts of a material substance, for the parts of a particle of this kind have a unity in virtue of their being inseparable.

Given the assumption that all individual substances are physical, at least the following two types of compound physical objects seem to exist and be subject to creation and destruction by assembly or disassembly: (i) mereological compounds, for instance, a steel rectangular solid, and (ii) living things, for example, a human being, a fish, or an oak tree. For example, according to common sense, a rectangular solid is created when two cubes are glued together, and will be destroyed if those cubes are pulled apart, and an organism comes into being when a sperm fertilizes an egg, and will pass away if that organism is dismembered. It seems that the relations which unite or organize the parts of compound inanimate objects and organic living things are *causal* ones of some kind. In particular, a mereological compound consists of a number of material objects held together by an appropriate unifying causal relation, one whose instantiation by material objects is logically necessary and sufficient for those material objects to compose a mereological compound. In this chapter we defend an analysis of such a causal relation, thereby providing a principle of unity for the parts of a mereological compound. In the next chapter we defend an analysis of a causal relation whose instantiation by physical things is logically necessary and sufficient for those physical things to compose an organism, thereby providing a principle of unity or organization for the parts of an organism. By a principle of unity or organization for the parts of a mereological compound or an organism, we mean a principle which asserts that necessarily, material or physical things are united or organized into a mereological compound or an organism if and only if those things instantiate a causal relation of the sort in question.

2 TWO SENSES OF "SUBSTANCE"

We begin with the observation that some of our ordinary discourse about material substances is not about material objects. Some of this discourse concerns quantities of matter, or stuff, of various kinds, for example, water, gold, or beef. Consequently, it is vital to draw a distinction between "substance" in the stuff sense and "substance" in the count sense.

This distinction is nicely illustrated by a possible ambiguity in the sentence "Mary had a little lamb."[2] On one possible reading, this sentence means that Mary owns a small lamb, that is, Mary owns a certain sort of living thing or individual substance. On another possible reading, that sentence means that Mary ate a small amount, or quantity, of lamb. The count sense of "lamb" is employed in the first reading, and can be used to ask how many individual substances of a certain sort exist. For instance, how many lambs did Mary own? Answer: just one, whose fleece was white as snow, and so on. In such a case "lamb" functions as a count noun. The stuff sense of "lamb" is used in the second reading, and can be used to ask how much there is of a certain kind of stuff. For example, how much lamb did Mary have for dinner? Answer: just two ounces. Similarly, to say that there are elements and compounds such as gold and water is to employ "gold" and "water" in the stuff sense. In other words, it is to employ "gold" and "water" as mass terms. In such a case one is talking about a quantity of matter of a certain kind, and the parts of such a quantity of matter (like the parts of a collection or mereological sum) need not be (but may be) united into a complex material object.

The applicability of a substance term, *T1*, in the stuff sense presupposes the applicability of a substance term, *T2*, in the count sense. In other words, there could not be a quantity of material stuff of some sort unless there were one or more material objects of some kind. On the other hand, it seems that the applicability of a substance term, *T1*, in the count sense does *not* presuppose the applicability of a substance term, *T2*, in the stuff sense. That is, it appears that there could be a substance of some sort, the existence of which does not imply that there is a quantity of stuff of some kind. This is because it is apparently possible for there to be an individual substance which has no proper parts, for example, a soul (which is a nonphysical substance), or a point-particle (which is a physical substance, but is not material in any robust sense), and it seems that neither a soul nor a point-particle is made of stuff of any sort. Another powerful reason for thinking that "substance" in the count sense is ontologically prior to "substance" in the stuff sense is that stuff cannot be formless: any quantity of stuff must be ultimately analyzed in terms of one or more objects. For example, a quantity of water consists of a certain number of hydrogen and oxygen atoms and a quantity of gold consists of a certain number of gold atoms. Thus, it seems that "substance" in the count sense is more fundamental than "substance" in the stuff sense.

There is at least one prominent metaphysician who disagrees, arguing that "substance" in the stuff sense is more fundamental than "substance" in the count sense. This is Michael Jubien, who says that:

> I am taking it as a fundamental ontological doctrine that the raw material of the physical universe is *stuff*, not *things*, and that the organization of (some or all of) this stuff into things is done by *us*.[3]

This conclusion follows from his claim that something's having the status of a material object is a function of how we view the stuff occupying certain regions, whereas something's having the status of material stuff is not a function of how we view anything. Jubien's argument depends on his claim that ordinary thinghood is the relational property, being a thing for us, and that what has this relational property is material stuff. According to Jubien:

> To believe that there is nevertheless some independent, non-relational property of *thinghood* . . . is surely too much to believe.[4]

In our view, ordinary thinghood *is* such an independent nonrelational property. We answer Jubien's argument as follows.

First of all, our analysis of the ordinary notion of thinghood in terms of ontological independence implies that ordinary thinghood is not a relational thinker-dependent property. Moreover, Jubien's account of ordinary thinghood in terms of being a thing for us seems to be unacceptable. In particular, it appears that his account is inadmissibly circular in two ways. First, it plainly employs the notion of a thing, the very notion Jubien is trying to explain. Second, it obviously employs the notion of *us*, or the notion of *ourselves*, or the notion of *people*, all of which are notions of *things* (in this case living things) in the very sense Jubien is seeking to explain. Furthermore, Jubien's account of thinghood seems to generate a paradox. Insofar as *we* are things, Jubien's account of thinghood implies that we exist *because* we hold the view that we exist. Yet, surely, it is only *because* we exist that we hold the view that we exist. Thus, given Jubien's account of thinghood, it seems to follow that, paradoxically, we exist because we hold the view that we exist, and we hold the view that we exist because we exist! Circular explanations of this sort are unintelligible. For these reasons, we conclude that Jubien has not provided a good reason to think that "substance" in the stuff sense is ontologically prior to "substance" in the count sense.

3 SKEPTICISM ABOUT THE COMMONSENSE VIEW OF COMPOUND OBJECTS

According to our commonsense intuitions about the creation or destruction of compound material objects by assembly or disassembly, it is essential to a material object that its parts have some principle of unity or organization (for instance, one which involves some kind of adherence). But it is *not* essential to a collection or mereological sum that its parts have a principle of unity of this sort. Hence, if the aforementioned commonsense intuitions are correct, then it is impossible for a material object to be identified with a collection or sum of other material objects (its parts). Such an identification would in that case be a category mistake.

However, our commonsense intuitions about the creation and destruction of compound material objects have been called into question. Let us call the intuitive datum that there are material objects which can be created or destroyed by assembly or disassembly the commonsense view. This commonsense view has been disputed in at least three ways.

First, monadism attacks the commonsense view on the ground that only true atoms or indivisibles exist.[5] Monadism has the radical implication that there are no compound material objects, either living or nonliving. Second, collectivism denies the commonsense view on the ground that any two material objects, no matter how scattered, compose a material object.[6] According to the collectivist, for any two material objects, x and y, there is a third material object, z, which is the collection or sum of x and y, and which has no proper parts which are not parts of either x or y (or both). Collectivism has the rather startling implication that there is a material object composed of the Moon, Mount Everest, and a particular platypus in Australia. It should be noted, however, that accepting that there are *collections* of such widely separated and apparently disconnected objects does not commit one to *collectivism*, since, as we have seen, if the commonsense view is correct, then a material object cannot be identified with a collection of this kind. Third, monism disputes the commonsense view on the ground that there is only one object, namely, the universe as a whole.[7] Each of these three alternatives to the commonsense view implies that if an object is created or destroyed, then it is created *ex nihilo* or destroyed *in nihilum*. In fact, in many instances these views are motivated by the idea that substances can neither be created nor destroyed.

Of course, monadism, collectivism, and monism are likely to strike ordinary folk as counterintuitive, if only because they are incompatible with the commonsense belief that material objects can be created or destroyed by assembly or disassembly. Furthermore, monism has an additional very serious disadvantage: it is inconsistent with something that appears to be an evident datum of experience, namely, that there is a plurality of things. We shall assume that a plurality of material things exists, and hence that monism is false.

Monadism, collectivism, and the commonsense view are consistent with there being a plurality of things. However, since monadism and collectivism are incompatible with the intuitive data concerning the creation or destruction of material objects, neither of these views is acceptable unless there are other intuitive data that lend it some support. Skepticism about the intelligibility of the relations which are commonly thought to unify or organize the parts of material objects, or claims of ignorance about the exact nature of those unifying or organizing relations, might be thought to provide such an argument in favor of monadism or collectivism. Such skepticism or claims of ignorance might be fueled by developments in modern science, developments which are themselves well confirmed by experiential data. For example, the laws of physics imply that in all but extremely exceptional circumstances, no two physical objects touch (strictly speaking) because of the presence of repulsive forces between fundamental particles. That is, physics implies that in at least the great majority of cases, any two material objects are at a positive distance from one another. In the absence of a clear account of the relations which are commonly thought to unite the parts of material objects, the monadist might argue that two material objects compose a third object only if they are at a zero distance from one another. The monadist could then appeal to the aforementioned implication of modern physics, and conclude that the common belief that there are nonfundamental material objects is mistaken. Given that there are fundamental particles (which are indivisible), it would follow that such particles are the only material objects. On the other hand, the collectivist may accept both the commonsense belief that there are nonfundamental material things, and the scientific belief that no two material objects are at a zero distance from one another, and conclude that there *are* nonfundamental things whose parts are at a positive distance from one another. Generalizing from this conclusion, the collectivist may infer that *any* two things, regardless of their distance from one another, compose a third thing. The collectivist might even admit that two things cannot compose a third thing unless there is a force which unites those two things. For the collectivist might argue that mutual gravitational attraction is a force which unites any two objects in the universe.

As we have noted, the commonsense view presupposes that mereological compounds and organic living things can be created or destroyed by assembly or disassembly. Thus, the skeptical attacks of the monadist and the collectivist upon the commonsense view can be answered if one can provide a satisfactory analysis of the causal relations that unify or organize the parts of mereological compounds and organic living things which is consistent with this presupposition of the commonsense view. In particular, skeptical attacks of these kinds are answerable if one can provide an adequate analysis of these relations that meets two conditions. First, it must be less strict than the monadistic view that two things are united only if they are at a zero distance from one another. Second, it must be more stringent than the collectivist view that mutual gravitational attraction between things is sufficient for them to be united. In this chapter, and the one to follow, we shall defend the commonsense view by developing such analyses for mereological compounds, and for organic living things, respectively.

4 PRELIMINARY DATA FOR ANALYSES OF UNITY

Suppose that two steel cubes come into contact (in the ordinary sense) but are not joined (they fail to adhere to one another). Does the mere contact of these two cubes create a mereological compound of which these cubes are parts? Intuitively, the answer in such a case is that the two cubes are *not* united into a third, rectangular mereological compound.

Because the mere contact of two nonadhering material objects does not create a mereological compound, and because the material objects composing a typical liquid or a gas, even if in contact, do not seem to adhere to one another in the relevant sense, a typical liquid or gas does not appear to be a mereological compound. Such a liquid or gas seems to be a quantity of matter of some kind: it appears to be substance in the stuff sense, but not a substance in the count sense. Arguably, a liquid or gas of this kind can be identified with a collection or mereological sum of atoms or molecules. But as we have argued, a material object in the ordinary sense cannot be identified with such a collection or mereological sum. It remains to be seen, however, whether there is a satisfactory account of the relation that unifies the parts of a mereological compound and which supports these claims about liquids and gases.

With respect to organic living things, notice that there is a way in which they resemble mereological compounds: the coming into contact of two organic living things is insufficient for the creation of an organic living thing which is composed of those two living things. Thus, given a pair of organic living things (or a pair of mereological compounds), something other than contact between the members of the pair is necessary in order for those members to be united into a third organic living thing (or a third mereological compound). In the case of the two inanimate steel cubes, what seems to be necessary is that the cubes *adhere* to one another in some way. For instance, the cubes can be united into a third noncubical substance with glue or screws or hooks or by melding the two cubes together into a seamless whole. By contrast, it is clear that two organic living things can be attached to one another by using glue or screws or hooks, or fused together in the manner of Siamese twins, without those two living things thereby being united into a third living thing. Hence, the unifying relation that organizes two or more organic living things, for example, two or more cells, into a more complex or multicellular organic living thing is *other* than the unifying relation which binds two or more inanimate material objects into a more complex inanimate mereological compound. As we have seen, the relevant unifying relation between nonliving material objects obviously involves adherence of some kind, although the nature of this unifying relation stands in need of clarification. But the nature of the relevant unifying relation among parts which compose an organic living thing is more difficult to characterize. For as we have seen, it is not adherence of a straightforward sort, and yet there are processes of assembly or disassembly, such as fertilization or dismemberment, which can result in the creation or destruction of organic living things.

5 AN ANALYSIS OF THE UNITY OF A MEREOLOGICAL COMPOUND

We turn next to the task of analyzing the causal relation which unifies the parts of a mereological compound. This task will be carried out in three stages. First, we develop an informal account of this causal relation and explain certain preliminary concepts which will be utilized in our final formal analysis. Second, we discuss the nature of bonding forces according to currently accepted theories of empirical science. Third, we present and defend a formal analysis of the causal relation in question which is compatible both with currently accepted empirical science and with the existence of mereological compounds.

To start, let us reflect upon the way in which the parts composing a mereological compound are causally interrelated. Consider, for example, this mereological compound: a piece of solid oak in the shape of a cylinder, six inches long and one quarter inch in diameter. On first thought, it seems relevant that in a wide range of normal circumstances, if we pull or push one half of the cylinder in any direction, then this results in the other half of the cylinder being pulled or pushed in that direction. Yet, it must be admitted that this result fails to occur even under some quite ordinary conditions. For instance, if a sufficiently powerful force is applied to one half of the cylinder, while the other half of the cylinder is held rigidly in a vise, then this results in the cylinder's snapping in half, with one end remaining at rest in the vise, and the other half moving away from the vise.

But there is another way of thinking about the causal relation among the cylinder's parts which avoids this difficulty. Roughly speaking, it is that this causal relation's being instantiated by the halves of the cylinder consists in there being a causal relation, R, that holds between these halves, such that either half of the cylinder *may* be pushed or pulled in any direction by pushing or pulling the other half of the cylinder in that direction in virtue of R's holding between the halves in question. (In this context, "may" means "it is physically possible that" or "it is compatible with the laws of nature that," and "in virtue of" means "because of.")

However, this proposal seems subject to another related problem. Even if R holds between the halves of the wooden cylinder, it is clear that it does *not* hold between every pair of parts which compose a mereological compound. For example, consider a mereological compound, W, consisting of a short and flimsy piece of cotton thread, T, that is glued with household cement to an object, M, that weighs several tons. We may assume that if we try to pull M in some direction, d, by pulling T in d with sufficient force, then either T, or the bond between T and M, will break, and in either case, M is not pulled in d by pulling T in d. Thus, it may be wondered whether our second way of thinking about the interrelationship of the wooden cylinder's parts is any more fruitful than the first.

Here is a preliminary sketch of a solution to this problem. To begin with, notice that although, as we have seen, T does *not* bear the causal relation, R, to M, T *does* bear R to some suitably small and lightweight part, P, of M, to which T is glued. That is, P may be detached from the rest of M, and under such conditions, either T or P may be pushed or pulled in any direction by pushing or pulling the other in that direction in virtue of a causal relation holding between T and P. This suggests that when a number of material objects $P_1 \ldots P_n$ compose a mereological compound it need not be true that any two of $P_1 \ldots P_n$ bear R to one another, but rather it must be true that each one of $P_1 \ldots P_n$ (or a part thereof) bears R to *some* other one of $P_1 \ldots P_n$ (or a *part* thereof), yet in such a way that all of $P_1 \ldots P_n$ (or *parts* thereof) are connected to one another through a finite number of instances of R. A formal account of the principle of unity for the parts of a mereological compound in terms of this concept of connectedness will be developed and defended later.[8]

But what is the nature of the causal relation R? A hint about how to answer this question was provided by the stoic philosopher Nemesius. As he observed:

> To activate the body, there is an inward motion balanced with an outward motion (which accounts for the tension), thus giving rise to the equilibrium of anything.[9]

Following this hint, we analyze the causal relation, R, as follows:

> (D1) R is a relation of *dynamic equilibrium* holding between discrete[10] material objects O_1 and O_2 = df. (i) R is a relation which holds between O_1 and O_2, and (ii) R is necessarily such that, for any x and y, R holds between x and y if and only if (a) there are attractive forces between x and y, and (b) there are repulsive forces between x and y, and (iii) the attractive forces of (ii)(a) and the repulsive forces of (ii)(b) are in equilibrium.

Metaphorically speaking, any relation of dynamic equilibrium holding between material objects O_1 and O_2 composing an object must balance the elements of "love" and "hate" between O_1 and O_2.[11] If an object composed of O_1 and O_2 were to lose the attractive elements, while retaining the repulsive elements, then that object would be apt to disintegrate, and if an object composed of O_1 and O_2 were to lose the repulsive elements, while retaining the attractive elements, then that object would be apt to collapse into a zero-dimensional entity lacking parts altogether.[12] This appears to be a necessary truth knowable *a priori*. Thus, it seems that the characteristic stability of a nonbasic material object could only result from a balance of the elements of "love" and "hate" between its parts.

As we have defined the notion of a relation of dynamic equilibrium, it can be the case that some such relations are weak, some strong, and some of intermediate strength. In analyzing the unifying causal relation that holds among a set of parts which compose a mereological compound we aim to identify an adherence relation, viz., a relation of dynamic equilibrium of the right strength. The notion of a relation of dynamic equilibrium which we have defined in (D1) is a technical one. We shall utilize this technical notion in our explication of the causal relation which unites parts that compose a mereological compound. The relation of dynamic equilibrium in question is not to be confused with the yet to be defined causal relation or with any of the other, more intuitive, concepts of adhesion, bonding, attachment, fastening, or the like.

According to currently accepted scientific theory, which seems to have originated with the work of Ludwig Seeber in 1824,[13] the adherence relation instantiated by parts that compose an actual mereological compound results from an equilibrium of attractive and repulsive forces of certain kinds among those parts. The particular nature of such an adherence relation is an empirical question to be decided by scientific investigation of the mereological compound in question. For example, it has been discovered that there is a relatively long-range attractive force between atoms or molecules as well as a relatively short-range repulsive force which comes into play when the atoms or molecules are close to one another. Current scientific theory implies that an equilibrium must obtain at some middle distance at which the net force is zero.[14]

What does physics have to say about the nature of these forces? Physics recognizes four fundamental forces, and if material objects are attached to one another, by gluing, fastening, linking, interlocking, fusing, grasping, suction, and so on, then this attachment can ultimately be explained in terms of one or more of these four forces.[15] These four fundamental forces are: (1) gravitational attraction, (2) the electromagnetic force, manifested in various kinds of chemical bonds and magnetic forces, (3) the strong force, which is stronger than any other known force, and (4) the weak force, which affects elementary particles and causes some cases of particle decay, nuclear beta decay, and the ejection and absorption of neutrinos. On any intuitive conception of bonding, the weak force is too feeble to bond objects together, and likewise for gravitational forces unless very large masses are involved. In contrast, the strong force is responsible for the binding together of neutrons and protons in the atomic nucleus. Finally, the forces between atoms and molecules are electromagnetic in nature, and include the forces associated with ionic bonds (bonds in which atoms "couple" through electron transfer), the forces associated with covalent bonds (bonds in which atoms "couple" through sharing electrons), Van der Waals forces, repulsive forces, and the forces associated with metallic bonds.[16]

Thus, the parts of the mereological compounds found on Earth are held together in virtue of the strong force (which is operative only at the subatomic level) and the electromagnetic force (which is involved at the interatomic and intermolecular levels).

It seems that if two material objects x and y physically bond with one another to form a mereological compound at a time t, then at t there must be a definite distance d such that if x were farther than d from y at t, then x and y would not bond with one another. But, as noted earlier, physics implies that x and y are at a positive distance from one another because of repulsive forces between fundamental particles. However, the assumption that $d > 0$ does not entail that there is no distance d of the sort that appears to be required. Physics implies that there is a precise positive distance (or at least a definite spatial region) at which (or within which) the attractive forces which bind x and y together and the repulsive forces which keep x and y apart come into balance or equilibrium, and it would be plausible to identify d with this distance (or with the maximum width of the region in question). We shall understand the attachment or bonding of two pieces of matter x and y, or the bonding of a surface or edge of x to a surface or edge of y, in such a way that it is compatible with, but does not require, x's being at a zero distance from y.

We can now provide an account of the principle of unity for the parts of a mereological compound. The first step is to construct a suitable technical conception of *joining* between material objects in terms of the notion of a relation of dynamic equilibrium and other ideas presented earlier.

(D2) Discrete material objects x and y are joined at a time t = df. at t, there is a relation of dynamic equilibrium, E, holding between x and y such that for any direction, d, it is both (i) physically possible that x is pulled or pushed in direction d thereby pulling or pushing y in direction d in virtue of E's holding between x and y, and (ii) physically possible that y is pulled or pushed in direction d thereby pulling or pushing x in direction d in virtue of E's holding between x and y.

For example, consider the right and left halves of our wooden cylinder. From our earlier discussion of this example, it is clear that (D2) implies that these two halves are joined. That is, these two halves are an x and a y that meet conditions (i) and (ii) of (D2). In contrast, the wooden cylinder, and an inclined plane upon which it rolls downward, are material objects which are not joined: they are an x and a y that meet neither condition (i) nor (ii) of (D2). Nor is the cylinder joined to the Earth, since in that case only *one* of the two conditions set forth in (D2) is satisfied: although it is physically possible to pull or push the Earth in any direction thereby pulling or pushing the cylinder in that direction in virtue of the forces which hold between the Earth and the cylinder, it is not physically possible to pull or push the cylinder in any direction thereby pulling or pushing the Earth in that direction in virtue of those forces. Similarly, a piece of flimsy cotton thread that is glued to a massive object weighing several tons is not joined to that massive object, because just one of the two conditions set forward in (D2) is met: while it is physically possible to pull or push the massive object in any direction, thereby pulling or pushing the piece of thread in that direction in virtue of the forces which hold between the massive object and the piece of thread, it is not physically possible to pull or push the piece of thread in any direction, thereby pulling or pushing the massive object in that direction in virtue of those forces. Since, intuitively, the piece of thread is attached to the massive object, thereby forming a mereological compound, the joining relation specified in (D2) cannot be identified with the relation commonly thought to attach one part of a material object to another. The latter relation is transitive, whereas the joining relation specified in (D2) is not. Finally, suppose that a nut-shaped piece of iron is threaded onto a bolt-shaped piece of iron: are they joined or not? The answer depends upon the exact circumstances. On the one hand, suppose that the nut-shaped piece of iron is loose, and that turning it in some direction doesn't cause the bolt-shaped piece of iron to turn in that direction. In that case, at most one of the two conditions in (D2) is satisfied, and therefore the nut and the bolt are not joined. On the (D2) is satisfied, and therefore the nut and the bolt are not joined.

other hand, suppose that the nut-shaped piece of iron has been tightened up, so that by turning the nut-shaped piece of iron one thereby turns the bolt-shaped piece of iron, and vice versa. If so, then both of the conditions in (D2) are satisfied, and the nut-shaped piece of iron and the bolt-shaped piece of iron are joined.

By making use of the concept of joining defined in (D2), and the standard formal notion of connectedness, we can define the following notion of material objects $P_1 \ldots P_n$ being connected via the joining relation (or joined and connected for short).

(D3) Discrete material objects $P_1 \ldots P_n$ are connected via the joining relation at a time t = df. at t, for any two of $P_1 \ldots P_n$, P_x and P_y, there is some finite number of joinings, each of which joins one of $P_1 \ldots P_n$ (or a part thereof) to another one of $P_1 \ldots P_n$ (or a part thereof), by which a path can be traced from P_x (or a part thereof) to P_y (or a part thereof).

The promised principle of unity for the parts of a mereological compound can now be expressed as the following necessary equivalence.

(P_{MC}) (Discrete material objects $P_1 \ldots P_n$ are united into a mereological compound at a time t) ⇔ (at t, $P_1 \ldots P_n$ are connected via the joining relation).

In the light of our earlier explanations, we can see that (P_{MC}) has the desirable implication that each of the following pairs of material things is united into a mereological compound: the right and left half halves of our wooden cylinder, a bolt-shaped piece of iron and a nut-shaped piece of iron which is tightened on the bolt-shaped piece of iron, and a piece of flimsy cotton thread and a very heavy object to which it is glued. For in each of these cases, the pair of objects in question satisfies (D3), i.e., they (or some parts of them) are connected via the joining relation, even though in the third case they fail to satisfy (D2), i.e., they are not joined. It is also clear, given our previous discussions, that (P_{MC}) has the welcome implication that the following pairs of material things are *not* united into a mereological compound: the wooden cylinder and the inclined plane that it is rolling down, the wooden cylinder and the Earth, and the bolt-shaped piece of iron and the nut-shaped piece of iron which turns freely on the bolt-shaped piece of iron. Because (P_{MC}) has the correct implications in these cases, and in many other similar ones that the reader is invited to imagine, (D3) seems to provide a satisfactory analysis of the causal relation which is intuitively thought to unite the parts of a mereological compound.

It was argued earlier that typical liquids and gases are not mereological compounds. Thus, if our account of the relation that unifies the parts of a mereological compound is compatible with this argument, then there is further confirmation of our account. Accordingly, let us see why our account is consistent with our claim that typical liquids and gases do not qualify as mereological compounds.

To begin with, when a body of water is in the liquid state, any two of its water molecules are electromagnetically bonded or joined to one another for only some trillionths of a second before they shift partners and electromagnetically bond or join to other water molecules. This pervasive and frenetic promiscuity among water molecules ensures that the molecules which compose such a body of water are not joined and connected. The standard model of this situation likens a liquid mass of water molecules to a mass of ball bearings which slide more or less freely past one another. This model may help one to understand why it is that the water molecules which compose a body of water in the liquid state are not joined and connected. Moreover, there is some reason to think that in a liquid mass of water there are gaps between water molecules opening up here and there at random, a phenomenon that is not represented in the foregoing model, even though that model is useful in other respects.[17] Notice that the latter phenomenon implies as well that a liquid mass of water molecules are not joined and connected. We conclude that a liquid mass of this kind is not a mereological compound.

Liquids and gases can both be classed as *fluids* in the sense that their atoms or molecules move with great ease among themselves, or freely over one another, so as to give way before the slightest pressure. However, unlike liquids, the atoms or molecules of a gas have a tendency to separate from one another. Since the atoms or molecules of a liquid such as a body of water are not joined and connected, and since the atoms or molecules of a gas are even less closely associated with one another, we conclude that the atoms or molecules comprising a gas are not joined and connected. Therefore, a gaseous mass of this kind does not qualify as a mereological compound.

Consider the case of a mereological compound that is solid, hollow, and filled with a liquid or gas such as water or oxygen, for example, a hollow iron sphere filled with liquid water or gaseous oxygen. Our account of the relation which unites the parts of a mereological compound implies that there does not exist a mereological compound composed of the sphere's iron atoms and the molecules of water or oxygen inside the sphere, inasmuch as it is not the case that all of these atoms and molecules are joined and connected. Thus, in general, a *container* is a material object that is discrete from any liquid or gaseous matter it contains, and there does not exist a mereological compound composed of a container *and* any liquid or gaseous matter it contains.

As we have stated, in our view it is an *a priori* truth that stability entails a dynamic equilibrium of the specified kind. This view might be questioned as follows. Consider, for example, a chain-like structure consisting of (fairly tightly fitting) links extending in three orthogonal directions. Such an entity would move as a unitary whole, though at rest, there would be no strong attractive forces between the links keeping them from moving apart, and no strong repulsive forces between them making them tend to move apart. That is, there would not be a "dynamic equilibrium" between the links of the sort we require. The difference between such a chain-like structure and the sort of structure we require for stability is that in the former, the relevant forces only come into operation shortly after various parts of the object are pushed or pulled, so that there is some "give" between these parts, whereas in the latter, the forces are constantly in operation, so that there is no "give." However, it is possible for there to be a macroscopic object whose microstructure is a chain-like structure of the sort described. And it is possible for our observations of such an object's macroscopic behavior when it is pushed or pulled to give us every reason to believe that it is a paradigm case of a "solid" object. It might be inferred from this that stability does *not* entail a dynamic equilibrium of the sort we have described.

We answer this objection in two ways. First, if we were able to see (what are in fact) microscopic objects, then the structural difference between the two types of objects under discussion *would* result in observable differences in the behavior of each type of object, when various of their parts were pushed or pulled. That is, we would observe some "give" in one case and not in the other. Since the principle of unity for the parts of a material substance cannot be logically dependent on the resolving power of the sense-organs of human (or other) observers, no reason has been provided to doubt that stability entails a dynamic equilibrium of the sort we require. Second, it is clear that a *macroscopic* chain-link structure of an ordinary sort does not display the characteristic stability of a "solid" object. Thus, it is intuitive that an ordinary chain is not such an object. This is true as well of a corresponding microscopic chain. Hence, in the case of a macroscopic object with a chain-link microstructure, there is a set of nonsolid parts, i.e., microscopic chains, which compose that macroscopic object. Yet, it seems that if an object is composed of parts which are not solid, then it itself is not solid.

Thus, in the light of the foregoing two replies, it appears that a macroscopic object with a chain-link structure is not "solid." We conclude that the objection under discussion does not succeed.

All material substances which do not perceptibly flow are commonly regarded as *solids*, but between an ordinary solid and an ordinary liquid there are many intermediate forms, for instance, viscous solids, semi-solids, and viscous liquids. We have argued that typical solids, unlike typical liquids, are mereological compounds. But given the gradations that exist between typical solids and typical liquids, can a precise distinction be drawn between mereological compounds and masses of atoms or molecules which are not mereological compounds? We believe that such a distinction can be drawn. After all, for *any* material objects $P_1 \ldots P_n$, (D1), (D2), (D3), and (P_{MC}) together provide a precise and determinate answer as to whether or not $P_1 \ldots P_n$ are united into a mereological compound. In other words, there is always a fact of the matter as to whether or not $P_1 \ldots P_n$ are joined and connected at some time. Determining in a particular case whether or not some $P_1 \ldots P_n$ are joined and connected at a particular time is an empirical question that is to be decided by scientific means. Of course, we readily admit that there might be an instance of some form of matter intermediate between typical solids and typical liquids with respect to which making such a determination is a daunting task. However, although we admit that in some cases there might be *empirical* difficulties in ascertaining whether or not certain objects are united into a mereological compound, no reason has yet surfaced for thinking that there is any *conceptual* difficulty in drawing a precise distinction between those masses of atoms and molecules which are so united and those which are not.

We are now in a position to respond to the arguments for monadism and collectivism stated earlier. These skeptical arguments were based on modern science and raised doubts about there being mereological compounds or inanimate objects which can be created or destroyed by assembly or disassembly. On the one hand, the monadistic argument implied that two things are united only if they are at a zero distance from one another. On the other hand, the collectivistic argument implied that mutual gravitational attraction between things is sufficient to unite them. Our analysis of the causal relation that unites the parts of a mereological compound seems to answer these monadistic and collectivistic arguments, since our analysis of this causal relation appears to have found the appropriate middle ground between the overly restrictive monadistic account and the excessively permissive collectivistic account. Accordingly, our analysis of the causal relation in question is compatible both with the existence of mereological compounds or inanimate objects which can be created or destroyed by assembly or disassembly and with current scientific theory about the structure of such compounds.

Chapter 4

On the unity of the parts of organisms

1 THE CONCEPT OF ORGANIC LIFE

We believe that we have provided an understanding of the unity of the parts of a mereological compound, but as yet the nature of an organizing causal relation for the parts of an organism remains something of a mystery. As indicated earlier, understanding the organization of the parts of an organism promises to be a more challenging problem than that of understanding the unity of the parts of a mereological compound, given the complexity of the former. Before turning our attention to solving this difficult problem, let us discuss the notion of organic life that this problem presupposes.

Many biologists deny the possibility of providing a satisfactory definition of organic life in terms of attributes that are empirical in character. They argue that the question "What is organic life?" cannot be answered by identifying a logically necessary and sufficient condition of organic life which is both empirical and explanatory.

It must be admitted that many difficulties stand in the way of providing such a definition of organic life, and that no definition of this kind is generally agreed upon by biologists or philosophers today.[1] Nor do we ourselves propose to construct such a definition of organic life.[2]

However, some biologists have even argued that because it is impossible to define organic life empirically, organic life is an unintelligible notion.[3] This should strike us as somewhat paradoxical, since we naturally understand the job of biologists to be the study of organic life, and because we view those who have this job as organic living things themselves! In any event, the argument of these skeptical biologists is invalid, for it might be the case that organic life is a coherent but primitive notion. Although it would be somewhat surprising should the notion of organic life turn out to be an undefined or primitive concept, it would be better to say this than to deny the existence of all organic living things, including ourselves.

Moreover, and more importantly, it is by no means a settled matter that an empirical definition of the notion of organic life is impossible. The chief obstacle thought to stand in the way of the construction of such a definition is the unavailability of a *precise* empirical criterion for distinguishing between organic living things and nonliving things. Obviously, we have no difficulty distinguishing living from nonliving things in a great many cases. But, supposedly, there is a continuum of intermediate cases which stand between organic living things and typical nonliving things, and consequently, we have no way of drawing a sharp line between the living and the nonliving. Viruses are often given as examples of borderline cases which we can neither classify as living nor classify as nonliving in any principled way.[4] But just how serious is this apparent obstacle?

On the one hand, although our talk about things may be vague, and our knowledge of things may be incomplete, it appears that the things themselves must be fully determinate. This observation seems just as applicable to living things as it is to any other sort of things. Thus, simply put, our lack of an exact empirical criterion for distinguishing between organic life and nonlife might be due to our ignorance of the precise empirical criterion. This possible explanation of our lack of such a criterion is compatible with there being a way, in principle, to define the concept of organic life in purely empirical terms. It might be just that this way of defining the concept has yet to be discovered.

On the other hand, even if a term, concept, or attribute is vague or indeterminate, it may be definable in terms of some other vague term, concept, or attribute. For instance, even if the concept of organic life is vague, it may still be definable in terms of a mix of empirical concepts some of which are equally vague and some of which are less so. These empirical concepts may include a vague concept of "reproduction" understood as a thing's causing something resembling itself to exist, a precise concept of "growth" understood as a thing's increasing in mass, and so on. Analogously, even if it is indeterminate when a boy becomes old enough to qualify as a bachelor, we can nonetheless say that a bachelor is an unmarried man, since it is equally indeterminate when a boy becomes old enough to qualify as a man. Hence, another possible explanation of our lack of a precise empirical criterion for distinguishing between organic life and nonlife is the inherent vagueness of the organic life/nonlife distinction. But, as we have seen, this possible explanation is also compatible with there being a way to define the concept of organic life in empirical terms.[5]

We conclude that our lack of a precise empirical criterion for distinguishing organic life from nonlife does not imply the impossibility of an empirical definition of organic life. And in fact, as far as anybody knows, an empirical definition of organic life is possible. Surely, it is premature to despair of discovering such an account merely because one has not been forthcoming so far. It may be the case that a combination of intellectual insight and advances in the biological sciences will someday result in a satisfactory empirical definition of organic life. Thus, although we currently lack such a definition of organic life, we have no reason to doubt the intelligibility of that notion. Accordingly, we assume that the philosophical questions we have posed concerning the principle of organization for the parts of organic life-forms are meaningful ones.

2 ORGANISMS AND ARISTOTELIAN FUNCTIONS

We now turn our attention to the problem of providing a principle of organization or unity for the parts of an *organism*. Our investigation into the unity of the parts of a mereological compound involved discussions of ideas from physics and metaphysics. Both empirical scientific theories and *a priori* methods of philosophical analysis played a role in solving the problems addressed in that investigation. Similarly, our inquiry into the organization of the parts of an organism will involve discussions of ideas from biology and metaphysics. In this case, too, theories of empirical science and *a priori* techniques of conceptual analysis will each have a part to play.

Examples of organisms are tigers, trees, paramecia, bacteria, algae, and mushrooms. Necessarily, something is an organism only if it is an organic living entity which is not a *part* of another organic living entity. On the other hand, it seems that a nerve cell, a brain, and a central nervous system are organic living entities which typically *are* parts of another organic living entity, for example, a tiger. Thus, organic living parts of these kinds typically do not qualify as organisms.[6]

There are at least two reasons to think that *qua* living things, full-fledged organisms are ontologically more fundamental than other organic living entities. First, although organic living parts of an organism have their own life-processes, there is a sense in which they do not have a life of their own: their life-processes subserve those of the organism of which they are parts. Second, since it is possible for there to be a unique first organism lacking *any* living parts, which dies before it has a chance to reproduce, there could be an organism even if no other organic living entity ever exists. In contrast, because living entities which are not organisms can only exist in virtue of the existence of organisms which evolve specialized functions, there could not exist an entity of the former sort unless there were a preexisting organism. This asymmetrical dependence of living entities which are not organisms upon organisms suggests that the former are not genuine substances. Typically, at least, living entities which are not organisms are proper parts of organisms, and the latter *are* genuine substances even if the former are not. In any case, our main goal is to provide a satisfactory principle of organization for the parts of an *organism*, an entity which is an organic living thing in a robust sense of *thing*.

As far as we know, Aristotle was the first figure to pursue systematic scientific studies in the areas of biology and metaphysics. He is also the first thinker to see a clear connection between the two areas. Moreover, Aristotle was particularly interested in the parts of living things and their principle of organization. He discusses these matters primarily in *Parts of Animals*, and to a lesser extent in his other biological treatises.[7] On becoming acquainted with *Parts of Animals*, no less a figure in the history of modern biology than Darwin wrote that Linnaeus and Cuvier, two biologists he had absolutely idolized, "were mere schoolboys to old Aristotle."[8] As we shall see, Aristotle's insights remain valuable for those who seek to understand the nature of living things.

According to Aristotle, the parts of living things exhibit purpose or function. Speaking perceptively of such bodily parts, Aristotle says:

> It is from a consideration of their functions that alone we can derive any knowledge of them.[9]

This idea seems to be no less important for biology today than it was in Aristotle's day. More specifically, any realistic account of the epistemology of biology presupposes that there is an intuitive sense in which the parts of organisms have natural functions. As the following citation illustrates, Aristotle argues that the functions of the parts of living things derive from Nature:

> Nature creates nothing without a purpose, but always the best possible in each kind of living creature by reference to its essential constitution.[10]

He also realizes that artifacts have functions:

> Every instrument and every bodily member is for the sake of something, viz., some action. . . . Thus, the saw is made for sawing, for sawing is a function, and not sawing for the saw.[11]

Together, these two citations imply that in Aristotle's view, there is a single, intuitive sense of "function," a sense in which artifacts as well as certain parts of organisms have functions, that is to say, a sense in which things of both of these sorts are *for*, or *for the sake of*, some end.[12] In this sense of "function," φing is a function of *x* just provided that *x* is *for* φ-ing.

However, there are two species of function, artificial and natural. Artifacts can be said to have artificial functions. For example, knives have an artificial function; they are *for* cutting things. This appears to be true because we are intelligent beings, and we designed the knife to cut things. In other words, a knife is capable of cutting things *because* it was designed and produced by human beings to do so.

On the other hand, certain parts of organisms can be said to have natural functions. For instance, a heart has a natural function: it is *for* pumping blood. Assuming, as we do here, that there is no evidently acceptable candidate for the role of an intelligent designer in the case of the heart, we may be puzzled as to *why* it is the case that the heart is for pumping blood. Aristotle hypothesizes that it is a basic fact about the nature of the heart that it is for the sake of a good end, i.e., for pumping blood. Generalizing from this case, and innumerable other examples of bodily parts and organs that have natural functions, Aristotle concludes that functions or purposes, in the sense of being "for the sake of" something, are ubiquitous in nature:

> Whenever there is plainly some final end, to which a motion tends should nothing stand in the way, we always say that the one is for the sake of the other; and from this it is evident that there must be something of the kind, corresponding to what we call nature. . . .[13] Absence of haphazard and conduciveness of everything to an end

are to be found in nature's works in the highest degree, and the end for which those works are put together and produced is a form of the beautiful. . . .[14] Invariably she brings about the best arrangement of such as are possible. . . .[15] Nature never makes anything superfluous or in vain.[16]

For example, Aristotle believes that purpose and function are involved in such varied phenomena as the vital organs of animals, the motions of celestial bodies, and the tendency of heavy objects to fall toward the center of the Earth.

Like most contemporary philosophers, we do not accept Aristotle's idea that it is a fundamental fact that certain natural things or processes are for the sake of (good) ends. Nor do we think that function and purpose are as pervasive in the natural world as Aristotle thinks. For example, near the Earth's surface we observe that an unsupported stone falls toward the center of the Earth. Although falling in this direction is something that a stone *does*, it is not plausible that a stone's doing this is a function of the stone in the relevant sense. That is to say, it is not intuitively plausible that a stone's doing this is *for* something. Nevertheless, Aristotle believes that a stone's falling toward the center of the Earth *is* for the sake of something. In particular, he thinks that a stone is a heavy object, the center of the Earth is the center of the universe, and the falling of heavy objects in the cosmic scheme of things is for the sake of reaching the center of the world. Aristotle believes that this is something that Nature causes heavy objects to do for some good end. But modern science can explain why an unsupported stone near the Earth's surface falls toward the center of the Earth in terms of ordinary efficient causation,[17] i.e., natural laws and physical conditions that do not involve any reference to function or purpose, and there seems to be no reason to accept Aristotle's purposive or teleological description of this sort of motion.[18] In the same way, modern scientific explanations of the motions of the heavenly bodies undermine Aristotle's descriptions of these motions as having natural functions or purposes. Thus, Aristotle's assumption that Nature is purposive or teleological receives no support from either the physics of terrestrial motion or astronomy.

More plausible evidence for this assumption derives from biology: it is indeed intuitively plausible that a heart, for example, is *for* pumping blood. Aristotle is aware of the possibility of explaining a heart's having this function in terms of developmental or evolutionary processes of a nonpurposive sort, but he maintains that no explanation of this kind is correct. Thus, he remarks that:

> When we are dealing with definite and ordered products of nature, we must not say that each *is* of a certain quality because it *becomes* so, rather that they *become* so and so because they *are* so and so, for the process of becoming attends upon being and is for the sake of being, not *vice versa*.[19]

But unfortunately for Aristotle's philosophy of biology, it seems that modern science can explain why hearts pump blood in terms of natural selection and evolution without assuming that Nature is fundamentally purposive or teleological. Thus, there appears to be no good reason to accept Aristotle's contention that it is a *fundamental* fact about the nature of hearts that they are for pumping blood.

Aristotle believes that a part of an organism, say, a heart, is in one key respect quite analogous to an artifact, for example, a knife. He would say that a knife is sharp *because* its being sharp is something which suits it to an end or purpose for which it was intended by its human creator, viz., cutting, and that a heart is muscular *because* its being muscular is something which suits it to an end or purpose for the sake of which it was created by Nature, viz., pumping blood. As Aristotle says:

> Just as art is present in the products of art, so in the things themselves there is evidently an analogous cause or principle derived like the hot and the cold from the environing universe.[20]

But although Aristotle incorrectly believes that the source of functionality in living things is the fundamental purposiveness of Nature, his comments about the functions which living things have which we have quoted remain largely true, even if the functionality of living things is ultimately the result of the nonpurposive processes of natural selection and evolution. Moreover, the last quotation implies that a creature's structure and powers are the (more immediate) effect of a substantial or formal principle within the creature. According to Aristotle:

> The principle object of natural philosophy is not the material elements, but their composition, and the totality of the substance, independently of which they have no existence.[21] ... In order of time, then, the material and the generative process must

necessarily be anterior; but in logical order the substance and form of each being precedes the material.[22]

Aristotle's notion that the powers and structure of an organism are determined by an internal "form" of the organism anticipates the currently accepted theory in biology that the information which directs an organism's development is encoded by organic macromolecules within the organism. Our account of the principle of organization for the parts of an organism will presuppose this theory.

We have argued against the Aristotelian view that natural function can be understood in terms of the idea that there are irreducibly teleological explanations of natural objects, processes, or powers. Notoriously, Aristotle's account does *not* provide a naturalistic reduction of natural function in terms of efficient causation. Nor do characterizations of natural function in terms of an irreducibly emergent purposive principle, or an unanalyzable emergent property associated with the biological phenomenon of life, provide such a reduction. Theistic and vitalistic approaches that try to explicate natural function in terms of the intentions of an intelligent purposive agent or principle are also nonnaturalistic. Another form of non-naturalism attempts to explicate natural function in terms of non-natural evaluative attributes such as intrinsic goodness, for example, the view that ϕ-ing is a natural function performed by a part, x, of an organism, O, just in case x ϕs, and x's ϕ-ing does x good by promoting things that are intrinsically good for O.[23] The only other sort of approach that we need to consider here is both reductionistic and naturalistic, and seeks to provide a reductive account of the natural functions of the parts of organic life-forms wholly in terms of nonpurposive phenomena such as natural selection and evolution.

We do not accept the anti-reductionist and anti-naturalistic theories about natural function listed above. Without entering into a detailed critique of these ideas, one can see that they either posit immaterial entities whose existence is in doubt, or make it utterly mysterious how it can be true that a part of an organic living thing manifests a natural function.

However, since there is such a strong intuition that eyes, ears, hearts, kidneys, and so on are *for*, or *for the sake of*, things, viz., inputting visual data, inputting auditory data, pumping blood, cleaning blood, and so forth, one might be forced to accept this mystery if all attempts to provide a reductive account of such natural functions prove to be unsatisfactory. Clearly, though, the theoretical unity of biology would be better served if the natural functions of the parts of organic life-forms could be given a reductive account completely in terms of nonpurposive or nonfunctional naturalistic processes or conditions. For in that case, we would avoid all of the dubious entities and mysteries referred to earlier. Accordingly, for our working hypothesis, we place ourselves squarely within that school of thought that endeavors to provide a reductive account of such natural functions wholly in terms of the nonpurposive naturalistic conditions or processes involved in natural selection and evolution.[24]

It will be helpful to clarify further what we mean by a non-functional/nonpurposive naturalistic condition or process in this context. Recall the difference between saying that the heart pumps blood, and saying that the heart is *for* pumping blood. To say that the heart pumps blood is to describe the heart in nonfunctional/nonpurposive terms. It is not to attribute a *telos*, function, or purpose to the heart. In contrast, to say that the heart is *for* pumping blood is to attribute a function to the heart, and it is not obvious how this functional description of the heart can be reductively defined just in terms of nonfunctional/nonpurposive processes or conditions. Accordingly, by such a naturalistic condition or process we mean a condition or process that can be fully described in terms of nonfunctional or nonteleological concepts as employed in the core natural sciences of physics, chemistry, and biology.

3 WHAT IS THE CAUSAL RELATION THAT UNITES THE PARTS OF AN ORGANISM?

As we argued in the preceding chapter on the unity of parts of mereological compounds, material objects $P_1 \ldots P_n$ being joined and connected is logically necessary and sufficient for $P_1 \ldots P_n$ to compose a mereological compound. Every organism is either unicellular or multicellular, and a multicellular organism is composed of a multiplicity of nonorganismic living entities. Yet, a set of atoms or molecules composing a functioning organism, whether unicellular or multicellular, are *not* joined and connected. This is implied by the following two facts. First, any *functioning* organism is in large measure composed of organic solids and liquid water intermingled. Second, since liquid water consists of molecules which are not joined and connected, liquid water cannot be joined and connected to a surrounding container, for example, a cell wall or membrane.

Thus, atoms or molecules which compose an organism can be joined and connected only if that thing is in a *nonfunctioning* state, for instance, a dormant state in which it is totally desiccated, or a state in which it is frozen solid. Since organisms are not usually in such a state, it is apparent that the principle of organization for the parts of an organism should *not require* that parts which compose an organism be joined and connected. This fact serves to distinguish sharply the unity of the parts of an organism from that of the parts of a mereological compound. It is clear from the fact that all or most living things are in part liquid that the unity of their parts requires instead that parts which compose an organism be interconnected via some causal relation other than that of being joined and connected. Thus, the central question confronting us has to do with the nature of this other causal relation.

4 ARISTOTLE'S ACCOUNT OF UNITY

As we have seen, the nature of a principle of organization for the parts of an organism cannot be understood just in terms of the parts being causally interrelated in the ways that we have discussed in connection with mereological compounds. What, then, is this principle of organization? Aristotle's answer is that this principle is functional in nature, and can only be understood in terms of the natural functions had by the parts of a living thing. We find Aristotle's answer to be a perceptive one, and the reader will be able to discern later the ways in which it anticipates the principle of organization for the parts of an organism that we shall provide. In Aristotle's formulation:

> The fittest mode, then, of treatment is to say, a man has such and such parts, because the essence of man is such and such, and because they are necessary conditions of his existence, or if we cannot quite say this . . . then the next thing to it . . . that it is good that they should be there.[25]

> When a function is ancillary to another, a like relation manifestly obtains between the organs which discharge these functions; and similarly, if one function is prior to and the end of another. . . . Thirdly, there are functions which are the necessary consequences of others. Instances of what I mean by functions and affections are

Reproduction, Growth, Copulation, Waking, Sleep, Locomotion, and other similar animal actions. Instances of what I mean by parts are Nose, Eye, Face, and other so-called members; and similarly for the rest.[26]

In what follows, we take note of a number of the significant points which Aristotle makes about the principle of organization for the parts of animals, and then begin to develop our own proposed principle of organization for the parts of an organism.

Aristotle, of course, recognizes that some parts of an organism are vital for, or essential to, the organism's existence, for example, the heart of a human being.[27] He also distinguishes these vital parts from other bodily parts which are not necessary for an organism to exist, but which nonetheless have a natural function, for example, the limbs of a human being.[28] Moreover, Aristotle observes that some other parts of an organism are causally necessary antecedents or consequents of vital parts or parts which have natural functions.[29] In addition, he recognizes functionally interrelated levels of composition within organisms. He distinguishes heterogeneous parts, for example, the kidneys, the bladder, and so forth, homogeneous parts, for example, flesh, bone, and the like, and even more basic material constituents.[30] Furthermore, he admits that a part may exist because of nonpurposive natural laws, or "blind necessity," but may come to be used by nature with a function.[31] Additionally, in Aristotle's view, certain parts of an organism are united in virtue of jointly performing some natural function, and therefore compose a single part of the organism in question.[32] This view suggests, for example, that a human's right lung is a part of a human, a human's left lung is a part of a human, *and* a human's respiratory *system* is a part of a human. Finally, Aristotle recognizes that a principle of organization for the parts of an animal should give the correct verdicts on whether or not a part belongs to an animal in certain problem cases, for example, cases involving imperfect or mutated animals of various sorts.[33]

Our principle of organization for the parts of an organism will be generically similar to Aristotle's account of this principle, and will be adequate as well to the other relevant remarks of Aristotle's that we have cited. Our account, like Aristotle's, sees the key to understanding the organization of the parts of organisms in their *functional unity*, that is to say, in logical and causal interrelationships among the natural functions of those parts. However, we shall place our principle of organization for the parts of an organism within a scientific framework that is compatible with currently accepted biological theory, and free from the now implausible Aristotelian doctrine that a complete account of natural phenomena, or of the natural functions of the parts of organic living things, requires the use of irreducibly teleological descriptions of those phenomena or functions. For we shall attempt to provide a *reductive* analysis of the natural functions of the parts of organisms in terms of natural selection and evolution.[34]

5   EVOLUTION, NATURAL SELECTION, AND NATURAL FUNCTION

In order to pave the way toward our reductive analysis of natural functions, let us begin with a brief description of evolutionary theory in contemporary biology. This theory has four main elements. The first consists of the interrelated factors of variation, mutation, and inheritance. Not all living things of a given species are inherently alike, and some of the differences or variations among them are heritable by their offspring. Moreover, sometimes the heritable traits of a living thing are sudden fundamental changes in heredity or mutations. The second element is competition. Given the limited power of organisms to obtain the necessities of life, as well as the relative scarcity of these necessities, there is a competitive struggle for existence among living things. The third element is natural selection. Only those organisms that survive the competition pass on their heritable traits to their offspring. Certain heritable traits of organisms which are likely to result in survival and reproductive success eventually become predominant, or are naturally selected. An organism that possesses these traits is in a sense better adapted for survival given its environment than an organism which lacks them. Accordingly, traits of this kind may be said to have survival value.

There are three relevant senses of "survival value" that evolutionary biologists have employed. First, a heritable trait of an organism may causally contribute to the survival of that organism. Second, a heritable trait of an organism may causally contribute to the survival of the species (or a population) to which that organism belongs. Third, a heritable trait of an organism may causally contribute to the replication of the genes which that organism possesses.[35] For the purposes of our argument it will be convenient to have a single expression that is neutral among these three senses of "survival value." Accordingly, when we say that a heritable trait of an organism has survival or reproductive value for that organism we shall mean that it has survival value in *one or more* of these three senses.

What traits are heritable? Intuitively, one might think of such traits as having brown eyes, having blond hair, and having a heart as being heritable. Strictly speaking, however, evolutionary biology implies that the heritable traits are genotypic or hereditary features which are *expressed* in certain environmental conditions as having brown eyes, having blond hair, and having a heart. Nevertheless, as a matter of convenience, we shall feel free to speak in the intuitive way indicated, with the understanding that what has been said can be rephrased in terms of the strict or correct account implied by evolutionary biology.

The fourth and final element of evolutionary biology is that of evolutionary descent. A limited variety of primitive life-forms have evolved into the huge variety of sophisticated life-forms we see today as a result of billions of years of natural selection.

Let us now turn to the task of developing a reductive account of the natural functions of the parts of organisms in terms of natural selection and evolution. The intuitive idea behind such an account may be understood in terms of the following analogy between the *artificial function* of an artifact, for example, a piston, and the *natural function* of a bodily organ, for example, a heart. A piston has a function because it has a certain design, and it has this design because of a purposive selective process of an intellectual kind carried out by human engineers. Analogously, a heart has a function because it has a certain design, and it also has this design because of a selective process, but it is a nonpurposive process of natural selection.[36]

Accordingly, if an object has a function, then the fact that the object's structure is suited to its function cannot be an accidental or coincidental one: this fact must be explained by the existence of some natural process, purposive or nonpurposive, which designs or selects that structure because it is suited to performing that function. Thus, in general:

(P1) Necessarily, for any x, x has a function, ϕ-ing, only if there is some level of composition, L, such that x has the structure, S, that it has at level L because x has the function of ϕ-ing (or, in nonfunctional language, because x possesses the capacity to ϕ).

That is, necessarily, an item, x, is *for* ϕ-ing only if there is some level of composition, L, and some structure, S, such that at level L, x's structure is S, and x's having S at level L is explained by x's having the function of ϕ-ing. (Examples of levels of composition are the macroscopic, cellular, subcellular, molecular, and atomic levels.)

For example, a piston has the function of moving a rod only if the piston has the macroscopic structure that it has, i.e., its being a rigid cylinder, *because* it has the function or capacity to move a rod. Likewise, a heart possesses the function of pumping blood in a body of a certain kind only if this heart's having the macroscopic or cellular structure that it has, i.e., its being a compressible sac of muscular tissue, is *explained by* this heart's having the function or capacity to pump blood.

The piston's macrostructure is explained by its having the capacity to move a rod in the following way: human engineers designed the piston in such a way that its macrostructure gives it the capacity to perform that function. Thus, pistons are produced or manufactured in such a way that their structure conforms with a *preexistent* design, a design selected because an object which has that design can perform a certain function. Analogously, the heart's macroscopic and cellular structure is explained by its having the capacity to pump blood. Here the explanation is that a process of natural selection resulted in the heart's having a macroscopic and cellular structure that gives it the capacity to perform this function. Accordingly, hearts are produced or generated in such a manner that their structure is in conformity with the results of an antecedent process of natural selection.

The explanatory relation between an object's (O's) having a certain structure, S, and O's having a function or a capacity to perform a certain activity is an *historical* one, inasmuch as the process of selection, whether purposive or nonpurposive, which explains O's having S in terms of O's having the function or capacity in question, occurs *prior to* O's existence.

It should be observed that, in another sense, the piston's or the heart's having the capacity to move a rod or pump blood is explained by the piston's or the heart's having a certain structure. This latter explanatory relation is *nonhistorical*, since in this sort of explanation a capacity of an object and the structure of this object which explains its having that capacity exist *at the same time*. But this second sort of account fails to explain *why* the object in question has the structure which enables it to function in a certain way. Because this second explanatory relation and the historical explanatory relation mentioned earlier are of different kinds, explanatory relations of *both* of these kinds can hold in a given case and not result in explanatory circularity.[37]

6 THE EMERGENCE OF LIFE AND NATURAL FUNCTION

A naturalistic reduction of the functionality of the parts of organisms presupposes some understanding of the level of structural complexity in organic objects at which such functionality emerges or appears in the world. It is evident that the existence of an organic object having a part with a natural function presupposes the existence of organic life.[38] We can think of no better way to begin acquiring the requisite understanding of the structural level at which functionality emerges in organic objects than by inquiring about the nature of the very *first* organic living things, or protobionts.[39]

Although scientists working on the problem of the origin of organic life have a variety of opinions about the attributes of protobionts, there is broad agreement that protobionts were composed of organic macromolecules, the notion of which we explain in what follows. In chemical theory, an atom is the smallest possible unit of an elemental stuff, for example, gold, iron, or carbon, whereas a molecule is the smallest possible unit of a compound stuff, for example, water, salt, or glucose. An organic macromolecule is a large organic molecule, that is, one that is composed of a very large number of atoms. In other words, an organic macromolecule is a carbon-based molecule which has a high molecular weight, for example, a molecule of a protein or a nucleic acid. For instance, proteins are macromolecules generally made up of hundreds or thousands of amino acid molecules, and have molecular weights in the range of ten thousand to several million.

One possible view is that the first living things were self-replicating organic macromolecules, for example, nucleic acids. Such molecules lack the ability to engage in the causally interrelated activities of absorption, excretion, metabolism, or growth, and for this reason, do not seem to have a comprehensive enough variety of fundamental life-processes to count as living entities. A parallel case is that of modern-day viruses, which appear *life-like* to the extent that they have reproductive powers. But because they lack the ability to metabolize or grow, and *a fortiori* lack the ability to engage in the processes of absorption or excretion which causally contribute to metabolism or growth, they also do not seem to be alive.

A more plausible view of the nature of protobionts is that they were primitive cells that contained *both* self-replicating organic macromolecules *and* catalytic organic macromolecules, for example, proteins, and which generally *did* possess the abilities to participate in causally interrelated activities of absorption, excretion, metabolism, growth, reproduction, and synthesis. This view is defended by Oparin, who argues that life originated when cell-like organic structures having the abilities to engage in causally interrelated processes of absorption, excretion, metabolism, growth, and reproduction, incorporated self-replicating organic macromolecules into their activities.[40]

A conflicting view is held by Sidney Fox, the discoverer of proteinoid microspheres.[41] Fox was familiar with the results of sparking experiments, in which electrical discharges, similar to lightning, occurring under atmospheric conditions thought to duplicate those on primitive Earth, had produced amino acids, the basic building blocks of life. He took this two steps further. First, he demonstrated that amino acids that are heated to 130 degrees centigrade by being placed on a slab of hot volcanic rock can copolymerize into a primitive or mini-protein he called *proteinoid*. (Although Fox's proteinoid molecule is large compared to typical inorganic molecules, it is considerably smaller than the typical proteins and nucleic acids found in contemporary cells.) Second, he found that when proteinoid was placed in cool liquid salt water, like that in oceans, it self-assembled into numerous proteinoid microspheres.

Fox has shown that these microscopic spheres are life-like in a number of significant ways. First, proteinoid microspheres are primitive cell-like structures that possess a membranous outer layer which permits the entry and the exit of materials in its watery surroundings, for example, proteinoid, other organic substances, dissolved minerals, and so forth. Second, proteinoid microspheres are extremely stable and durable, and are known to last up to six or seven years. Third, proteinoid has catalytic or enzymatic properties. Accordingly, microspheres can engage in metabolic activity, grow via the absorption of proteinoid present in their surroundings, and then reproduce, typically by budding, though in some cases by binary fission. Third, it seems that microspheres have a feature which prefigures the associative activities of contemporary organisms. This is because some microspheres are positively charged, and others are negatively charged: oppositely charged microspheres attract, and similarly charged microspheres repel. When two microspheres with the right chemistry meet, they "mate" or become attached to one another for some time, directly interchange portions of their contents via an open connecting channel at the point of contact, and may either bond for "life" or separate later. Fourth, Fox observed that asymmetrical pairs of "mating" microspheres of different sizes can engage in nonrandom courses of circular motion. Thus, it appears that microspheres have a characteristic which prefigures the motility of today's organisms. Fifth, Fox has experimentally determined that the electric action potentials for proteinoid microspheres are strikingly similar to that of contemporary nerve cells. He has also noted several other interesting similarities and affinities between certain types of proteinoid microspheres and nerve cells, including the projection of tubular outgrowths resembling those of neurons, and that the memory of mice is enhanced when they are given proteinoid. Sixth, electron microphotographs of what are reputed to be the earliest microfossils do not reveal anything that distinguishes the microorganisms that left these imprints from proteinoid microspheres. On the basis of the similarities between proteinoid microspheres and contemporary living things, and on these other suggestive facts, Fox hypothesizes, with some evidence, that proteinoid microspheres were the first living things.

One interesting aspect of Fox's advocacy of the thesis that proteinoid microspheres are living things is the way in which it appeals to both conceptual, or *a priori*, and empirical premises to support this thesis. Microspheres engage in activities intuitively associated with organic life, such as absorption, excretion, growth, and reproduction. We know *a priori*, from our intuitive understanding of the concept of an organic living thing, that species of organisms could not exist unless some organisms have the capacity to engage in such activities. Thus, since microspheres have the capacity to engage in activities of this kind, microspheres meet certain logically necessary conditions for organic life. The empirical premise is an inductive one which suggests that proteinoid microspheres are the best available candidates for the first living things, given that contemporary life evolved from first living things of some kind. According to this inductive premise, since microspheres can easily arise under primitive conditions, and reputed microfossils of very ancient cells cannot be distinguished from microspheres, and since there are many significant ways in which microspheres resemble or anticipate the compositional, structural, and behavioral attributes of contemporary cells, microspheres seem to be the best available candidates for the first living things. Without committing ourselves to Fox's conclusions, we can see that his mode of argument in this case is perfectly legitimate. It appears that such a mode of argument, combining conceptual and empirical aspects, is possible in this case just because the concept of organic life is partly intuitive and partly empirical in nature. It seems intuitive that organic life-forms must generally engage in certain fundamental life-activities, for example, absorption, excretion, growth, and reproduction. It also appears that the essential compositional or microstructural nature of those organic life-forms can only be known by means of empirical inquiry within biology and the other fundamental natural sciences.

In this respect, our intuitive concept of organic life is analogous to our intuitive concept of a substance such as water. For it appears intuitive that water must satisfy certain conditions, for example, that it is physically possible for it to exist in a colorless liquid state. But the essential compositional or microstructural nature of water, for example, being H_2O, can only be known through inquiry in chemistry and physics. There are two senses in which water or organic life can be said to have an essential microstructural nature. According to the *de dicto* sense, for example, it can be said that the proposition that for any x, if x is a sample of water, then x is composed of H_2O is a necessary truth (i.e., a proposition whose falsehood is impossible). According to the *de re* sense, that thing which is a sample of water is necessarily such that it is composed of H_2O (i.e., it is composed of H_2O and couldn't exist otherwise). It would appear to be true in *both* of these senses that water as well as organic life have essential compositional or microstructural natures that are discoverable only *a posteriori* or through empirical scientific research. Saul Kripke is the leading recent defender of the thesis that things such as water have *de re* essential natures of this kind.[42]

George Bealer has observed that in these respects the concepts of organic life and of water seem to differ from the concept or category of Substance, a concept that is more general or basic than that of organic life or water.[43] As we have argued, the essential nature of individual substance can be known through purely *a priori* methods of philosophical analysis. Hence, such knowledge does not require empirical scientific investigation. Bealer also suggests that the concept of *life*, a concept that needs to be distinguished from the narrower concept of *organic life* that we are focusing upon, is a general categorical concept whose essential nature is likewise to be understood by means of *a priori* methods of philosophical analysis, rather than through empirical scientific investigation.

Thus, to ascertain if a proteinoid microsphere is an organic living thing, one needs to determine if a microsphere satisfies both some intuitive preconditions for organic life and some empirically discovered ones. Since there is controversy about the exact nature of these preconditions, it is not surprising that there is controversy over whether microspheres are alive.

In particular, Oparin and Fox have incompatible views about the necessary and sufficient conditions for organic life, as well as incompatible theories about attributes of protobionts. Microspheres do not incorporate nucleic acids or any other self-replicating organic macromolecules; and they are incapable of synthesizing the proteinoid of which they are made. Rather, proteinoid microspheres grow and reproduce heterotrophically by absorbing the necessary stuffs from the environment. According to Oparin, but not Fox, it is a necessary condition of organic life that a living thing incorporate into its activities an organic macromolecule which is capable of self-replication. Thus, the conditions Oparin puts forward seem sufficient for organic life, but are not *obviously* necessary, whereas the conditions that Fox sets forth seem necessary for organic life, but their sufficiency is questionable.

Unlike a virus, a proteinoid microsphere seems to have a wide enough range of activities to count as a living thing. Yet, a proteinoid microsphere lacks that feature of a virus which is ultimately responsible for a virus's life-like quality, viz., its incorporating into its activities an organic macromolecule which is capable of self-replication. Of course, the organic macromolecular components of viruses that possess the power of self-replication, i.e., nucleic acids, need to mobilize the life-processes of a "host" in order for them to replicate themselves. Therefore, some biologists have argued that a virus is not alive because *it* doesn't reproduce, rather it depends upon its "host" to produce copies of it. Similarly, when Maynard Smith explains why a fire isn't alive, despite the fact that it grows and multiplies, he says that it is because a fire's multiplication depends too much on external or environmental factors.[44] In particular, he argues that the traits of a fire's "descendants," for example, their color, size, and temperature, are more a function of meteorological conditions and what it is that is being burned or heated by those "descendants," than they are of the traits of the "parent" fire.

Maynard Smith uses what is basically the same criterion to argue that proteinoid microspheres are not alive. He maintains that "Fox's microspheres lack heredity, and so will not evolve by natural selection."[45] However, Maynard Smith's conception of heredity is problematic: the replication or reproduction of anything is *always* the result of a combination of external *and* internal factors. Thus, it is hard to understand how the distinction which Maynard Smith presupposes between mere multiplication and multiplication with heredity can be drawn or justified. For example, the fact that a nucleic acid needs something external, i.e., a "host," in order to produce copies of itself does *not* imply that viral nucleic acids do not really "self-replicate." Something external is always needed for a thing to replicate itself or reproduce, whether this something be an enzyme, a food stuff, an energy source, or a member of the opposite sex. Viruses and their nucleic acids can be said to reproduce or self-replicate because in each case the production of copies is controlled by the information coded in the nucleic acids of the viruses. By analogy, a proteinoid microsphere's production of a copy of itself is controlled by the information coded in the molecular structure of the molecules of proteinoid which compose it. Moreover, since a "child" of a microsphere will be composed of things that the "parent" has absorbed and incorporated into itself, microspheres can evolve by natural selection via the inheritance of certain acquired traits. For example, the next major evolutionary jump beyond microspheres might come about when a microsphere absorbs a self-replicating nucleic acid which then somehow gets incorporated into the microsphere's growth or reproductive activities, and these more sophisticated growth or reproductive mechanisms are then passed on to the microsphere's "children." Thus, notwithstanding Maynard Smith's contrary opinion, it would appear that proteinoid microspheres can evolve.

Although Maynard Smith's argument against the claim that proteinoid microspheres are alive is inconclusive, Oparin's idea that there is no life without self-replicating organic macromolecules has its attractions. Yet, Fox's case for thinking that proteinoid microspheres are alive also has its appeal. On the whole, therefore, we are unaware of any decisive argument which settles the question of whether or not Fox's proteinoid microspheres are alive. Thus, it remains unclear whether Oparin's, or Fox's, or some third view is the most plausible theory about the nature of first life.

Nevertheless, we can now introduce a device that will both assist us in accommodating the possibility of protobionts and help us to answer questions about the emergence of functionality in organic objects. This device consists in using a comprehensive set of naturalistic conditions, S, which is logically sufficient for organic life, and includes all of the fundamental activities of organic life which are logically necessary for organic life. It is possible to pick out such a set of conditions, S, because there is a family of fundamental, causally interrelated, activities of organic life (together with a structure for organic life) without a general capacity for which (or without the presence of which) species of organic life could not exist. This family consists of the activities of absorption, excretion, metabolism, growth, reproduction, and (perhaps) biosynthesis, in conjunction with a cellular structure. Some of these fundamental biological factors are intuitively or *a priori* general preconditions for the existence of organic life, for example, absorption, excretion, growth, and reproduction. Others have been *empirically* discovered, for example, cellular structure, metabolism, and biosynthesis.

Although we assume that the parts of protobionts had the capacity to engage in, or causally contribute to, *some* of the activities which belong to the set S, we take no stand, one way or the other, on the question of whether those parts had the capacity to engage in, or causally contribute to, *all* of the activities in the set S. In any event, the set S includes the naturalistic activities of living things without which biological evolution and natural selection could not occur.[46]

We are now prepared to specify the set, S, which plausibly includes all of the fundamental naturalistic conditions for organic life.

(D1) The elements of S are the following eight conditions: Where x is a persisting organism, (i) x has parts which are m-molecules, that is, organic macromolecules of repeated units which have a high capacity for selective reactions with other similar molecules, (ii) x has a layer or membrane made of m-molecules whose limit is x's exterior surface, (iii) x absorbs and excretes through this layer or membrane, (iv) x metabolizes m-molecules, (v) x grows through an increase in the number of m-molecules that compose it, (vi) x synthesizes m-molecular parts of x by means of m-molecular parts of x copying themselves, (vii) x reproduces, either by means of x's m-molecular parts copying themselves, or by means of another, more basic, process, (viii) x's absorbing and excreting causally contribute to x's metabolizing m-molecules; these jointly causally contribute to x's biosynthesizing m-molecules; these together causally contribute to x's growing and reproducing by means of the addition or copying of m-molecules; and x's growing causally contributes to x's absorbing, excreting, metabolizing, biosynthesizing, and reproducing.

Some of the important features of (D1) are explained in the following passages.

First, clause (viii) of (D1) shows the way in which the fundamental biological activities of an organism are causally interrelated, and we remind the reader that these activities are to be understood in purely naturalistic terms. In utilizing (D1), we understand the notion of a condition's figuring in (D1) in such a way that if a conjunction's contributing to some result figures in (D1), then the individual contribution of each conjunct figures in (D1) as well.

Second, clause (iv) of (D1), which concerns the metabolic activities of an organism, x, has the following two implications: first, that x has the capacity to alter many of its parts, while x's overall structure stays relatively intact; second, that in circumstances of this kind, x's maintenance demands a constant infusion of energy, but x's maintenance results in the depletion of this energy.[47] Although it is arguable that the capacity to metabolize m-molecules is a logically necessary condition of organic life, our argument does not require this assumption. Thus, we do not presuppose that (iv) of (D1) is a logically necessary condition for organic life in the arguments that follow.

Third, our claim is that (D1) is a logically *sufficient* condition for organic life which includes all of an organism's fundamental biological activities. Since we are *not* claiming that having a capacity to engage in *all* of the activities which figure in (D1) is a logically *necessary* condition for organic life, our claim is compatible with any plausible hypothesis about the character of the first organic life, including the hypotheses that protobionts were self-replicating organic macromolecules such as DNA or RNA, that protobionts were proteinoid microspheres, or that protobionts consisted of self-replicating organic macromolecules incorporated within proteinoid microspheres.

Turning again to the topic of natural function, it seems that a natural function, f, of a part, P, of an organic living thing is an emergent property of an organic complex in the minimal sense that P is a complex object having organic parts, P has f, and none of P's proper parts has f. Thus, f "emerges" or "appears" only when an organic object attains a certain *level* of structural organization or complexity. The following emergence-of-functionality principle can be inferred as a corollary. For any natural function f, and any part, P, of an organic life-form, if either P is inorganic, or P is organic but has less than the requisite level of structural or organizational complexity needed for the emergence of f, then P lacks f.

What is the minimum level of structural or organizational complexity needed for the emergence of a natural function in a part of an organic life-form? We propose the following answer. Necessarily, at a time, t, a physical thing, P, which is a part of an organic life-form, O, has a natural function only if, at t, either P or a part thereof is a molecule of at least the size of the largest macromolecular part of the simplest possible organic life-form. Since a proteinoid microsphere is arguably a living thing, and since anything whose largest macromolecular part is smaller than a molecule of proteinoid seems not to be an organic living thing, the following generalization is reasonable. Depending on whether the simplest possible organic life-forms were either proteinoid microspheres, or involved DNA, RNA, or the like, the smallest possible size of such a molecule is either as small as a molecule of proteinoid, or as large as a molecule of DNA or RNA, or of some intermediate size. Thus, there is a sense in which organic life and the functionality associated with it are emergent qualities that can appear only when the indicated (very high) threshold of structural or organizational complexity is reached. So, according to our proposal, a part of an organism which does not have a molecular part as large as that of a molecule of proteinoid, for example, a molecule of an amino acid, does not have a natural function: such a part lacks the requisite level of structural or organizational complexity for the emergence of natural functions.

Since a part of a living thing such as a calcium atom, a carbon atom, or a water molecule lacks the required level of structural complexity, the foregoing argument implies that a part of this kind does not have a natural function. This implication is an intuitively plausible one: it seems that a part of this sort could not be *for* anything.

But it might be suggested that some calcium atoms which are parts of organic living things *are* for something, for example, for transmitting signals from one nerve cell to another, for building strong bones, and so on. For example, according to Andrew Woodfield, if x has a natural function, f, then any part of x that causally contributes to x's performing f has some natural function: such a part of x is *for* causally contributing to x's performing f.[48] Since the activity of calcium atoms causally contributes to neurons using them to send signals to other neurons, and to bone cells using them to build strong bones, Woodfield's view implies what we have denied, namely, that calcium atoms are *for* causally contributing to neurons using them to send signals to other neurons, and *for* causally contributing to bone cells using them to build strong bones. However, there are three plausible arguments which imply that teleological descriptions of these kinds are inapplicable to objects such as calcium atoms.

First of all, Ockham's Razor appears to imply that we should not attribute natural functions to calcium atoms, since to do so is to multiply such functions unnecessarily. It is not parsimonious to make attributions of this sort, because for the purposes of biology we need (at most) to attribute natural functions only to much more complex structures.

Second, as we have seen, necessarily, a part of an organic entity has a natural function only if life exists. This suggests that the level of structural complexity in organic matter required for the existence of natural functions is roughly of that order of magnitude as that which is required for the emergence of life. Yet, it is extremely implausible to attribute *life* or any state approaching life to such parts of organisms as calcium atoms, carbon atoms, and water molecules. Evidently, these parts fall far short of the order of magnitude of structural complexity necessary for the emergence of life. Thus, analogously, it is highly implausible to attribute natural functions to parts of this kind.

Third, as we have argued, necessarily, an item, x, is *for* ϕ-ing only if there is some level of composition, L, and some structure, S, such that at level L, x's structure is S, and x's having S at level L is explained by x's having the capacity to ϕ. However, there is no level of composition L at which it is true of a water molecule, or an atom of carbon or calcium, that it possesses the structure that it has at level L *because* it causally contributes to some biological activity. Obviously, the structure of objects of this kind is prior to and independent of any biological activities in which they might be involved. In other words, it is evident that the biological realm emerges out of the realms of physics and chemistry. It follows that objects such as water molecules, calcium atoms, and carbon atoms are not *for* some biological activity. That is to say, objects of this sort do not have the performance of such an activity as a natural function.[49]

Thus, although it is a fact that nerve cells make use of calcium atoms to transmit signals to other nerve cells, and a fact that calcium is used to build strong bones, we deny that these facts imply that calcium atoms are *for* these things. On our account, these facts should instead be understood as implying that nerve cells are *for* transmitting signals to other nerve cells with calcium atoms, and that bone cells are *for* building strong bones out of calcium.

It should be noted, however, that our account is compatible with the apparent fact that some liquid *mixtures* containing water, inorganic minerals, *and* complex organic macromolecules, for example, blood and cytoplasm, have a natural function, for example, fluid transport, since such a mixture has an organic macromolecular component of sufficient structural complexity.

7 AN ACCOUNT OF NATURAL FUNCTION

The conception of an m-molecule can now be employed to analyze the notion of a natural function of a part of an organic living thing in wholly naturalistic terms:

(D2) ϕ-ing is a natural function had by a proper part, P, of an organism x = df. P is a proper part of x such that: (a) P has the capacity to ϕ, and (b) P is an m-molecule or P has a part which is an m-molecule, and (c) the trait, having a proper part with the capacity to ϕ, is either naturally selected for x, or naturally selected for one or more ancestors of x, from whom x inherited this trait via some line of descent.

It is instructive to understand why (D2) avoids a certain pitfall. Let G be an arbitrary gerrymandered region of an organism, x, which comprises a large portion of x's total mass and which has the property, P, of having some of its constituent atoms electromagnetically bonded to other of its constituent atoms. Although these atoms being bonded in such a way makes it more probable that x will survive and reproduce than their failing to be so bonded, it is intuitively unacceptable that G is *for*, or for the sake of, its constituent atoms being bonded in the way in question. Similarly, P

does not qualify as a *biological* activity or function of *G*. Fortunately, it is not possible that natural selection explains *G*'s having *P*. This is because having *P* is an attribute of a sort that is too simple or basic to be naturally selected. Thus, (D2) does not have the unwelcome implication that *G* is *for P*.

Only attributes of far greater complexity than having atoms that are electromagnetically bonded can be naturally selected. The minimum level of complexity required for an attribute of a part of an organism to be naturally selected, or to count as a biological trait, is commensurate with the level of structural or organizational complexity necessary for a part of an organism to exhibit functionality. In other words, the exemplification of such an attribute entails the existence of an m-molecule. For instance, *G*'s trait of having atoms that are electromagnetically bonded does not qualify as biological, since its exemplification does *not* entail that there is an m-molecule. On the other hand, a kidney's specific way of cleansing blood *is* a biological trait, and its exemplification *does* entail the existence of an m-molecule.

It should be noted that (D2) covers not only a natural function that is *performed* by a part of an organism, but also a natural function that is *had* (but not performed) by a part of an organism. An inactive or dormant organism, for example, a spore, has parts that have natural functions which are not being performed, although those parts remain capable of performing those functions.

Finally, three special sorts of cases of natural functions of the parts of organic life-forms deserve some comment. First, it is possible for an organism to have a part, *p*, that performs a certain specialized activity, *A*, as a result of a breeding program instituted by humans for the purpose of developing an organism having a part capable of such an activity.

Is this specialized activity a natural function of that part? One possible intuition about this case is that *A* is an artificial function of *p* rather than a natural one. This intuition can be accommodated if clause (c) of (D2) is understood in such a way that the activities of the breeders which result in the generation of living organisms do not count as environmental conditions which naturally select *p* to do *A*. However, our own intuitions in this instance run in the other direction, namely, that *A* *does* count as a natural function. We can accommodate this second intuition by understanding clause (c) of (D2) in such a way that the human activities which result in the creation of living organisms qualify as environmental conditions which naturally select p to do A.[50]

A second special sort of case is exemplified when favorable mutations of the parts of an organism, which enhance the survival or reproductive success of the mutated organism, *have just occurred*. For example, through what seems to be a mutation, there is a family of humans in Italy who have a gene that keeps their arteries from getting clogged with fat, thereby preventing heart disease. Is it *now* the case that this gene is *for* keeping their arteries unclogged with fat?

Our intuition about this case is that this gene does *not* presently have this function. To be sure, this gene now keeps their arteries from getting clogged with fat, but it is not really *for* that activity until it is naturally *selected* for it, something which will not occur, if it ever does, until some time in the future when this gene is widespread in a human population. Since our account is formulated in terms of natural selection, it is adequate to this intuition. However, there is another intuition to the effect that this gene *is* presently *for* keeping their arteries unclogged with fat. After all, this gene not only now keeps the arteries of individuals who have it from getting clogged with fat, but it presently has survival or reproductive value for these individuals. The trouble with such an intuition is that it runs afoul of our principle (P1). In particular, since there is no level of composition at which these genes have the structure that they do *because* they have the capacity to keep arteries from getting clogged with fat, it is a mistake to say that these genes are *for* that activity.[51]

Third, notice another implication of clause (c) of (D2). If a part, p, of an organism, O, has been naturally selected to perform a certain function, f, and retains the capacity to do so, but, because of changed environmental conditions, p no longer *performs* f, nevertheless p still *has* f. Moreover, (D2) has this implication even if f has not been maintained by natural selection in the recent past. We believe that these implications of (D2) are intuitively plausible ones.[52]

Peter Godfrey-Smith rejects an account of functions such as (D2) on the ground that a capacity for a certain activity counts as a function only if natural selection has maintained that capacity *in the recent past*.[53] Godfrey-Smith's position has two drawbacks. First, since there is no precise way to specify the notion of the recent past, his account of functions is vague in a certain respect. Though the use of vague temporal notions of this sort is not necessarily objectionable, it is still true that all other things being equal, an account of functions would be better off without such vagueness. Second, Godfrey-Smith's account of functions has unintuitive implications. For example, suppose that there is an artifact, A, such that A is obsolete, and A has not been utilized or maintained in the recent past, but A has the capacity to be utilized. Intuitively, natural functions and artificial functions are analogous. Thus, it seems that if Godfrey-Smith's account of natural functions were correct, then an analogous account of artificial functions would be correct, an account which would imply that A is no longer *for* what it was originally designed to do. Surely, this implication is implausible. It certainly appears that A retains its original function, even though A is not currently performing that function. Hence, Godfrey-Smith's account of natural functions, and the analogous account of artificial functions, seem to be mistaken.

8 THE DEGREE OF NATURALNESS OF AN INDIVIDUAL'S LIFE-PROCESSES

Now that the notion of a natural function of a part of an organism is better understood, we propose to utilize it to provide a principle of organization for the parts of an organism. Another, related, notion that will also be employed stands in some need of explanation. This is the notion of the degree to which an organism's life-processes or microstructure are natural, with maximal naturalness as a possible limiting case. To say that an organism's life-processes are maximally natural, or that an organism's microstructure is maximally natural, is to say that they are as natural as they could be, or, in common parlance, "that they are as Nature intended them to be."

The notions of the degree of naturalness of an organism's life-processes or microstructure presuppose the relational notions of x's life-processes or microstructure being less natural than y's. These relational notions are asymmetric, transitive, and irreflexive, and can be illustrated by the following examples. All other things being equal, with respect to life-processes or microstructure, those of a man with a heart transplant are less natural than those of a man without one; those of a man with both a heart transplant and a kidney transplant are less natural than a those of a man with only a heart transplant; those of a man with a liver transplant are less natural than those of a man with a corneal transplant; those of a man with an artificial heart are less natural than those of a man with an artificial ankle-joint; those of a man with an artificial heart are less natural than those of a man with a heart transplant; and those of a man with a heart transplant from a distant relative are less natural than those of a man with a heart transplant from an identical twin.

Since there are relatively clear relational notions of x's life-processes (or x's microstructure) being less natural than y's life-processes (or y's microstructure), there must be intelligible notions of the degree to which x's life-processes (or x's microstructure) are (is) natural. Generalizing from the foregoing examples, we define the latter notions as follows.

(D3) x's life-processes (or x's microstructure) are (is) *natural* to the degree that x's life-processes (x's microstructure) conform(s) to the information implicit (at x's first moment of existence) in x's hereditary make-up.

It should be noted that the conception of naturalness which we are employing here differs importantly from Aristotle's. The standard against which Aristotle measures the degree to which a trait of an individual organism is natural is the nature of *the species* to which that individual belongs. By contrast, our standard for measuring the degree to which such a trait is natural is the original hereditary nature of *that individual*. These two standards are quite independent of one another. Aristotle regards a creature as stunted, imperfect, or un-natural to the extent that it fails to conform to the nature of its species. On the other hand, we shall regard an organism as less than maximally natural to the extent that it fails to conform to its own original hereditary nature. Although modern biology may not em-brace the Aristotelian idea that species have a nature, it embraces with enthusiasm the idea that individual organisms have an original hereditary or genetic nature. According to this idea, the original hereditary or genetic nature of an organism is encoded in organic macromolecules which are parts of that organism at its origin. Contemporary organisms have all, or at least much, of their original hereditary nature encoded in DNA molecules which are originally parts of those organisms. On the other hand, a more primitive organism (not containing a DNA molecule) has its original heredit-ary nature encoded in other, less complex, organic macromolecules which are parts of such an organism at its inception.

The original hereditary nature of an organism can be identified with an attribute whose content specifies a microstructural "design" for that organism. (D3) presupposes that for every organism there must be an attribute of this kind, and that instructions for implementing the specifications in question are encoded in the organism's original hereditary make-up. The assumption that there are such attributes or microstructural hereditary blueprints is both plausible and compatible with current ideas in biology. A "blueprint" of this kind incorporates a *range* of structural specifications, including the permitted tolerances and allowances for an organism's functional parts. In other words, it includes the range of variation permitted in maintaining a specified dimension when a functional part is generated, and the allowed dimensional differences for functional parts having directly interrelated activities. This includes, for example, the range of sizes from minimum to maximum for the inner diameter of certain blood vessels, the greatest allowable difference in size between the heart and the kidneys, and so on. Implicit in such a "blueprint" is a parallel range of specifications pertaining to the character and interrelationship of an organism's life-processes at a microstructural level. In other words, a microstructural hereditary blueprint is equivalent to an indefinitely long disjunction of non-disjunctive microstructural attributes, a property of the form "P_1 or P_2 or P_3 or P_4 or . . .," where the first disjunct resembles the second, the second resembles the third, the third resembles the fourth, and so on. Thus, an organism's (O's) possession of a microstructural hereditary blueprint is compatible with the fact that the way in which O's heredity or genes are expressed in O's microstructure or life-processes is partly dependent upon environmental conditions.

A related notion is that of a norm of reaction for an organism, O, which may be thought of as the range of phenotypes (or body-types) generable by O's genotype (or hereditary-type) in the environmental conditions in which organisms with O's genotype (or hereditary-type) can exist.[54]

By utilizing the notion of a microstructural hereditary blueprint, we can now say that x's life-processes or x's microstructure is *natural* to the degree that it conforms to the information implicit in x's microstructural hereditary blueprint. We plan to employ both the notion of a natural function of a part of an organism, and the notion of the degree to which an organism's life-processes are natural, to provide a satisfactory principle of organization for the parts of an organism.

At this juncture we remind the reader that the fact that organisms have parts which lack the level of structural complexity required for the emergence of natural functions, for example, water molecules, creates a complication for such an account. Specifically, it appears that the organization of the parts of an organism which are below the level of structural complexity in question is not to be understood in terms of the natural functions of those parts. Fortunately, we can identify the relevant activities of such parts as those of either engaging in, or causally contributing to, fundamental biological activities of the sorts which figure in conditions (iii)–(viii) of (D1), for example, absorption, excretion, metabolism, growth, reproduction, and (possibly) biosynthesis. Thus, although certain parts of an organism must engage in, or causally contribute to, some of these fundamental biological activities, those parts need not be *for* performing, or causally contributing to, these activities. Nevertheless, we shall maintain that the organization of the parts of an organism which are below the level of structural complexity required for the emergence of natural function can be understood in terms of interconnections among the biological activities of the organism's parts in a way that parallels the functional interconnections of the parts of the organism which are above that level of structural complexity. Henceforth, we shall find it convenient to use such terms as "function" and "functional" (unmodified by the term "natural") to mean *either* a natural function, *or* a function which is not a natural one, of engaging in, or causally contributing to, one or more fundamental biological activities.

9 VITAL PARTS AND JOINT NATURAL FUNCTIONS

It is necessary for any organism to have one or more *vital* parts. For example, typically, a human being has vital organs such as a brain, heart, and liver. And it seems that organ-*systems* such as the nervous, cardiovascular, digestive, respiratory, and excretory systems are vital parts of an ordinary human being. Organs, or organ-systems, of these kinds have functions, for example, pumping blood, digesting food, oxygenating blood, and so forth. In common parlance, functions of this kind are also said to be vital.

A preliminary analysis of the concept of a vital part goes as follows:

(D4) v is a vital part of an organism O at a time t = df. (i) v is a proper part of O at t, and (ii) for some time t', later than t, but not so much later than t that O could not live from t until t', there is a function, f, such that under normal conditions, O's life cannot continue from t until t' unless v performs f at some time t^* ($t \leq t^* < t'$).

(D4) raises further issues. First, it would be desirable to have an explanation of the notion of normal conditions presupposed by (D4). Second, when (D4) says that a vital part is one which an organism *cannot* live long without under normal conditions, (D4) makes use of an unspecified modal or causal notion.

The notion of the degree of naturalness of an organism's (O's) life-processes can be used to provide an alternative account of the concept of a vital part which has some advantages. The former notion was explained in terms of O's original hereditary or genetic make-up (or microstructural hereditary blueprint) in the preceding section. As a first step toward the alternative account in question, we observe that v is a vital part of O just in case v is a proper part of O, and there is a function, f, such that: if O's life continues much longer, then O's life must be sustained by v's performing f, *unless* there is a proxy, v^*, which comes to perform f, in place of, or in addition to, v. For example, v^* might be a transplant, an artificial organ, a vital organ of another organism which sustains O's life via some unnatural connection, or an artificial life-support machine. But v^*'s coming to perform, or performing, f necessarily involves an artificial or un-natural aspect or element which is *not* implicit in O's microstructural hereditary blueprint. Thus, v^*'s coming to perform, or performing, f entails that the degree of naturalness of O's life-processes does *not* remain constant. Therefore, a second account of the concept of a vital part can be stated as follows:

(D5) v is a vital part of an organism O at a time t = df. (i) v is a proper part of O at t, and (ii) for some time t', later than t, but not so much later than t that O could not live from t until t', there is a function, f, such that so long as the degree of naturalness of O's life-processes remains constant, O's life-processes continuing from t until t' entails that O's life-processes are sustained by v's perform-ing f at some time t^* ($t \leq t^* < t'$).[55]

Notice that (D5), unlike (D4), does *not* use the notion of normal conditions, a notion which is notoriously difficult to define. Nor does (D5) presuppose an unspecified modal or causal notion. Instead, it utilizes the concept of the degree of naturalness of an organism's life-processes holding constant, the standard modal concept of broadly logical or metaphysical entailment,[56] and the notion of a sustaining cause. (D5) employs the ordinary or intuitive concept of a sustaining cause, a concept which we shall not attempt to analyze.[57] However, at least this much can be said about the nature of a sustaining cause: an event E_1 sustains an event E_2 only if event E_1 is causally necessary and sufficient in the circumstances for event E_2.

In addition to having one or more vital parts, it appears to be necessary for an organism to have *nonvital* parts, examples of which are an eye, an ear, a single water molecule, and so forth. Typically, parts of this kind perform nonvital functions, for example, inputting visual data, inputting auditory data, engaging in activities which causally contribute to fundamental biological processes, and so on. Some nonvital functions are natural functions, such as an eye's inputting visual data, and some are not, such as a single water molecule's causally contributing to fundamental biological processes.

Is a single kidney or lung of an organism a vital or a nonvital part of that organism? Typically, an organism has a pair of kidneys or lungs, and usually if one member of the pair ceases to function, then the life-processes of the organism in question are sustained by functional activities of the other member of the pair. Because a sustaining cause is causally necessary in the circumstances for its effect, neither member of the pair in question by itself sustains this organism's life-processes. Since under such conditions, a single kidney or lung does not sustain the organism, it follows that typically, a kidney or lung is a *nonvital* organ.[58]

However, as Aristotle thought, there is a sense in which organic living, or functional, parts of an organism may jointly act as a unitary functional part, a part which may be vital, or may be nonvital. For example, specialized living organelles and other functional items, for example, mitochondria, a nucleus, golgi bodies, a cell membrane, and so on, may compose a living cell with a specialized function, such as a lung cell; specialized living cells and other functional items, for example, lung cells and intracellular materials, may compose a living organ, such as a lung, with a specialized function, for example, inhaling air; and specialized living organs and other functional items, for example, lungs, nostrils, and so forth, may compose a living organ-system, such as a respiratory system, with a specialized function, for example, oxygenating blood. Parallel remarks apply to the composition of other organ systems, for example, the nervous, cardiovascular, digestive, and excretory systems. It appears that joint activities of the aforementioned kinds are a result of natural selection. Thus, it seems that the living and functional items which compose the relevant cells, organs, and organ-systems *jointly* have a natural function. Moreover, it is intuitively plausible that specialized cells, organs, and organ-systems of the kinds in question are organic living entities. Thus, we are prepared to accept the following principle.

(D6) Necessarily, if $P_1 \ldots P_n$ are organic living or functional proper parts of an organism, and at least one of $P_1 \ldots P_n$ is an organic living entity, and $P_1 \ldots P_n$ have the natural function of being jointly *for* φ-ing, then $P_1 \ldots P_n$ compose an organic living entity, x, that has the natural function of being *for* Ø-ing.

Let us summarize some of the important implications of the foregoing discussion. First, specialized organ-systems, organs, cells of multicellular organisms, and subcellular organelles (at least in some cases) are organic living parts of organisms. Thus, an organ-system, organ, cell, or organelle of this kind qualifies as an organic living entity for the purposes of the definitions which follow. Second, organic living parts of the foregoing kinds typically have natural functions.[59]

However, since an organism cannot be a proper part of an organic living entity, and since organ-systems, organs, cells of multicellular organisms, and some organelles *are* or *can be* organic living proper parts of an organism, such organic living proper parts, of course, do not qualify as full-fledged *organisms*. This point should be kept in mind in the discussions which follow.

By using the ideas of a vital part and of parts which have a joint natural function, we can sketch the outlines of a promising strategy for providing a principle of organization for the parts of an organism. To begin with, further reflection upon the notion of a vital part reveals that some vital parts have a more central role to play in the unification or organization of an organism's parts than others. Both the heart and the central nervous system are vital parts of a typical human being. Thus, in typical cases the central nervous system's functional activities sustain the heart's functional activities, and vice versa. But modern biology has discovered that in these cases the central nervous system's functional activities regulate or control the functional activities of the heart, but *not* vice versa. This seems to have been denied in ancient times by Aristotle. He apparently thought that the heart is the seat of centralized control, and that the brain's activities are controlled by the heart's.[60] Aristotle suggests that no animal has ever been born without a heart,[61] and that when a "monster" is born we can determine whether we have one creature with supernumerary organs or Siamese twins by seeing whether there is one heart or two. As Aristotle puts it:

> We must decide whether the monstrous animal is one or is composed of several grown together by considering the vital principle; thus, if the heart is a part of such a kind then that which has one heart will be one animal, the multiplied parts being mere outgrowths, but those which have more than one heart will be two animals grown together through their embryos having been confused.[62]

The principle of organization for the parts of an organism which we shall provide confirms the central thrust of this Aristotelian view, though, of course, it is the primitive central nervous system, or notochord-mesoderm, and not the heart, that is the regulative or controlling vital part in question.

It is plausible to suppose that a regulative vital part plays a more central role in the organization of an organism's parts than a nonregulative vital part. For example, it seems that a human's central nervous system plays a more prominent role in organizing a human's parts than does a human's heart. The principle of organization for the parts of an organism which we shall defend reflects this distinction between regulative and nonregulative vital parts.

We are now in a position to set forth the following idea as a promising basis for such a principle of organization. According to this idea, if x is a part of an organism, O, and e is any life-process or functional activity of x, then so long as the degree of naturalness of O's life-processes remains constant, e's continuing entails that there is a vital part, v, of O such that e is regulated by the functional activity of v. In this sense, there is at least one vital part, v, of O such that: the life-processes or functional activities of the organic living or functional parts of O are subordinate to v's functional activities. In every known case, v is a system of parts which have a joint natural function. It seems that organic living or functional entities compose O if and only if these entities are connected in this way. Hence, it appears that there is a sense in which all of O's organic living or functional parts are *united* in virtue of being so connected.

10 REGULATION AND FUNCTIONAL SUBORDINATION

In this section we explore in more detail the idea that an organism must have a vital part which regulates or controls that organism's life-processes.[63] We shall then define a technical concept of what it is for an organic living or functional entity to be functionally subordinate to such a vital regulative part. This technical concept will play a central role in the principle of organization for the parts of an organism which we shall propose.

It is in the nature of an organism to be self-sustaining and self-regulating: any organism must have some vital part whose functional activities *regulate* or *control* the life-processes or functional activities of the parts of that organism. In all known cases, the regulation or control of the life-processes of the parts of an organism is accomplished by means of the activities of a system of biological parts which jointly have a natural function, and this system may vary in its degree of centralization from one kind of organic living thing to another.

Animals appear to have a highly centralized regulatory system. Thus, an adult vertebrate seems to regulate its life-processes by means of the activities of a highly centralized system consisting of its brain and spinal cord, i.e., the central nervous system.[64] On the other hand, a plant appears to regulate its life-processes by means of the activities of a rather diffuse or decentralized system. For instance, a typical mature plant, P, may have a regulatory system consisting of P's roots, stem, and leaves. Although this regulatory system is decentralized, it cannot be identified with P as a whole. In particular, P's roots, stem, and leaves comprise much, though not *all*, of P. P also has the water and sugar molecules in its sap as parts, molecules which are discrete from P's roots, stem, and leaves.

A eukaryotic single-celled organism seems to have a highly centralized regulatory system, i.e., its nucleus, whereas a prokaryotic single-celled organism appears to have a centralized regulatory system involving its DNA and messenger RNA molecules.

In the light of the foregoing discussion, it seems that there could not be an organism which does not have a *vital proper part* which regulates or controls its life-processes. It appears that even the simplest possible organism, i.e., a protobiont, has such a vital proper part. For instance, assume for the sake of argument that a proteinoid microsphere qualifies as an organism. Even so, since a microsphere has proteinoid and water as parts, and since a microsphere's life-processes are regulated or controlled by information encoded in its proteinoid, its regulatory system is a proper part of itself. We conclude that, necessarily, an organism has a vital regulative proper part. Let us call a part of this kind a master-part.

The intuitive concept of a regulating or controlling cause employed in the foregoing discussion plays a role in both ordinary discourse and scientific reasoning. This intuitive causal concept is a concept of a stronger causal relation than either a contributing cause or a causal determinant. Moreover, being a regulating or controlling cause and being a sustaining cause are different relations. For example, the functional activities of a human's central nervous system regulate, directly or indirectly,[65] all of a human's life-processes, whereas the functional activities of a human's heart sustain, but do not regulate, these life-processes. In addition, possibly, the activities of y regulate or control the activities of x without the former activities sustaining the latter ones. For instance, it is logically possible that Jones's activities regulate or govern a corporation's activities even though Jones's activities do not sustain the corporation's activities.

We concede that the ordinary or scientific concept of a regulating or controlling cause is difficult to analyze. In this respect it resembles many other intuitive causal notions. Nonetheless, this ordinary or scientific concept is a legitimate one, and there is no reason to disallow its use in providing a principle of organization for the parts of an organism.[66]

We are now ready to define our technical conception of one functional thing being functionally subordinate to another.

(D7) x is functionally subordinate to y at a time t = df. at t, x is an organic living or functional entity, and y is an organic living or functional entity, and there exists an organism, O, such that: y is a vital proper part of O, and for some time t', later than t, but not so much later than t that O could not live from t until t', (the degree of naturalness of O's life-processes remaining constant from t until t') entails [that from t until t', y has a function, f, and any life-process or functional activity of x occurring at t' is regulated by y's performing f at some time t^* ($t \le t^* < t'$)].

Two observations about (D7) are in order.

First, (D7) defines a concept of a causal relation which must hold between a master-part of an organism and any part of that organism whose life-processes or functional activities are regulated by that master-part.[67] Ordinarily, in those cases in which y is a master-part which satisfies (D7), y is a system of parts having a joint natural function. For example, y might be the central nervous system of a living human being, O, and x *another* organic living part of O, for example, O's right lung, which is functionally subordinate to y. In another sort of case, x is *identical* with y. For instance, a human's central nervous system is a master-part of that human, one which is self-regulating. Thus, a human's central nervous system is functionally subordinate to itself, and is a limiting case of functional subordination in our technical sense.

Second, observe that in (D7) the term "function" applies not only to a natural function, but also to a fundamental biological activity of a part of an organism which is not the performance of a natural function. For example, it applies to the biological activity of certain parts, such as water molecules, inasmuch as these water molecules engage in, or causally contribute to, fundamental biological activities, for example, metabolism, growth, and reproduction. Of course, these water molecules do not literally have natural functions, because of their lack of sufficient structural complexity. But the term "function" in (D7) also applies (and more literally) to those biological activities of parts of organisms which are indeed performances of genuine natural functions: to the blood-cleaning activity of a kidney, to the food-digesting activity of a stomach, and so forth.[68]

In the latter case, (D7) utilizes natural functions in order to explicate the relation of functional subordination, as well as for the purpose of *identifying* some of the things which enter into this relation. Thus, (D7) is indeed a functional account, even if, as we have argued, the concept of a part of an organism having a natural function has a naturalistic analysis.

11 A PRELIMINARY ANALYSIS OF UNITY

As we argued earlier, an organic living thing is organic in the sense of having a chemical composition of a certain kind. In other words, an organism is a thing which has a certain compositional nature. We can discover such a compositional nature or essence only by engaging in an empirical study of organisms within the context of natural science. From the empirical study of organisms within this context, it is reasonable to conclude that this compositional essence involves the compositional attribute of having carbon-based macro-molecules and water molecules as parts.

We shall call anything which is possibly a part of an organism a *biotic entity*. Biotic entities may be either nonliving entities, for example, organic macromolecules and water molecules, or organic living entities, for example, heart cells and hearts.

But suppose that Jones's heart is successfully replaced with a pump made of plastic, rubber, and metal. Is this artificial heart a part of Jones? Does such an artificial heart count as a biotic entity? Such an artificial organ or device is not a biological entity: it is not an entity which is a proper object of scientific inquiry of a distinctively biological sort. An organism is an entity of a certain *natural kind* whose nature is investigated by an appropriate branch of natural science. Accordingly, it appears that the nature of an organism places certain limitations on what sorts of parts it can have. It seems that one of these limitations is that an organism cannot have an artificial organ or device of the sort in question as a part.[69] By this reasoning, an artificial heart made of plastic, rubber, and metal is not a part of Jones, any more than Jones's eyeglasses are a part of Jones: clearly, both are appliances that are in varying degrees useful to Jones, but Jones's nature precludes either of them being a part of Jones. On the basis of the foregoing argument, it appears that an artificial heart of this kind is not a biotic entity.

In contrast, given the nature of a human organism, it seems that a human's *biological* heart, kidneys, eyes, lungs, and so forth *are* parts of that human. It is evident that a human's *original* biological organs are parts of that human, and it would appear that a successfully transplanted biological organ, for example, a heart, is also a part of the recipient. But the claim that such an organ is a part of the recipient is not as obvious as the claim that an organism's original biological organs are parts of that organism. Nevertheless, since a biological organ that is successfully transplanted to an organism, O, is an organic living entity which is integrated into, or participates in, O's life-processes to a reasonably full extent, it is not implausible to suppose that a biological organ of this kind is a part of O. In any event, we aim to provide a principle of organization for the parts of an organism which is compatible with the possibility of an organism's having a transplanted part.

It might be hypothesized that it is necessary for every part of an organism to be either an organic living entity, a functional entity, or both. The class of organic living or functional parts of organisms includes organic living parts which have a natural function, for instance, a heart, nonliving parts which have a natural function, for example, DNA molecules, and nonliving functional parts which lack a natural function, for example, water molecules. It also includes organic living parts which lack a natural function. For instance, a human's appendix is an organic living part of the human in question, but it would appear that a human appendix is a vestigial organ which does not presently have a natural function. Second, male nipples are organic living parts of male mammals, but apparently do not have, and never did have, any natural function. Third, it is possible, through a mutation in the genes of a human, for a child to be born in 1997 with living tissue between its fingers. Although the webbing between its adjoining fingers would be an organic living part of this child, this tissue would lack a natural function.

For the sake of argument, suppose that it is necessary for every part of an organism to be either an organic living or a functional entity. In that case, it appears that the functional subordination relation can be utilized to provide a principle of organization for the parts of an organism in two steps, as follows.

(D8) Discrete biotic entities $P_1 \ldots P_n$ are *functionally connected* at a time t = df at t, $P_1 \ldots P_n$ are organic living or functional entities and there is a P_y, such that each of $P_1 \ldots P_n$ is functionally subordinate to P_y.

(D9) Discrete biotic entities $P_1 \ldots P_n$ are *functionally unified* at a time t = df. (i) at t, there is a P_y, such that $P_1 \ldots P_n$ are functionally connected in virtue of their being functionally subordinate to P_y, and (ii) at t, there does not exist a biotic entity discrete from $P_1 \ldots P_n$ which is functionally subordinate to P_y; and there does not exist a biotic entity discrete from P_y to which P_y is functionally subordinate.

(D9) is a preliminary attempt to use the relation of functional subordination defined in (D7) to analyze a causal relation which unifies the parts of an organism. In other words, (D9) attempts to analyze an organizing causal relation whose instantiation by biotic entities is logically necessary and sufficient for those entities to compose an organism. (D9) is relatively straightforward, and contains a key element of an adequate principle of organization of this kind.

The basic idea in clause (i) of (D9) is that the organic living or functional parts of an organism are unified in virtue of there being a vital part, P_y, of that organism, such that the life-processes or functional activities of the aforementioned parts are regulated by P_y's functional activities. We postpone the task of defending our technical formulation of this basic idea until the final version of our principle of organization for the parts of an organism has been stated.

Clause (ii) of (D9), henceforth known as the maximization requirement, is designed to guarantee that functionally unified biotic parts $P_1 \ldots P_n$ do not compose an organic living entity which is a mere proper part of an organism. Since (D9) is intended to provide the basis of a principle of organization for the parts of an *organism*, and since a proper part of an organism cannot qualify as an organism, a guarantee of this kind is required.

(D9) can be illustrated by using examples of organic living or functional parts of humans which are functionally connected, for instance, an eye, a liver cell, a heart, a kidney, the respiratory system, a blood cell, blood, mitochondria, cytoplasm, a cell nucleus, a strand of DNA, molecules of water, an appendix, male nipples, and webbed tissue between human fingers. According to (D9), a multicellular organism such as a human is composed of functionally connected organic living or functional parts, i.e., a heart, lungs, kidneys, blood, appendix, etc. These parts in turn are composed of further functionally connected organic living or functional entities, i.e., heart cells, kidney cells, brain cells, blood cells, appendix cells, etc. A cell which is part of a multicellular organism, or a unicellular organism such as a paramecium, is composed of functionally connected organic living or functional parts such as a nucleus, a cell membrane, mitochondria, golgi bodies, cytoplasmic fluids, and so forth. Organisms also have molecules, atoms, and subatomic particles as functional parts. Some of these microparticles have natural functions, for example, organic macromolecules such as proteins and nucleic acids, whereas others, which lack the complexity required for having a natural function, are still functional in the relevant sense, since they engage in, or causally contribute to, fundamental biological activities, for example, water molecules as well as their atomic and subatomic parts.[70] It appears that all of a human's organic living or functional parts are functionally subordinate to his or her central nervous system.

(D9) presents an attractive picture of the organization of the parts of an organism. Nevertheless, (D9) is subject to one serious difficulty. This difficulty is a consequence of (D9)'s requirement that every part of an organism be either an organic living or functional entity. Let us call an entity which is of either of these kinds a basic biotic entity. Unfortunately for (D9), it is possible for an organism to have as a part a functionless entity which is *not* an organic living entity. Accordingly, let us call an entity which is of this possible sort a nonbasic biotic entity. The possibility of a nonbasic biotic part is illustrated by the following two cases.

First, possibly as a result of a genetic mutation, in 1996 a horse is born that has on its back (as an expression of some of its genes) a functionless, nonliving hump, H. In such a case it is intuitively plausible to suppose that H is a part of the horse. But a nonliving part such as H neither has a natural function, nor engages in a fundamental biological activity, nor has activities which causally contribute to fundamental biological activities.

Second, intuitively, it is possible for there to be an organism, O, that has a nonliving organic macromolecule, M, as a part, where a large part of M has a function (call this part N), and a small part of M, i.e., a side chain joined to N, is nonliving and lacks a function (call this side chain C). We may assume that O's part M (which is a mereological compound) is composed of N and C. Because parthood is transitive, it follows from the fact that M is a part of O, and C is a part of M, that C is a part of O. But since C is a submolecular piece of "junk" or "garbage," it is a nonliving and functionless part of O.

Since it is possible for a *first* organism to have had a part such as *C from the start*, it is possible that O's having a part of this kind does not result from a mutation of an organism. And it could be the case that descendants of such protobionts inherit the trait of having a nonliving functionless part of this sort. Hence, it appears possible for protobionts as well as more advanced or evolved organisms to have or have had nonliving functionless parts independently of any mutation.

Inasmuch as C does not causally contribute to O's life-processes in any relevant way, there is a sense in which C's absence would not impede O's life-processes. How, then, is C's connection to other parts of O to be understood? There are two factors that seem to be relevant to understanding C's connection to other parts of O. The first is that C is joined to a functional part of O, that is, N.[71] The second is that necessarily, if O has a part such as C, then O, or some organic living part of O, possesses a hereditary trait for having such a part.

In the light of the two foregoing possible cases, we can see that it is possible for an organism to have a nonbasic biotic part. But unhappily for (D9), (D9) recognizes only basic biotic parts. Consequently, (D9) defines a causal relation, R^*, such that, possibly, parts which compose an organism fail to exemplify R^*. However, an analysis of the organizing causal relation for the parts of an organism defines a causal relation, R, such that, necessarily, parts compose an organism if and only if those parts exemplify R. Therefore, (D9) does not provide the basis of a satisfactory principle of organization for the parts of an organism.

12 A FINAL ANALYSIS OF UNITY

Despite this difficulty for (D9), we believe that it is possible to state a principle of organization for the parts of an organism which accommodates the possibility of nonbasic biotic parts and which is otherwise satisfactory. Our overall strategy for constructing such a principle is as follows. Building upon the idea of functional connectedness defined in (D8), we construct a more sophisticated analysis of an organizing causal relation for the parts of an organism. This enhanced analysis introduces a notion of functional unity that is somewhat broader than the notion of functional unification introduced in (D9). By using this broader notion we shall be able to provide a functional principle of organization for the parts of an organism which can accommodate the possibility of nonbasic biotic parts.

The broader notion of functional unity in question is defined partly in terms of a mereological relation which attaches a nonbasic biotic entity to a basic biotic entity. We specify this attachment relation in the following definition:

(D10) A nonbasic biotic entity, x, is attached to a basic biotic entity, y, at a time $t = $ df. (i) at t, x is a nonbasic biotic entity, and y is a basic biotic entity, and (ii) at t, either x (or a part thereof) and y (or a part thereof) compose a mereological compound in virtue of their being joined, or there is a material object, z, other than any of these entities, such that x (or a part thereof), y (or a part thereof), and z compose a mereological compound in virtue of their being joined and connected.

(D10) presupposes our principle of unity for the parts of a mereological compound in terms of the parts of that compound being joined and connected.[72]

By utilizing the concept of functional subordination defined in

(D7), and the concept of attachment defined in (D10), we formulate
the final version of our analysis of an organizing causal relation for
the parts of an organism as follows:

(D11) Discrete biotic entities $P_1 \ldots P_n$ are functionally united
at a time t = df. (i) at t, some or all of $P_1 \ldots P_n$ are basic biotic
entities, and there is a P_y, such that each of these basic biotic
entities is functionally subordinate to P_y, and (ii) at t, for any one
of $P_1 \ldots P_n$, P_x, if P_x is a nonbasic biotic entity, then P_x is
such that: [at t, or an earlier time, some part of P_y, or some part
of an organic living or functional entity that is functionally
subordinate to P_y, encodes hereditary information which, under
the environmental conditions obtaining up to t, is expressed at t
by P_x being attached to, or being inside of, some basic biotic entity
referred to in (i)],[73] and (iii) at t, there does not exist a biotic entity
discrete from $P_1 \ldots P_n$ which is functionally subordinate to
P_y; there does not exist a biotic entity discrete from P_y to which
P_y is functionally subordinate; and there does not exist a nonbasic
biotic entity discrete from $P_1 \ldots P_n$ which satisfies the condition
on nonbasic biotic entities in the bracketed portion of (ii).

The first clause of (D11) requires that functionally united basic biotic
entities are functionally connected as in (D8). But the first and
second clauses of (D11) also allow for the possibility that biotic
entities $P_1 \ldots P_n$ are functionally united even if some of $P_1 \ldots$
P_n are *not* basic biotic entities. The second clause of (D11) deals with
all of the possible cases of nonbasic biotic entities. The third
expresses a revised version of what we have called the maximization
requirement, suitably modified to cover both basic and nonbasic
biotic parts. This clause ensures that functionally united biotic parts
$P_1 \ldots P_n$ do not compose an organic living entity which is merely
a proper part of an organism, as is required.

We shall present a more detailed defense of (D11)'s adequacy as
an analysis of the organizing causal relation for the parts of an
organism in the following two sections. In the first of these sections,
we shall defend the thesis that clause (i) of (D11) is, together with
clause (iii), adequate for the purposes of uniting an organism's *basic*
biotic parts. In the second of these sections, we shall defend the
thesis that clause (ii) of (D11) is, together with clause (iii), adequate
for the purposes of uniting an organism's *nonbasic* biotic parts with
its basic biotic parts.

13 FUNCTIONAL CONNECTEDNESS AMONG BASIC BIOTIC PARTS

In this section we defend our claim that functional connectedness is a causal relation whose instantiation is, together with the satisfaction of the maximization condition, logically necessary and sufficient for the unity of the basic biotic parts of an organism. These are parts of the sort covered in clause (i) of (D11).

As we have argued, an organism, O, must have a master-part, i.e., a vital part which regulates O's life-processes, including the life-processes or functional activities of O's parts. Nevertheless, it might be possible for there to be an organism which survives the replacement of a master-part with a proxy. For example, it might be possible for there to be an organism which survives a master-part transplant. Although a central nervous system switch is currently not feasible, it would appear to be logically possible. Moreover, at the level of individual cells, successful nuclear transplants have been performed. One might worry that clause (i) of (D11) is not compatible with an organism's surviving a master-part switch, and hence that (D11) fails to provide a logically necessary condition of the unity of the basic biotic parts of an organism. In response to these doubts about (D11), we shall argue that clause (i) of (D11) is compatible with an organism's surviving a master-part switch. If this argument is correct, then the foregoing worry about (D11) is groundless.

Of course, it might be the case that a master-part switch is logically sufficient to cause the organism on the receiving end to go out of existence and be replaced by another. If so, then the worry about (D11) under consideration is groundless, since it assumes that it is possible for an organism to persist through such a switch. Nevertheless, for the sake of argument, we shall accept this assumption in dealing with this worry. In this book we remain neutral about whether or not the assumption in question is correct.

To simplify our argument, we shall suppress temporal indices throughout. As a part of this process of simplification we shall speak, somewhat loosely, of an organism's life-processes continuing *much longer*, where this refers to a temporal interval of relatively short duration and of suitable length for the basic biotic part in question per the condition in (D7).[74] This imprecise temporal interval can be eliminated in favor of existential quantification over times as in (D7).

For the purposes of our argument we shall assume that the central nervous system of a human is a master-part of that human,[75] and we shall take an example of this sort as representative. Let us instantiate (D11) with a typical human being's (S's) basic biotic parts, and S's central nervous system, P_y. In that case, this instance of [clause (i) of] (D11) is equivalent to the following entailment.

(E1) For any basic biotic part, x, of S, so long as the degree to which S's life-processes are natural *remains constant*, x's life-processes or functional activities continuing much longer entails that x's life-processes or functional activities are regulated by the functional activities of P_y.

Notice that (E1) is *de re* with respect to the entities specified in (E1). More specifically, the necessity expressed by (E1) is *de re* metaphysical necessity, and the attribution of necessity is with respect to certain particular *res* or entities, i.e., the life-processes or functional activities of any basic biotic part of S, S's life-processes, and S's central nervous system, P_y. It follows that an organism, for example, S, or S's central nervous system, has an essential nature or a *de re* essential attribute.[76]

Another extremely plausible proposition ascribing a *de re* essential nature to S is the following one. S is necessarily such that if S's life continues much longer, then S's life-processes are regulated by certain activities, activities which must either be performed by an original master-part, for instance, S's original central nervous system, or be performed by a replacement which assumes its function, for example, a central nervous system transplant. If these activities are not performed either by an original master-part or by a replacement, then S must die in the not too distant future. Parallel remarks apply to any organism (existing in any possible world).

We shall now demonstrate that (D11) is compatible with an organism's surviving a master-part switch by showing that the following *de re* entailment, (E2), holds with respect to the entities specified in (E2).

(E2) If P_{y*}, a replacement for P_y, assumes P_y's functional role in such a way that x's life-processes or functional activities are regulated by P_{y*}'s functional activity, but not by any functional activity of P_y, then this entails that it is *not* the case that the degree to which S's life-processes are natural remains constant, i.e., S's life-processes undergo either a decrease or an increase in their degree of naturalness, or cease to exist altogether, at some point in time.

It is apparent that if (E2) is true, then (E1) is compatible with S's surviving the replacement of P_y with P_{y*}. Since (E1) and the instance of (D11) under discussion are equivalent, (E2) implies that (D11) is compatible with S's surviving the replacement of its central nervous system with a proxy.

Let us call such a proxy or "functional equivalent," P_{y*}, a central nervous system *replacement*. Necessarily, such a replacement, P_{y*}, is either genetically identical with P_y, for example, a central nervous system transplant from an identical twin, or else not.

If P_y is replaced with a functional equivalent, P_{y*}, that is not genetically identical with P_y, then S acquires a microstructure that fails to conform entirely with the information implicit in S's micro-structural hereditary blueprint.[77] Hence, acquiring such a central nervous system replacement would result in a decrease in the degree to which S's microstructure conforms to the information implicit in S's microstructural hereditary blueprint. Consequently, acquiring a central nervous system replacement of this kind would produce a decrease in the degree to which S's life-processes are natural.

Moreover, even if P_{y*} and P_y were genetically identical, since the central nervous system replacement, P_{y*}, would have to be joined in some artificial or unnatural way to the appropriate nerves at some time, and since this is *not* implicit in S's microstructural hereditary blueprint, the result would be an overall decrease (at least for a time) in the degree to which S's life-processes are natural. Furthermore, S's central nervous system, P_y, being *replaced* by a *different* central nervous system, P_{y*}, would itself be an intrinsic change in S's structure of a kind that is at variance with the sorts of intrinsic changes in S's structure that are implicit in, and can occur as a result of, S's microstructural hereditary blueprint. For these reasons, whether P_{y*} and P_y were genetically identical or not, the replacement of S's central nervous system would have to result in a net decrease (at least for a time) in the degree to which S's life-processes are natural.

As we have seen, if a central nervous system replacement, P_{y*}, were to assume P_y's functional activities, then this would cause the degree of naturalness of S's life-processes to undergo a decrease at some time. It follows that S is necessarily such that if P_{y*} assumes P_y's functional activities, then this results in the degree to which S's life-processes are natural *failing to remain constant*. Therefore, (E2) is true. And as we have seen, if (E2) is true, then (D11) is compatible with S's surviving the replacement of its central nervous system, P_y, with a functional equivalent, P_{y*}. Consequently, (D11) is compatible with S's surviving such a switch.[78] Furthermore, a parallel argument applies to any organism (existing in any possible world), and to any master-part of that organism (in the possible world in question). Hence, the possibility of an organism's surviving a master-part switch does not cast any doubt upon (D11). Thus, this possibility does not undermine our claim that the functional connectedness of the organic living or functional parts of an organism is a logically necessary condition of their unity.

It is evident that this is true of any organic living part of an organism, O, regardless of whether that part has a natural function. It is also apparent that it holds for any nonliving part of O which has a natural function, for example, a DNA molecule. But does it hold true of a nonliving part of O, for instance, a water molecule, which lacks a natural function (in the full sense of that term)? Recall that it is our view that this question should be answered in the affirmative. Such a nonliving part of O (but not necessarily every nonliving part of O) engages in, or causally contributes to, one or more fundamental biological activities of O, for example, absorption, excretion, metabolism, growth, synthesis, or reproduction. We maintain that a nonliving part of this kind is functionally subordinate to a master-part of O in virtue of its participating in, or causally contributing to, one or more of these fundamental biological activities. For example, consider a particular water molecule, m, which is a part of O. Surely, so long as the degree of naturalness of O's life-processes remains constant, m's causally contributing to O's fundamental life-activities for much longer entails that m's activity in this regard is regulated by a master-part of O.

Did protobionts have parts with natural functions? If, as appears possible, a protobiont were to come into being because of a pre-biological natural selective process involving multiplication, variation, and (in some sense) the inheritance of traits which have reproductive or survival value, then it seems that this protobiont would have parts with full-fledged natural functions. We are prepared to understand the notion of natural selection employed in our account of natural functions broadly, so as to include a nonbiological natural selective process of this kind. On the other hand, if, as also seems possible, a protobiont were to come into existence as a result of a spontaneous process of self-assembly among organic molecules, then the structures of its parts would be suited to engage in the activities in question wholly by accident, and not because of a process of design or selection. In that case, none of the parts under discussion would have a full-fledged natural function. In either case, a protobiont must have had parts with the capacity to engage in, or causally contribute to, some fundamental life-processes or activities, for example, absorption, excretion, metabolism, growth, or reproduction. In other words, a protobiont must have had parts with functions in our extended sense. This is all that is required in order for our account to explain the unity or organization of a protobiont's parts.

Our thesis that the functional connectedness of basic biotic parts is logically necessary for their unity also has a number of desirable implications in a variety of typical and atypical cases. In what follows we illustrate this point.

Typically, two organisms, for instance, two humans, are such that neither has a vital part, p, such that p's functional activities regulate the life-processes or functional activities of a part of the *other* organism. Thus, the thesis that the functional connectedness of basic biotic parts is logically necessary for their unity has the welcome consequence that in typical cases, a basic biotic part of a human, for example, his or her heart or right ear, is not a basic biotic part of any *other* human.

However, there is a class of atypical cases in which an organism has a vital part whose functional activities sustain the life of *another* organism. One such atypical case is that of an unnatural arrangement in which one organism's life-processes sustain another organism's life via some artificial connection between them. Another is a case in which a host's life-processes sustain the life of a parasite. A third is a case in which a symbiont and its host or partner are mutually sustaining, respectively. Three representative cases of this kind are discussed below.

First, it is logically possible, by using highly sophisticated medical technology, for the appropriate arteries and veins in the chest of a human baby with heart failure to be connected to the heart of a strong, healthy, adult human, in such a way that the adult's heart pumps blood for both of them. In such a case, the functional activities of the adult's vital organs sustain the baby's life. Intuitively, the baby is not a part of the adult, but why not?

Second, consider the phenomenon of parasitism, in which one organism (the parasite) lives on or in another organism (the host) to the host's detriment. To cite one example, some humans have parasitic tapeworms living inside of them, and the functional activities of the human's vital organs sustain the tapeworm's life. Intuitively, the tapeworm is not a part of the human, but why not?

Third, there is the phenomenon of symbiosis, in which two organisms (symbionts) live together for mutual benefit. Symbiosis is also a case in which life-processes of one organism sustain life-processes of another organism. For instance, termites cannot digest their food without the protozoa that live in their intestines, but these protozoa cannot live independently of the termites under natural conditions. Thus, the termites and the protozoa are interdependent: typically, neither of them can live without the other. In a possible case in which two symbionts, A and B, are interdependent, the functional activities of A's vital organs sustain B's life, and the functional activities of B's vital organs sustain A's life. Intuitively, A is not a part of B, and B is not a part of A, but why not?

It is desirable that a principle of organization for the parts of an organism be able to provide informative answers to the three questions we have posed. Let us see how the analysis of an organizing causal relation for the parts of an organism we have proposed provides such answers.

In each of the three cases in question, there is a pair of organisms such that one (or both) of them has (have) a vital part whose functional activities sustain both of their lives. Yet, in none of these cases does either member of the pair have a master-part whose functional activities regulate the life-processes or functional activities of *both* its own organic living or functional parts and the organic living or functional parts of the other member of the pair. For example, there is not a central nervous system whose functional activities regulate the life-processes or functional activities of the parts of *both* the adult and the baby. Similar remarks apply in the case of the parasitic tapeworm and its human host, and in the case of the interdependent symbionts. But in order for there to be a multicellular organism whose parts are functionally connected, there must be a master-part whose functional activities regulate the life-processes or functional activities of the parts of that organism. Hence, in none of the three cases under discussion is there a multicellular organism whose parts are functionally connected and which include the basic biotic parts of both members of the pair of organisms in question. Therefore, the claim that the functional connectedness of basic biotic parts is logically necessary for their unity has the desirable implication that in atypical cases of the sorts we have discussed one organism is not a part of another. In addition, it seems that the functional subordination of functionally connected basic biotic parts to a master-part, together with the satisfaction of the maximization condition, is a logically *sufficient* condition of their unity. It will be instructive to see why the following possible case does not prove otherwise.

Imagine that there are two humans, Smith, a physician, and Jones, a patient of Smith. Jones is being kept alive by artificial life-support machines whose activities are under the control of Smith. Let us assume that through the operations of these machines the activity of Smith's central nervous system sustains Jones's life and regulates the life-processes or functional activities of Jones's basic biotic parts. In this case, would Jones's basic biotic parts be functionally subordinate to Smith's central nervous system, and therefore functionally connected with it? If so, then the functional connectedness of basic biotic parts, together with the satisfaction of the maximization requirement, would not be logically sufficient to unite them, because, presumably, in this instance there is not an organism which has as parts both Smith's central nervous system and Jones's basic biotic parts. But as the following line of reasoning shows, Jones's basic biotic parts would *not* be functionally subordinate to Smith's central nervous system, and hence would not be functionally connected with it. It is possible for control of the life-support machines to pass from Smith to another, equally capable, physician, and for Jones's life-processes to continue after this switch. But since it would not be implicit in Jones's microstructural hereditary blueprint that Smith's central nervous system regulates Jones's life-processes, the switch in question does *not* entail that there is a *change* in the degree to which Jones's life-processes are natural. It follows that Jones's basic biotic parts would not be functionally subordinate to Smith's central nervous system. Hence, Jones's basic biotic parts would not be functionally connected with Smith's central nervous system. We conclude that the case in question does not militate against our claim that the functional connectedness of basic biotic parts, together with the satisfaction of the maximization requirement, is logically sufficient to unite them.

We cannot think of any other cases which undermine this claim of logical sufficiency. And as we have argued, the functional connectedness of basic biotic parts is logically *necessary* for their unity. We conclude, therefore, that the functional connectedness of basic biotic parts, together with the satisfaction of the maximization condition, is logically necessary and sufficient to unite them.

14 NONBASIC BIOTIC PARTS

Clause (ii) of (D11) specifies a relation which, together with the maximization condition, is logically necessary and sufficient for connecting a nonbasic biotic part of an organism with a basic biotic part of an organism. This clause requires that a nonbasic biotic part is either attached to, or inside of, a basic biotic part. One thing's being inside of another is a familiar two-term relational spatial concept which we shall not attempt to define or analyze. Attachment was defined in (D10).[79] Clause (ii) of (D10) implies that necessarily, a nonbasic biotic part, $p1$, is attached to a basic biotic part, $p2$, just when $p1$ (or a part thereof) and $p2$ (or a part thereof) are joined and connected.[80] Clause (ii) of (D11) requires that this attachment or containment be an expression (in the environmental conditions) of hereditary information encoded by an appropriate organic living or functional part. Clause (ii) of (D11) secures reference to an appropriate encoding part in a recursive manner. That is, this clause recursively characterizes such an encoding part as one which is either a part of the master-part, P_y, referred to in clause (i) of (D11), or a part of an organic living or functional entity which is functionally subordinate to that master-part.

Earlier, we described two possible cases of organisms which have nonbasic biotic parts.[81] In describing how clause (ii) of (D11) applies to these and three other possible cases, we shall speak of hereditary information being encoded in a part, or in genes, of an organism. When we speak in this fashion, we presuppose that this is to be cashed out in terms of the aforementioned recursive characterization.

First, there is the possible case in which a horse has a nonliving functionless hump on its back that is a part of the horse. In this case, the hump is attached to the horse's hide in virtue of hereditary information encoded in the horse's genes. Thus, a nonbasic biotic part of the horse, the hump, is attached to a basic biotic part of the horse, the hide, in virtue of the fact that hereditary information encoded in the genes of the horse is expressed (under the environmental conditions) as the hump's being attached to the hide. Hence, the hump satisfies clause (ii) of (D11), and (D11) has the intuitively correct implication that the hump is united with a basic biotic part of the horse.

Moreover, the hump's being attached to the horse's hide as a genetic expression of the sort required entails that the hump's *parts* are attached to the horse's hide as such a genetic expression. Therefore, (D11) implies, as it should, that each of the hump's parts is united with a basic biotic part of the horse.

Second, there is the possible case in which an organism, O, has as a part a nonliving functionless side chain, C, such that C and a functional entity, N, compose an organic macromolecule M. In the case in question, C is attached to N in virtue of hereditary information encoded in O's genes. Accordingly, a nonbasic biotic part of O, C, is attached to a basic biotic part of O, N, in virtue of the fact that hereditary information encoded in O's genes is expressed (in the environmental circumstances) as C's being attached to N. Therefore, C satisfies clause (ii) of (D11), and (D11) has the desirable consequence that C is united with a basic biotic part of O.

In addition, C's being attached to N as a genetic expression of the requisite sort entails that C's *parts* are attached to N as such a genetic expression. Accordingly, (D11) implies, as it ought to, that each of C's parts is united with a basic biotic part of O.

On the other hand, if a nonbasic biotic entity is attached to an organism, but not in virtue of hereditary information of the requisite sort, then, intuitively, this nonbasic biotic entity is *not* a part of that organism. (D11) captures this intuition. For instance, intuitively, if a molecule of glucose is attached to the left hand of a human with Superglue, then that molecule does not count as a part of that human. After all, if a glucose molecule is glued to a human in this way, then it is not attached to that human in virtue of hereditary information of the sort required. In other words, a glucose molecule's being attached to a human in this manner is not an expression (under the environmental circumstances) of hereditary information encoded in a part of that human, as clause (ii) of (D11) requires. Consequently, such a glucose molecule fails to satisfy clause (ii) of (D11), and (D11) has the welcome implication, intuitively speaking, that a glucose molecule of this kind is *not* united with a basic biotic part of a human.

As we mentioned earlier, clause (ii) of (D11) allows for the possibility of an organism's having a nonbasic biotic part which is not attached to a basic biotic part, provided that the nonbasic biotic part is inside of a basic biotic part in virtue of hereditary information encoded in a part of the organism in question. A possible example of such a part is a nonliving functionless molecule floating in the cytoplasm of a paramecium, where this molecule's being located within the perimeter of the paramecium's cell membrane is an expression of the paramecium's genes in the environmental conditions. It is intuitively plausible that the molecule under discussion is a part of the paramecium. It is also apparent that a molecule of this sort satisfies clause (ii) of (D11). Thus, (D11) has the welcome consequence that such a molecule is united with a basic biotic part of the paramecium.

Furthermore, if such a molecule is inside the paramecium's cell membrane as a genetic expression of the sort required, then this entails that the *parts* of that molecule are inside this cell membrane as a genetic expression of this kind. Hence, (D11) implies, as it should, that each part of such a molecule is united with a basic biotic part of the paramecium.

The foregoing example stands in sharp contrast to the following possible case. Suppose that a human, Jones, ingests an indigestible nonbasic biotic entity, for example, a molecule of cellulose which is nonliving and functionless. Although this molecule is inside of a basic biotic part of an organism, for instance, Jones's stomach, it is intuitively plausible that the molecule in question is *not* a part of Jones. (D11) does justice to this intuition. After all, the cellulose molecule is not inside of Jones's stomach in virtue of hereditary information encoded in a part of Jones: this nonliving functionless molecule's being inside of Jones's stomach is not an expression (under the environmental conditions) of hereditary information encoded in a part of Jones. Nor is this cellulose molecule attached to a basic biotic part of Jones as an expression (in the environmental circumstances) of such hereditary information. It is clear that such a molecule does not satisfy clause (ii) of (D11). Hence, (D11) has the desirable implication that the molecule under discussion is *not* united with a basic biotic part of Jones.

It should be noted that although we allow for the possibility of functionless parts of organisms, our analysis of an organizing causal relation for the parts of an organism in (D11) *is* a functional one. This is because (D11) allows for the possibility of a functionless part by relating it (directly or indirectly) to a basic biotic part which *is* functional, i.e., to a master-part or to a part that is functionally subordinate to a master-part.

Let us summarize. In the preceding section, we defended our claim that the first clause of (D11) specifies a connecting relation whose instantiation, together with the satisfaction of the maximization condition, is logically necessary and sufficient for the unity of all of an organism's (O's) basic biotic parts. And as we have argued in this section, the second clause of (D11) specifies a connecting relation whose instantiation, together with the satisfaction of the maximization condition, is logically necessary and sufficient for uniting a nonbasic biotic part of O to a basic biotic part of O. Furthermore, it is a necessary truth that every part of O is either a basic biotic part or a nonbasic biotic part. We have also argued that the maximization requirement in the third clause of (D11) is adequate to the task for which it was designed.[82] We conclude that a satisfactory principle of organization for the parts of an organism is expressed by the following necessary equivalence.

(P_O) (Discrete biotic entities $P_1 \ldots P_n$ are organized into an organism at a time t) $\Leftrightarrow$ (at t, $P_1 \ldots P_n$ are functionally united).

15 PROBLEM CASES

There are nonstandard cases in which uncertainty may arise about whether an organic living entity is a part of an organism. Intuitions about whether an organic living entity is a part of an organism in these problem cases tend to be unclear.

The first case concerns a living cell (of a multicellular organism) which undergoes a mutation. As a result of repeated acts of binary fission, this cell may give rise to an association of living cells. Our discussion will cover four possible examples: (i) a malignant cell, (ii) a malignant growth or association of malignant cells, for example, a cancerous tumor, (iii) a benign cell, and (iv) a benign growth or association of benign cells, for instance, a benign mole.

If a multicellular organism, O, is afflicted with a malignancy, then is this malignancy a *part* of O? Intuitively, such a malignancy is a "renegade," a living cell, or association of living cells, which does not belong to the association of cells which is O. This intuition is predicated on the idea that the life-processes of a malignancy are not under the regulation or control of the organism afflicted with that malignancy. Thus, it is intuitively plausible to suppose that a malignancy is not a part of O. Our principle of organization for the parts of an organism has the merit of cohering with this intuition. In particular, this principle of organization requires that the life-processes of a living part of an organism are regulated or controlled by a master-part of that organism, but it is necessarily true that a malignancy's life-processes are not under the regulation or control of a master-part of the afflicted organism.

On the other hand, an autoimmune disease, for example, one in which cells of the immune system destroy cells of the nervous system, appears to be a case in which the activities of the former cells continue to be regulated by an organism's master-part, but in an abnormal, self-destructive way. Thus, unlike a malignancy, it seems that the aforementioned cells of the immune system qualify as parts of an organism.

Are the life-processes of a typical benign growth regulated or controlled by a master-part of an organism in the necessary way? Unlike the cells in a malignant growth, the cells in a typical benign growth exhibit a rather orderly and regular pattern. Perhaps, then, unlike the life-processes of a malignancy, the life-processes of a typical benign growth are regulated or controlled in the requisite way by a master-part of the organism. If so, then it seems that a benign growth counts as a living part of an organism. Nevertheless, it is not completely clear to us that the life-processes of such a growth are regulated or controlled by a master-part of the organism in the required manner. If these life-processes are not regulated or controlled in this manner, then a typical benign growth does not, after all, qualify as a part of an organism. In sum, although there is some reason to think that a typical benign growth is a living part of an organism, at the present time it is not evident to us that this is the case.

It seems that with sufficient empirical evidence, the foregoing questions, and a host of related ones, can be answered one way or the other. Yet, there are atypical cases which are intermediate between the case of a typical benign growth and the case of a malignant growth. In these intermediate cases, cell growth is partly ordered and partly disordered. In some of these cases it may be doubted whether we can have sufficient empirical evidence for determining whether the life-processes of these cells are under the regulation or control of an organism's master-part in the requisite sense. Thus, it is questionable whether we can discern whether such growths or cells are a part of an organism by appealing to our principle of organization. But cases of this kind are marginal, and if we cannot ascertain whether growths or cells of this kind are parts of an organism by using our principle, then this does not detract significantly from its utility.

Another sort of case concerns endosymbionts or symbionts that live inside of a host organism. It seems possible for what was *once* a species of endosymbiont to evolve to a point at which the natural functions of the parts of its descendants are so intimately and completely coordinated with the natural functions of its host's parts, to the host's benefit, that these descendants *cease* to belong to a distinct species of organism, and become organic living functional *parts* of the host organism. Thus, an organic living functional part of this kind, like a specialized functional cell which is a part of a heart or a kidney, is not a full-fledged *organism*. There is considerable evidence that mitochondria are examples of organic living functional parts of this kind.

As the examples of parasites and symbionts discussed earlier illustrate, for any two organisms, O_1 and O_2, if O_1 and O_2 belong to *different* biological species, then O_1 and O_2 are discrete from one another, and there is no organism which has both O_1 and O_2 as parts. Although O_1 and O_2 depend upon one another, they do not depend upon one another in as intimate a fashion as is required, i.e., there is no master-part which sustains and regulates the life-processes of both O_1 and O_2. Thus, organisms of different species belonging to the same ecosystem are not united into a single organism.

In many cases, protista (nonmulticellular *organisms*) of the *same* species form associations which have survival or reproductive value for those protista. Still, it seems that, typically, these associations of protista cannot be identified with multicellular organisms. But how is the distinction between a multicellular organism and a more casual association (or colony) of protista to be drawn? A plausible way to draw this distinction is as follows. A multicellular organism must have at least one vital proper part which regulates the life-processes of all of the associated cells, whereas a colony of protista does *not* have such a part. We suggest that every multicellular organism must have such a master-part. If we are right, then the distinction between a multicellular organism and a mere colony of protista can be drawn in a principled fashion.

Parallel arguments imply that for any two multicellular organisms, O_1 and O_2, if O_1 and O_2 belong to the *same* species, then O_1 and O_2 are not united into a third organism, and neither of them is a part of the other. Accordingly, multicellular organisms of the same species belonging to an ecosystem, for example, bees in their hive, and ants in their colony, are not united into an organism. Parallel remarks apply to a pregnant woman and her fetus, and to Siamese twins.

There is a continuum of possible cases of Siamese twins, ranging from those in which the twins are so superficially connected that the vital life-processes of neither of them are causally necessary in the circumstances for the continuance of the life-processes of the other, to those in which the twins are so intimately connected that the vital life-processes of each sustain the life-processes of the other. For example, they range from a case in which the twins are attached by only a thin piece of connective tissue, which can be disconnected easily, to a case in which the life-processes of the twins are sustained by the activities of one or more of the *same* vital organs, for instance, a heart or a liver which is a part of one or the other of them. Such twins either resemble two humans who are artificially glued together, or resemble a human whose heart engages in functional activities which sustain another human's life-processes via some unnatural connection between those humans. If one human is glued or connected to another in such an artificial or unnatural way, then there does not exist an organism which has both of these humans as parts. Since in such a case there does not exist a master-part which regulates the life-processes of both humans, two humans of this kind are not functionally united in the manner required by our principle of organization for the parts of an organism.

Among chordates (a classification which includes all vertebrates), how are Siamese twins to be distinguished from a creature with supernumerary organs? For example, what is the basis for distinguishing between Siamese twin turtles and a turtle with two hearts?

These questions can be answered as follows. Siamese twins and a creature with supernumerary organs are produced by the blastula in different ways. Siamese twins result from a division (or fusion) of one (or two) portions of the primitive notochord-mesoderm, where each of these portions contains a primary organizer for an entire creature. In contrast, a creature with supernumerary organs is produced by a secondary field organizer (or an organ organizer) which is formed under the influence of a primary organizer and which is not located in the same part of the blastula as a primary organizer. Because the genesis and formation of Siamese twins is distinct from that of a creature with supernumerary organs, it seems possible to distinguish between them in a principled way.[83]

The developmental history of a Siamese twin is mirrored in the organization of its parts. Each part of the twin develops from a primary organizer in the notochord-mesoderm, and that organizer eventually develops into a Siamese twin's central nervous system.

Other vital parts, for example, the circulatory, digestive, respiratory, and excretory systems, are formed under the influence and control of that primary organizer via the activities of a functionally subordinate secondary organizer. The upshot is that eventually these vital parts are regulated or controlled by just one central nervous system, viz., the one which developed from the primary organizer in question. That is, the brain and spinal cord of a Siamese twin is a master-part, and while the life-processes of a Siamese twin's vital parts are functionally subordinate to that master-part, these life-processes are not functionally subordinate to the corresponding master-part of its twin, viz., its twin's brain and spinal cord. Thus, for example, if Siamese twins "share" a single liver, L, then, strictly speaking, L will be a proper part of only one of the twins, i.e., the one whose primary organizer is ultimately responsible for L's existence. The activities of L are functionally subordinate to the central nervous system of the twin in question, but are not functionally subordinate to the central nervous system of the other twin. Since a parallel argument applies to any of a Siamese twin's vital parts, it follows that Siamese twins do not have any of their *vital* parts in common.

If Siamese twins have some *nonvital* basic biotic part in common, then the life-processes or functional activities of this nonvital part must be regulated by two central nervous systems at the same time. This implies a kind of causal overdetermination which appears to be possible. Thus, it seems possible that there are Siamese twins which have a part in common. It appears that the most likely example of a shared part of this kind is skin or bone where the Siamese twins in question are connected.

Chapter 5

What kinds of physical substances are there?

1 ATOMS, MEREOLOGICAL COMPOUNDS, AND ORDINARY PHYSICAL OBJECTS

In this chapter, we shall consider in general what sorts of physical objects can plausibly be said to exist. We begin by distinguishing four kinds of physical objects. The first three are types of inanimate objects: (1) atomic objects; (2) compounds which have their parts essentially; and (3) nonliving compounds which can undergo mereological change. The fourth kind, organisms, are animate compounds which can undergo mereological change.

By an atom we mean a physically simple substance, i.e., a physical substance which has no other physical substance as a part. There is a further distinction to be drawn here. First, there is the possibility of unextended point-particles. Second, there is the possibility of a different sort of physically simple substance, viz., Democritean atoms, or indivisible voluminous particles.

Leibniz argues against the possibility of Democritean atoms as follows: (i) necessarily, any compound is composed of simples (things which lack parts); (ii) necessarily, any extended substance is compound (has parts); therefore, (iii) necessarily, since a Democritean atom is extended, it is compound, and hence composed of simples. But, (iv) a Democritean atom is by definition a physical simple, and consequently cannot be composed of simples. Thus, (v) a Democritean atom is impossible. We reject premises (i) and (iv). Premise (i) is false because it implies that an extended entity can be built up out of unextended entities, and this is impossible.[1] Premise (iv) is false as well, because a Democritean atom is not a simple in Leibniz's sense. Rather it is a simple in the sense stated in the preceding paragraph, viz., it has no other *physical substance* as a part. The parts of a Democritean atom are not physical substances because they are not detachable and cannot exist independently of the substance of which they are parts.[2]

There seems to be no conceptual problem standing in the way of the existence of atoms, and there may be conceptual arguments supporting their existence. Some have argued, for example, that there cannot be compound physical substances unless there are simple or atomic physical substances. We are prepared to assume that physical objects exist. Thus, if we may also assume that the existence of compound physical objects entails the existence of simple physical objects, then we may conclude that there are atoms. We find such an argument fairly persuasive, but not conclusive. Jonathan Lowe has argued along similar lines that physical compounds have to be composed of physical simples on the basis of a principle of "well-foundedness."[3] On the other hand, both Aristotle and Descartes held that physical objects are infinitely divisible. Since the existence of infinitely divisible physical objects seems conceivable, there is some doubt about whether the existence of compound physical objects entails the existence of physical simples. In any case, there are sufficiently strong empirical reasons to affirm the existence of voluminous atomic particles, for example, Democritean atoms in the form of electrons and photons. We doubt that there is at present good empirical evidence for the existence of point-particles.

The existence of compound inanimate and animate objects is supported by both science and common sense.[4] For example, common sense recognizes objects such as ships, rocks, statues, snowballs, frogs, flowers, and so forth, and science recognizes objects such as water molecules, crystals, organic compounds, frogs, flowers, and so forth. Moreover, some philosophers would distinguish between a statue, for instance, and the piece of marble which constitutes it. We can indicate the sort of object which constitutes the statue by describing it as a statue-shaped piece of marble. Let an object such as a statue be called an ordinary physical object. The aforementioned philosophers hold that an ordinary physical object can undergo a change in its parts, i.e., can undergo mereological change. However, they also hold that the piece of marble, which is a material object spatially coincident with the statue, cannot undergo a change in its parts. In other words, it has its parts essentially, and anything which is not a part of it could not be a part of it. We have called such objects mereological compounds.[5] For example, it is intuitively the case that the statue-shaped piece of marble ceases to exist if it loses even a *tiny* part. It would then be succeeded by a slightly smaller statue-shaped piece of marble which was a proper part of the original statue-shaped piece of marble. Likewise, intuitively, if a minuscule piece of matter is added to the statue-shaped piece of marble, then a larger statue-shaped piece of marble comes into being that is composed of the original statue-shaped piece of marble and the minuscule addition. The original piece of marble would then be a proper part of the newly created statue-shaped piece of marble. On the other hand, such philosophers would argue, a statue can persist even though the original matter has been partly or even completely replaced (as long as the replacement has been gradual).[6] In such a case, it is clear that the piece of matter or mereological compound that originally constituted the statue no longer exists, even though the statue still exists.[7]

Usually, the philosophical defenders of ordinary physical objects (rocks, statues, ships, etc.) would concede the primacy of the constituting mereological compounds, and would describe the former as *depending* upon the latter. A plausible rationale for this stance is that a change in, or the stability of, the former can be understood and explained only in terms of a change in, or the stability of, the latter. Scientific research has revealed that ordinary physical objects are not the kinds of objects in terms of which explanations of the behavior of such objects can be framed. These explanations must be stated in terms of constituting mereological compounds whose parts are essential to them.

Eli Hirsch has expressed an opposing view.[8] According to Hirsch, ordinary physical objects like rocks and ships are more basic than mereological compounds. He infers this from the premise that the concepts of the former are observational and less abstract, while the concepts of the latter are theoretical and more abstract. We fail to see the connection between being more basic ontologically and being more observational and concrete. Why should we think that relations of dependence among physical objects correspond to how directly such objects are observed or known? Has not science taught us that this assumption is false?

However, the doctrine of mereological essentialism with respect to physical objects implies that *no* such object can undergo a change in its parts, i.e., that every object of this kind has each of its parts essentially. Thus, such a view presents a challenge to the common-sense and philosophical belief in the reality of ordinary physical objects. For example, according to Roderick Chisholm, a prominent mereological essentialist, a physical thing that undergoes mereo-logical change is nothing but a logical construction upon a succes-sion of mereological compounds.[9] In Chisholm's view, a ship, for example, which "persists" through the gradual replacement of its parts is what Chisholm calls an *ens successivum*. With this de-scription, he means to imply that such a ship has identity over time in a "loose and popular sense" only, and not in a "strict and philosophical sense." Thus, he appears to set out to *eliminate* any physical thing which can putatively undergo mereological change in favor of mereological compounds which succeed one another over time in a certain way.

This view, however, gives rise to a problem in the case of organisms, for example, plants, worms, and humans. In particular, since organisms are physical things which putatively undergo mereo-logical change, Chisholm's view implies that organisms are logical constructions, and hence eliminable. But since it seems that *we* are living things, and since it is a very powerful datum that we ourselves are *ineliminable*, it seems that at least some living things are not eliminable. Because Chisholm would agree with this conclusion about the ineliminability of the self, it seems that in order for him to hold a consistent set of principles, he must hold that selves are substantial things which have identity in a strict and philosophical sense over their lifetimes and which are incapable of mereological change. Evidently, such a substance is not an organism. It appears instead that a substance of this kind is either a soul or a microparticle of some kind that possesses psychological properties. Needless to say, each of these alternatives is quite difficult to defend empirically.

Thus, those who subscribe to mereological essentialism about physical objects would argue that putative inanimate objects like rocks, statues, and ships do not really exist, and likewise for putative organisms like frogs, flowers, and cats. The only compound physical objects which actually exist, on this view, are the mereological compounds which have been thought by some to constitute or compose such putative objects or organisms. Of course, mereological essentialism is radically at odds with common sense in implying that organisms do not exist. But the mereological essentialist would maintain that there are convincing conceptual, or *a priori*, arguments against the existence of organisms and other ordinary physical objects. He would say correctly that, in general, common sense should give way when convincing conceptual or *a priori* arguments come into conflict with it. Therefore, to evaluate his view, we must ask, what are the conceptual arguments that the mereological essentialist can bring to bear against the existence of ordinary physical objects, both animate and inanimate, and are they convincing?

2 THE PROBLEM OF INCREASE

A first conceptual argument of the mereological essentialist against the reality of ordinary physical things is based upon what is known as the problem of increase.[10] According to this argument, there is an incoherence in the idea of a material thing's growing or increasing by the addition of a part (and a parallel argument can be constructed for decrease). Thus, the problem of increase is meant to be a challenge to the very possibility of mereological change.

Suppose that there is a material thing, *a* (see Figure 2). Necessarily, if *a* increases by the addition of a part, *b*, then there exists the

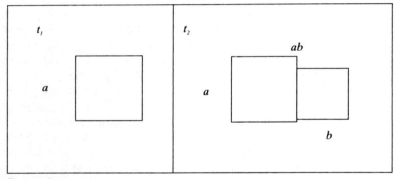

Figure 2

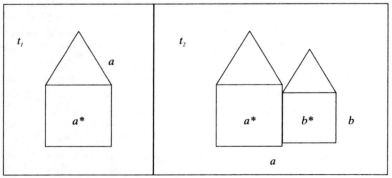

Figure 3

compound material thing *ab*. (We assume in this and in later, parallel, examples that what constitutes or composes *a* before the addition of *b* also constitutes or composes the thing which is labeled "*a*" after the addition of *b*.) In that case, what has increased? Not *a*, for it has remained the same. Not *b*, which (we assume) is no larger than before. And, finally, not *ab*, which has not increased, since it did not even exist before. This argument appears to be a *reductio ad absurdum* of the hypothesis that a material thing can increase by the addition of a part.

One reply that the defender of ordinary inanimate physical objects may give is that the foregoing argument equivocates between ordinary physical objects and the mereological compounds which constitute them. At time t_1, let *a* be an ordinary physical object, for example, a house (see Figure 3).

At time t_2, let *b* be a room added to that house. In that case, the house *has* increased, even though the mereological compound, a^*, which constituted the house before the addition, has *not* increased. At t_2, the house, *a*, is constituted by a mereological compound composed of a^* and the mereological compound, b^*, which constitutes the addition, *b*. At t_2, it is not *a*, or the original house, but a^*, the mereological compound that had constituted *a* at t_1, that is identical with (or constitutive of) a proper part of the enlarged house. This response implies, of course, that the house *is other than* the mereological compound which constitutes it at any given time, and therefore, that at any time at which the house exists, there are *two* physical objects in the same place, the house *and* the mereological compound.

Thus, there are two costs which the defender of ordinary inanimate physical objects such as houses must pay to avoid the problem of increase. First, he must concede that more than one physical object can occupy the same space at the same time. Second, he must accept that there is a peculiar *constituting* relation which holds between mereological compounds and ordinary inanimate physical objects.

Parsimony may seem to militate against the belief that there are two objects in the same place at the same time. But more needs to be said in order to show that in this case commonsense beliefs in ordinary physical objects are outweighed by considerations of parsimony.

One additional reason for abandoning these commonsense beliefs is that the constituting relation is a mysterious or vacuous one. This, in turn, may elicit the reply that the constituting relation is a relation of *supervenience*. In particular, it is a dependence relation of a supervening entity (an inanimate ordinary physical object) upon a more basic entity (a mereological compound), such that, necessarily, if any two more basic (constituting) entities share all of the same intrinsic qualities, then the two corresponding less basic (constituted) entities which supervene upon them will share all of the same intrinsic qualities. This reply helps to clarify the nature of the constituting relation, but doubts remain about why one should suppose that the relation actually holds in any case. After all, what is the necessity of positing the existence of ordinary inanimate physical objects in addition to mereological compounds? Why should it be thought that the former objects somehow emerge from the latter? Isn't this emergence rather mysterious?

In the light of the foregoing discussion, we find that the argument based on the problem of increase raises serious difficulties for the proposition that ordinary inanimate physical objects actually exist. We shall supplement this challenge to the existence of ordinary inanimate physical objects with further arguments below, and eventually we shall come to the conclusion that ordinary inanimate physical objects are indeed unreal.

The argument based on the problem of increase can also be applied to organisms. But in that instance, the reply to the argument is different than in the case of ordinary inanimate physical objects. Applied to organisms, this argument claims that a (an organism) cannot increase. This claim presupposes that there is an organism, a^*, after the alleged increase, at time t_2, such that at t_2, a^* is a proper part of the allegedly enlarged organism, a; at t_2, a^* is identical with a less the added part, b; and at t_2, a^* is identical with a at time t_1 (see Figure 4).

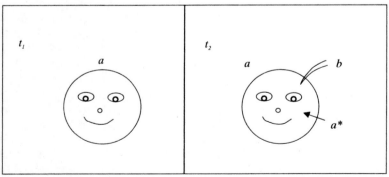

Figure 4

There is a reply to this argument which refutes this presupposition based on the following two premises. First, as we argued in Chapter 4, necessarily, an organism is not a part of another living thing. Second, any entity which is an organism is essentially an organism.[11] These premises seem unproblematic. Given the first premise, on the hypothesis that $a*$ is a proper part of an enlarged organism, it follows that $a*$ is not an organism. Moreover, since a is an organism, a is essentially an organism. It follows that $a* \neq a$. Therefore, the presupposition that there is a living thing, $a*$, after the alleged increase, which is a proper part of the allegedly enlarged organism, and which is identical with a, is false. Hence, the argument based on the problem of increase does not appear to pose any real threat to the reality of organisms.

We further observe that in replying to the problem of increase for organisms we did not need to appeal to the existence of constituting mereological compounds. There seem to be no such compounds constituting living organisms, since, as we saw in Chapter 4, it is always or almost always the case that the parts of living organisms are *not* joined and connected. Thus, the defense of living organisms against the problem of increase does not seem to involve a commitment either to there being two physical objects in the same place at the same time, or to there being a constituting relation holding between mereological compounds and living organisms.

Still, it might be denied that in replying to the problem of increase for organic living things one would never need to appeal to the existence of constituting mereological compounds, on the ground that there are some living things whose parts *are* joined and connected. If the parts of a living thing at a given time are joined and connected, then those parts compose a mereological compound at that time. Moreover, if there could be an organic living thing whose parts were joined and connected, then (at least in some cases) the living thing could undergo mereological change, while the mereological compound in question could not. Given all this, it follows that the living thing would not be identical with the mereological compound which existed in the same place at the same time. In this case, we would have an instance of a mereological compound constituting a living thing.

Putative cases of such living things are of two kinds. The first sort of instance is of alleged life-forms of an extremely primitive nature, for example, self-replicating molecules of nucleic acids, and crystals of tobacco mosaic virus. The second sort of example is of allegedly living things of a more sophisticated nature that are frozen solid or desiccated, for example, a freeze-dried insect which is inactive but capable of being revived through rehydration. We concede that the parts of such putative living things are joined and connected. However, we maintain that organic macromolecules, viruses, and freeze-dried insects are nonliving or inanimate objects. As we argued in Chapter 4, organic macromolecules and viruses do not have a comprehensive enough variety of fundamental biological activities to count as being alive. Moreover, it seems that an insect which is freeze-dried, and can be revived later, is not currently alive. Strictly speaking, the commonsense description of such a case as one of suspended animation implies that the insect in question is no longer an animate object or a living thing. It lacks a "life" in the sense that it is not engaged in any life-processes or activities.[12]

Furthermore, it is evident that there cannot be something which is simultaneously living *and* inanimate, as this implies a contradiction. In addition, since the parts of a freeze-dried insect are joined and connected, they compose a mereological compound. Because a mereological compound has its parts essentially, and a living insect does not, this mereological compound cannot be identified with a living insect. Thus, if a freeze-dried insect is a living thing, then (as we noted earlier) both it and a corresponding mereological compound are in the same place at the same time, with the latter constituting the former. Since parsimony militates against the notion that there are two objects in the same place at the same time, and since the judgment of common sense is that a freeze-dried insect is not a living thing, there are good reasons to reject the claim that a freeze-dried insect is a living thing which simultaneously occupies the same place as a mereological compound. Therefore, it seems that a freeze-dried insect is an *inanimate* mereological compound,[13] and that its existence does not stand in the way of our general conclusion that living things are not constituted by mereological compounds. Nor we do see how there could be any kind of living thing whose parts were joined and connected, because, being so constructed, such entities could not engage in the range of activities necessary for life.

The only barrier to holding that material objects $P_1 \ldots P_n$ being joined and connected is logically sufficient for $P_1 \ldots P_n$ to compose an inanimate object is the possible existence of living entities such as self-replicating organic macromolecules, viruses, and freeze-dried insects, together with the assumption that there cannot be two things in the same place at the same time. If one were to grant all this, there could be cases where joined and connected material objects $P_1 \ldots$ P_n compose a living thing but not a mereological compound. But, as we have just seen, there cannot be a living thing composed of material objects $P_1 \ldots P_n$ that are joined and connected, and self-replicating organic macromolecules, viruses, and freeze-dried insects are not alive. Hence, material objects $P_1 \ldots P_n$ being joined and connected *is* logically sufficient for $P_1 \ldots P_n$ to compose an inanimate mereological compound.

Because any living thing, x, is essentially a living thing, and because a freeze-dried insect, y, is not a living thing, if x exists at a time, t_1, and y exists at another time, t_2, then $x \neq y$. In particular, a freeze-dried insect is not identical with either a living insect before freeze-drying or a living insect revived after freeze-drying. However, it seems that a particular living insect can be freeze-dried and revived later. Thus, it appears that there are living things that can have intermittent existence. The possibility of a thing's having inter-mittent existence is unproblematic, as the following example illus-trates. Possibly, material atoms a, b, and c are joined and connected at times t_1 and t_2, and at a time, t^*, between t_1 and t_2, a, b, and c are not joined and connected. In this case, it is clear that the mereological compound abc exists at t_1 and t_2, but that this mereological com-pound does not exist at t^*. Thus, it is possible for a thing to have intermittent existence.

The denial of this possibility has been frequently attributed to John Locke on the basis of his assertion that "one thing cannot have two beginnings of existence."[14] However, we think that this is a mis-interpretation of Locke and that he never intended to reject the possibility of intermittent existence.[15] Acceptance of this view, mistakenly attributed to Locke, that a thing cannot exist inter-mittently, has led some philosophers to defend what to our minds are bizarre and wildly unintuitive positions.[16] In particular, David Wiggins, noting that a clock exists both before and after its dis-assembly and reassembly, and assuming that nothing can exist intermittently, infers that the clock also exists while disassembled! This is surely wrong, for no physical substance can consist of a collection of disassembled, scattered, parts which no longer stand in the requisite unifying causal relation. Not only do the parts of the disassembled clock fail to exemplify this unifying causal relation, but these scattered parts lack the *form* of a clock, and there cannot be a clock that lacks this form. Furthermore, Wiggins view implies that a clock exists while disassembled, *if* the clock happens to get reassembled in the future, but *not* otherwise. The supposition that the present existence of a physical object is contingent upon future happenstance is bizarre. For an object, *o*, must have an intrinsic nature, and a nature of this sort cannot involve a relation to a future contingent event, or, in general, to any entity whose existence is not entailed by *o*'s existence. It should be noted that in another case Wiggins himself argues that an object must have an intrinsic nature that does not involve such a relation. In particular, he criticizes the "best candidate" account of the identity of artifacts over time on the ground that it entails that artifacts lack an intrinsic nature of the sort required.[17]

3 ANOTHER CONUNDRUM: DOES MEREOLOGICAL INCREASE IMPLY THAT A THING IS A PROPER PART OF ITSELF?

A second argument of the mereological essentialist against the existence of ordinary physical things is related to the problem of increase (see Figure 2 above). Suppose that at time t_1 there is a compound material thing, *a*, which at some later time, t_2, undergoes mereological change, in this case by adding a part, *b*, resulting in a compound material thing, *ab*, at t_2. There are two principles which generate this second argument. The first is that necessarily, $(x)\,(y)$(if *y* is a proper part of *x*, then $x \neq y$). The second is that necessarily, $(x)(y)(t_1)(t_2)[(x$ at time $t_1 = y$ at $t_2) \rightarrow (\text{at } t_2, x = y)]$. The proponent of this argument assumes that necessarily, if *a* exists at t_1, and *a* undergoes mereological change by *b*'s being added to *a* at t_2, then *a* at $t_1 = ab$ at t_2. This, together with the second principle, implies that at t_2, $a = ab$. But necessarily, if *ab* exists at t_2, then at t_2 *a* is a proper part of *ab*. Hence, the first principle implies that at t_2, $a \neq ab$. Thus, we have arrived at a contradiction, namely, that at t_2, $a = ab$ and $a \neq ab$. On the assumption that the only other premises employed in reaching this contradictory conclusion are necessary truths, the argument is a *reductio ad absurdum* of the original hypothesis, viz., that *a* undergoes mereological change (through the addition of a part *b*). In other words, if this argument is sound, then this original hypothesis is impossible.

There are various replies to this argument in the case of ordinary physical objects, depending on whether they are living or nonliving. A first reply applies just in case they are nonliving. Suppose that *a* is such an object, for example, a house (see Figure 3 above). Then at t_1, house a is constituted by $a*$, while at t_2, a is constituted by $a*b*$, where $b*$ is what constitutes the room addition b at t_2. Accordingly, the house which exists at t_2 should retain the label "a," and that which is constituted at t_2 by $a*$ is not a but a proper part of a. Thus, it has not been shown that if a increases by the addition of b at t_2, then at t_2 a is a proper part of itself. (This reply shows that if, in Figure 2, at time t_1, a is a house, then the house which is constructed by adding room b at time t_2 is mislabeled as ab: it should still be labeled house a. It also shows that the proper part of this house at time t_2 which is labeled a in Figure 2 is mislabeled.)

A second response applies to both nonliving and living things. This reply is based upon two premises. First, an ordinary physical thing of a certain substance-kind is essentially of that substance-kind, and an organism is essentially an organism. For example, a house is essentially a house, a snowball is essentially a snowball, and a tiger is essentially an organism. Second, necessarily, neither an ordinary physical thing of a certain substance-kind nor an organism is a proper part of an ordinary physical thing of that substance-kind or another organism. For example, necessarily, a house is not a proper part of a house, a snowball is not a proper part of a snowball, a tiger is not a proper part of any other organism, and so on.

The first premise expresses a form of "Aristotelian essentialism" about ordinary physical things. Ordinary physical things have both formal aspects, for example, structural or functional aspects, and material aspects, for example, compositional aspects, and it seems that the nature or essence of such a thing is determined by one or more of these aspects. Our conceptions of various kinds of ordinary physical things, for example, houses, snowballs, and organisms, seem to be conceptions of such essences. The first premise concerning ordinary physical things is a plausible one.

Aristotle and some of his followers seemed to have believed that a biological species is essential to whatever organisms instantiate it, for example, that a tiger is essentially a tiger. However, serious challenges to this view have been raised in more recent discussions of this issue. For example, one possible objection to the claim that biological species are essential to whatever instantiates them arises as follows. It seems to be possible for an organism, O, to belong only marginally to a species, s, such that either s recently evolved from a prior species, $s-$, or s is, or recently was, in the process of evolving into a new species $s+$. However, it would seem that O could have existed even if its genotype were slightly different in certain ways from its actual one. Moreover, arguably, a possible consequence of some such slight difference in O's genotype is that O would belong to $s-$ or to $s+$. Thus, it might be argued that it is possible for O to have belonged to $s-$ or to $s+$, instead of to s. This argument implies that O's species is not essential to it, and hence that biological species are not essential to whatever instantiates them. It should be noted, however, that such an argument is consistent with the claim that if an organism, O, belongs to a species, s, then O is essentially s-like, for example, that a tiger is essentially tiger-like.

The foregoing argument raises important questions about what sorts of natural kinds organisms fall under.[18] But even if the argument that an organism does not essentially belong to its species is sound, it is safe to assume that every organism is an instance of at least one biological category that is essential to whatever instantiates it, namely, the category of being an organism; this is the summum genus of all biological categories, and it is a natural kind given the premise that biology is a natural science. Moreover, this assumption will suffice for the purposes of the main argument in this chapter.

To evaluate the second premise about ordinary physical things, we shall use the example of a house as a representative case. It can be argued plausibly that a proper part of a house cannot itself be a house. If a house could have another house as a part, then the best candidates for such a part of a house are those of its proper parts which most resemble a house. These proper parts are those which are composed of all of a house's atomic parts less one. Since the subtracted atomic part can be *any* of the atomic parts of a house, there are innumerably many such good candidates. Thus, if a house, $H1$, has another house, $H2$, as a part, then $H1$ has as proper parts innumerable other houses $H3$, $H4$, etc., each of which is composed of nearly all of the atomic parts of $H1$. Moreover, parallel arguments imply that $H2$ has as parts innumerable other houses composed of almost all of the atomic parts of $H2$, $H3$ has as parts innumerable other houses composed of almost all of the atomic parts of $H3$, $H4$ has as parts innumerable other houses composed of almost all of the atomic parts of $H4$, and so on. In other words, if a house, $H1$, has another house, $H2$, as a part, then there will exist a vast number of partially overlapping houses within the boundaries of an ordinary house. Since it is intuitively implausible that this multitude of houses exists, and since to posit all of those houses would be to multiply entities unnecessarily, there are good reasons to reject their existence. It follows that a house cannot have a house as a proper part. An exactly parallel argument applies to organisms. In that case, the argument implies that an organism cannot have an organism as a proper part. We conclude that our second premise about ordinary physical things is also a plausible one.

We are now prepared to answer the mereological essentialist's second argument based upon the two premises we have defended about ordinary physical things. Let us assume that at t_1, a is a house (or an organism). However, a house (organism) is essentially a house (organism). Thus, a is not possibly a nonhouse (nonorganism). Furthermore, necessarily, a house (organism) is not a proper part of a house (organism). Therefore, the label "a" cannot correctly be used to designate both the house (in Figure 3) which exists at t_1, and the *part* of that same house which exists at t_2, and which part is constituted by the mereological compound we have labeled a^*. Nor can it correctly be used to designate both the human being (in Figure 4) which exists at t_1, and the *part* of that same human being which exists at t_2, which part we have labeled a^*. Consequently, the absurd conclusion that at t_2, a is a proper part of a can no longer be derived, and the mereological essentialist's *reductio* against the possibility of mereological change by the addition of a part is blocked.

Let us survey the conclusions we have reached. As we have seen, the mereological essentialist's arguments do not pose a serious threat to the reality of organisms. However, there appears to be a difference on this score between the case of living things and the case of ordinary inanimate physical objects. Specifically, in the latter case, but not in the former one, the replies to all the mereological essentialist's arguments presuppose that there are physical things which supervene upon spatially coincident mereological compounds. Since this presupposition is questionable, it seems that the arguments of the mereological essentialist raise a serious worry about the reality of ordinary inanimate physical objects.

4 THE PROBLEM OF THE SHIP OF THESEUS

The class of ordinary physical objects is commonly thought to include artifacts, i.e., objects having artificial functions. Examples of artifacts are ships, tables, and hammers. The classic problem of the ship of Theseus raises further questions about whether artifacts are genuine entities over and above mereological compounds.

Here is the problem, as stated by Plutarch in his life of Theseus:

> The ship wherein Theseus and the youth of Athens returned had thirty oars, and was preserved by the Athenians down even to the

time of Demetrius Phalereus, for they took away the old planks as they decayed, putting in new and stronger timber in their place, insomuch that this ship became a standing example among the philosophers, for the logical question of things that grow; one side holding that the ship remained the same, and the other contending that it was not the same.[19]

Thus, the problem of the ship of Theseus is generated by a possible scenario of the following kind. At a time t_1, a ship, $S1$, comes into existence. At t_1, $S1$ is composed of parts, for example, planks, $P_1 \ldots P_n$ arranged in way $W1$. As a consequence of $S1$'s regular program of maintenance, these parts are gradually replaced with other similar ones. In due course, this results in a ship, $S2$, at a time t_2, all of whose parts are discrete from $P_1 \ldots P_n$. But at t_2 another ship, $S3$, comes into being that is composed of $P_1 \ldots P_n$ arranged in way $W1$. The question now arises of whether $S1 = S2$ or $S1 = S3$.[20]

A parallel question arises for organisms in the following situation, which seems to be (remotely) possible. At a time t_1, an organism, $O1$, comes into existence. At t_1, $O1$ is composed of parts, for example, atoms, $B_1 \ldots B_n$ organized in way $W2$. In the course of $O1$'s natural processes of self-maintenance these parts are gradually replaced with other similar ones. Eventually, this results in an organism, $O2$, at a time t_2, that is discrete from $B_1 \ldots B_n$. Finally, at t_2 an organism, $O3$, comes into being that is composed of $B_1 \ldots B_n$ organized in way $W2$. Is $O1$ identical with $O2$ or is $O1$ identical with $O3$?

Intuitively, the life-processes of organisms $O1$ and $O2$, including their metabolic or mereological changes, are parts of the same life-history, whereas $O3$'s life-processes are not parts of that life-history. For this reason, it seems that $O1 = O2$ and $O1 \neq O3$. Hence, in a case of this kind there is a plausible answer available to the question posed about whether $O1 = O2$ or $O1 = O3$.

In the case of ships, however, there are a number of relevant intuitions which seem to be in conflict. On the one hand, there is an intuition that $S1$'s and $S2$'s mereological changes are parts of the same history of maintenance, whereas neither $S3$, nor any change in $S3$, is a part of that history of maintenance. Thus, it might appear that $S1 = S2$ and $S1 \neq S3$. On the other hand, while the course of an organism's life-history is typically controlled or regulated by that organism's internal nature, and this internal nature is a proper object of scientific investigation, a parallel claim is not true of the course of an artifact's history of maintenance. Thus, the notion of an artifact's history of maintenance is far less robust than the notion of an organism's life-history. So, it is not surprising that there are cases in which there are intuitions which are opposed to the ones which supported the claim that $S1 = S2$ and $S1 \neq S3$. For example, if $S1$ is a ship of great historical importance, for example, the *Mayflower*, then it is more intuitively plausible to suppose that $S1 = S3$ and $S1 \neq S2$. This suggests that the identity conditions of artifacts, for instance, ships, are pragmatically determined. In other words, these identity conditions seem to be relative to our interests, and there appears to be no fact of the matter as to whether $S1$ is identical with $S2$ or $S3$. If the identity conditions of ships and other artifacts are conventional in this way, and if a genuine substance has a nature which is independent of human convention, then it seems that artifacts are not genuine substances. However, there is an alternative view available. Specifically, it might be claimed that an ordinary ship and an historical ship are diverse objects which have different conditions of identity over time. According to this view, an ordinary ship and an historical ship can be constituted by the very same mereological compound at one time, and yet be constituted by different mereological compounds at another time. This implies that there can be *more* than two physical objects in the same place at the same time. However, considerations of parsimony militate against this alternative view, and the claim that common sense actually distinguishes between two physical objects, an historical ship and an ordinary ship, is problematic. For these reasons, the claim that an ordinary ship and an historical ship are diverse beings with different conditions of perdurance seems implausible. Thus, it is doubtful that this alternative view provides a plausible defense of the reality of ships and other artifacts.

We conclude both that the problem of the ship of Theseus gives rise to a serious difficulty for the view that artifacts are genuine substances, and that the view that organic living things are genuine substances does not face a parallel difficulty.

5 THE SCIENTIFIC ARGUMENT AGAINST THE REALITY OF ARTIFACTS AND TYPICAL NATURAL FORMATIONS

We believe that there is an additional and weighty argument which implies that artifacts, as well as typical inanimate natural formations, are not genuine substances. But as we shall see, this argument no more threatens the reality of organisms than did the arguments we have already examined.

To begin with, if the identity over time of a putative compound physical thing, P, is conventional, then P is not a real thing. That which is conventional logically depends upon the beliefs or decisions of one or more psychological subjects. But the identity through time of any genuine physical thing must derive (in a strong sense) from that thing's intrinsic nature over time, and cannot logically depend on the beliefs or decisions of any psychological subject. Thus, the identity of a real compound physical thing through time is due to *nature* rather than to *convention*.

In the case of compound physical objects, the question of what is due to nature, as opposed to convention, is a proper object of investigation in natural science. Moreover, to have a scientific understanding of the intrinsic nature of a compound physical thing over time is to understand its composition and structure over time as a function (in a robust sense) of its intrinsic nature. Hence, a real compound physical thing has an internal nature which is in a strong sense a determinant, and a factor limiting the structure and composition, of that physical thing through time, and which is a proper object of investigation in natural science. Two examples of kinds of compound physical things which have internal natures of this sort come to mind.[21]

First, there is the case of mereological compounds. Since it is of the nature of such a compound to be incapable of mereological change, a mereological compound's internal nature logically or metaphysically determines its composition over the course of its existence. In particular, the nature of a mereological compound metaphysically determines that it persists only as long as it retains all of its parts. Furthermore, the internal nature of a mereological compound is a causal determinant of its structure over time in a suitably strong sense, strictly determining the extent (if any) to which it can be stretched or compressed.[22] It should also be observed that the internal nature of a mereological compound is a proper object of scientific inquiry, for example, in solid-state physics.

Second, there is the case of organisms. In the light of the argument we presented in Chapter 4, we can see that an organism, O, has an internal nature, or microstructural hereditary blueprint, N, such that: (i) N determines the range of alternative structural properties and compositional natures possible for O so long as the degree of naturalness of O's life-processes remains constant, i.e., the range of sizes, shapes, masses, order and arrangements of parts, and so on, that O can have so long as O retains N, and (ii) so long as the degree of naturalness of O's life-processes remains constant, N controls or regulates O's structure and composition. Such an internal nature of a living thing is a proper object of inquiry in the natural sciences of biology and chemistry. Moreover, another feature of organic living things is that there are rather strict limits, even when the degree of naturalness of O's life-processes does not remain constant, to the extent to which an organism can undergo compositional or structural alteration. For example, an artificial organ which takes the place of a living part of an organism does not become a part of that organism, as we have argued in Chapter 4. Moreover, even if an artificial organ were to be counted as a part of the living thing under discussion, there is a limit to the extent to which the parts of an organism could be replaced with artificial organs. If the replacements were too extensive, then the result would be either a living cyborg, or an inorganic living thing, or else a nonliving automaton, and in all three cases it is extremely plausible to suppose that the result would not be identical with the original organism. After all, intuitively, the entity resulting from these replacements neither would have the same intrinsic nature as the original organism, nor would be a member of the natural kind to which the original organism belongs. And there is a limit to the amount of hereditarily different living matter which could be successfully transplanted to an organic living thing, were that organic living thing to retain its identity over time. For instance, if too much genetically different living matter were successfully transplanted, then this would produce a new creature that would not be identical with the original one. Although an organism apparently can survive the replacement, by transplantation, of *some* of its vital organs with genetically different ones, it seems that if *all* of an organism's vital organs were replaced with genetically different organs via successful transplants, then the resulting organism would not be identical with the one with which we began. Intuitively, the identity of an organism over time is constrained by its heredity in at least this way.

Any physical substance which can undergo mereological change can undergo alteration of its parts in three ways: it can lose a part, it can gain a part, and a part of it can be replaced. It is commonly thought that artifacts and typical inanimate natural formations, as well as an organisms, are compound physical objects which can undergo mereological change. Yet, a compound physical object, O, which can undergo mereological change is real only if O has an internal nature, N, which has the ability to determine causally (in a robust sense) O's increase or replacement of parts. However, N's ability to determine causally O's increase or replacement of parts is sufficiently robust only if N can *control* or *regulate* O's increase or replacement of parts over time. But, unlike organic living things, artifacts and typical inanimate natural formations do not have an internal nature of the sort that is required. Artifacts, for instance, ships, do not have an internal principle which can control or regulate their increase or replacement of parts over time. Rather, all ships can do is passively react to the environment by losing parts, undergoing weathering, rusting, and so forth.[23] In contrast, living things actively grow and repair themselves. Moreover, we can bring it about that a ship which retains its identity over time nevertheless undergoes a radical alteration in its composition, for example, from cedar to oak, or even from wood to aluminum, by having its cedar planks gradually replaced with oak ones, or its wooden planks with aluminum ones. Thus, a ship need not have any particular compositional nature. But as we argued earlier, the range of repairs that can be made to a living thing is rather strictly limited by its compositional nature, even when the degree of naturalness of its life-processes does not remain constant. Because a real thing which can undergo mereological change has an internal principle which controls or regulates its increase or replacement of parts, and which strictly limits both its compositional nature over time, and the extent to which it can undergo compositional change, and because a ship has no such internal principle, a ship is not a real thing. We remind the reader that our position here is only that a *ship* is not a real thing. We affirm the reality of the *mereological compound* which some believe to be spatially coincident with and constitutive of a ship.[24]

Similarly, a snowball, which presumably must be roundish and made of snow,[25] although capable of mereological change, lacks an internal principle which can govern or regulate its growth or replacement of parts. This parallels the case of an artifact like a ship, and has the same implications for the ontological status of the snowball as for the ship. Thus, a snowball is not a real thing.

Finally, typical inanimate natural formations also lack an internal nature of the requisite sort. For example, a crystal, a glacier, a lake, or a planet does not possess any internal principle which can control or regulate its increase or replacement of parts over time. Because any real thing has such an internal principle, a crystal, a glacier, a lake, or a planet is not a real thing.[26]

Of course, a crystal is more life-like than a ship, a snowball, or a lake, since unlike the latter, but like an organic living thing, it has an internal nature which governs its shape. But there is this relevant difference between a crystal and an organic living thing: an organic living thing has a nature which governs its growth or replacement of parts, and cannot survive without growth or replacement of parts, while a crystal can persist without growth or replacement of parts. Thus, in this sense a crystal does not naturally grow or replace parts, and any growth or replacement of parts it undergoes is fortuitous, whereas a living thing naturally grows or replaces parts. Another relevant difference is that a living thing has an internal principle that governs its size, whereas a crystal has no such principle. For instance, a human cannot grow to a height of more than one thousand miles, whereas there is no inherent limit to the size to which a crystal can grow. An interesting possible case of a crystal that has grown to extreme proportions is the recent, apparently plausible, geological theory that there is a single gigantic crystal of iron at the center of the Earth whose width is roughly fifteen hundred miles.[27]

Since an argument of the foregoing kind applies to all artifacts and to typical inanimate natural formations, and since doubts about the reality of such objects are also raised by the problem of the ship of Theseus and by the problem of increase, there is good reason to think that artifacts and typical inanimate natural formations are not real things. We propose their elimination from any reasoned ontology.

At this point, one might be tempted to conclude that the class of real things does not include *any* inanimate natural formations. However, it seems that this conclusion is unwarranted, for the following reasons. As we explained in Chapter 4, we are unable to decide whether a proteinoid microsphere, m, that is engaged in metabolic activities is animate or inanimate. So, for all we know, m is a life-like inanimate natural formation that undergoes mereological change. It might nevertheless be true, though, that m has a rudimentary microstructural hereditary blueprint of the requisite sort, and an internal principle which can control or regulate the structure and composition of m over time, where this hereditary blueprint and that internal principle are proper objects of investigation in natural science. Thus, m might have an internal nature of the kind required for a real compound physical thing. Hence, as far we know, some inanimate natural formations, for example, proteinoid microspheres such as *m*, are real things. However, it seems to follow that any such inanimate natural formation is bound to be strikingly life-like. On the other hand, for all we know, a proteinoid microsphere that is engaged in metabolic activities is alive, and hence does not provide an example of an inanimate natural formation which undergoes mereological change. In that case, it may be true that the class of real things does not include any inanimate natural formations.

So far, the argument against the reality of artifacts and typical inanimate natural formations has focused on the identity of ordinary physical things over time. We shall set forth two other related arguments which together undermine the reality of artifacts and certain inanimate natural formations. These arguments focus upon the status of the substance-kinds that are commonly thought to be instantiated by such physical things. Both of these arguments make use of the notion of a natural kind.

The notion of a natural substance-kind appears to have originated with Aristotle. According to him, artifacts, i.e., ships, chairs, beds, and so on, differ from organisms, i.e., lions, tigers, bears, and so forth, because the latter, but not the former, have an essence or nature whose exemplification is logically independent of the existence of human beliefs or decisions. For this reason, Aristotle counts biological species, for example, lion, tiger, and bear, as natural substance-kinds, but does not count artifact-kinds, for example, ship, chair, and bed, as natural substance-kinds. If he is right, then there seems to be a sense in which artifact-kinds are artificial substance-kinds.

In recent years, interest in the topic of natural kinds has been rekindled by the work of philosophers such as Kripke and Putnam, who have argued that science investigates the structural or compositional essences of naturally occurring chemical elements or compounds such as iron, gold, and water. The notion of a natural kind has also figured prominently in attempts to answer Goodman's new riddle of induction.[28] This literature tends to emphasize natural kinds which are not natural substance-kinds, for example, kinds of *stuffs* such as gold, water, and blood (substances in the stuff sense), or inductively projectible qualities, for example, yellowness, sweetness, and hardness, rather than kinds of *things* such as pieces of iron, portions of ice, and organisms (substances in the count sense).

One important exception to this trend is David Wiggins.[29] He applies the ideas of Kripke and Putnam to natural-kind predicates which refer to individual substances. Wiggins describes their main idea as follows:

> Frege said that the sense of an expression determined its reference, and not the reference the sense. If Putnam's theory is correct, this is not normally true of natural kind words. Just as the sense of a proper name (contrast definite description) is best explained by saying what its reference is, so in the process of the teaching and elucidation of the sense of a natural kind predicate everything depends upon the actual extension of the predicate (viz. all past, present, and future compliants of the predicate), or on what Frege would have called its reference – the *what it is to be an f*.[30]

In the light of the foregoing discussion, let us now proceed to characterize the relevant notions of a natural and an artifactual substance-kind. K is a natural substance-kind if and only if it is a physical substance-kind that meets three conditions.

First, K must be essential to whatever instantiates it: K is the essential nature of a physical substance of a certain sort, for example, being a piece of gold.[31] On the other hand, although it might be said that yellowness is a natural kind, it is *not* a natural substance-kind, since some physical things instantiate yellowness accidentally. In other words, to say that something is a piece of gold is to say *what* it is, whereas to say that something is yellow is not to say what it is.

Second, K is a proper object of inquiry in natural science and figures in one or more natural laws. As T. E. Wilkerson puts it:

> Members of natural kinds, and the corresponding real essences, lend themselves to scientific investigation. It is possible to have a science of gold, water and cellulose, or of tigers, oaks and sticklebacks, because it is possible to make suitable theoretical generalizations about their behaviour. . . . By the same token, natural kind predicates are inductively projectible, whereas other predicates are not.[32]

In a similar vein, Wiggins defines the notion of belonging to a natural substance-kind as follows:

> A particular continuant x belongs to a natural kind, or is a natural thing, if and only if x has a principle of activity corresponding to the nomological basis of that or those extension-involving sortal identifications which answer truly the question "what is x?".[33]

With respect to the lawlike principles in nature whose truth is presupposed by the existence of an instance of a natural-kind concept, f, Wiggins remarks perceptively that:

> They must determine ... the typical history, and the limits of any possible development or history of any compliant of f.[34]

Our account of the notion of an organism's microstructural hereditary blueprint is consonant with this remark.

The third condition which must be met by a natural substance-kind, K, is that K is possibly instantiated without its being instantiated because of any belief(s) or decision(s) of any psychological subject(s).[35]

Finally, any two physical things which belong to the same natural kind of compound substance must do so in virtue of their structural and compositional similarity. Moreover, if K is a natural kind of compound substance, for example, if K = Organism, then K must supervene on structural and compositional properties: necessarily, for any x, and for any y, if x instantiates K, and x and y are indistinguishable in their qualitative structural and compositional properties, then y instantiates K; otherwise K would not seem to be a proper object of scientific inquiry.[36] It should be noted that nothing we have said here implies that biological species, for example, Tiger, are natural compound substance-kinds. As we shall see, there are reasons for doubting this.

A natural kind, for instance, Organism, or Material Object, is distinguished from an artificial kind, for example, Knife, or Ship, in that only a kind of the former sort is a subject of natural or scientific laws. For while there are natural laws about organisms *qua* organisms, or about material objects *qua* material objects, there are not natural laws about artifacts *qua* artifacts.

An artificial substance-kind, A, is a nonnatural substance-kind such that, necessarily, whatever instantiates A has an artificial function. Hence, it is impossible for A to be instantiated unless it is instantiated because of some belief(s) or decision(s) of one or more psychological subject(s).

Of necessity, something which belongs to an artifactual substance-kind, for example, a knife, essentially has an artificial function or purpose, for example, cutting. And by definition, an artifact has an artificial function or purpose because of some belief(s) or decision(s) of some purposeful intellect(s). Hence, it is not possible for an artifact to exist unless it exists because of some belief(s) or decision(s) of some psychological subject(s). For example, it is impossible for a knife to exist in a universe that never contains a purposeful intellect, though of course it is possible for a mereological compound that could constitute a knife to exist in such a possible universe.

On the other hand, an organism, O, unlike an artifact, has a nature which is a natural kind, and whether O is artificially created or naturally generated, it is theoretically possible for O to exist without existing *because of* any belief(s) or decision(s) of any psychological subject(s).[37]

The first argument that utilizes the notion of a natural kind to argue against the reality of artifacts goes as follows. As we have seen, if an ordinary physical thing instantiates a substance-kind, then it does so necessarily or essentially: for example, a house is essentially a house, a tiger is essentially an organism, a snowball is essentially a snowball, and so on. If such a substance-kind is a *conventional kind*, then that substance-kind is not instantiated by a real thing. The character of a conventional kind logically depends on the beliefs or decisions of psychological subjects. But a substance-kind whose instantiation is essential to the existence of any of its genuine physical instances must express the intrinsic nature of those instances, and the character of that substance-kind cannot logically depend upon the beliefs or decisions of any psychological subject. Thus, a genuine substance-kind must be a *natural kind* rather than a conventional kind. If a kind of compound physical substance is a natural kind, then this substance-kind is a proper object of investigation in natural science. Thus, a putative compound physical substance of a particular substance-kind is real only if that substance-kind is a proper object of scientific inquiry. Moreover, a substance-kind is a proper object of such inquiry only if this substance-kind is a natural kind. Therefore, a putative compound physical substance is real only if it instantiates a natural kind. Moreover, since whatever instantiates an artifactual kind, for example, a rug, or a statue, must do so essentially, and since it is not possible that a thing which instantiates a natural kind, for example, a bear, or a piece of copper, also essentially instantiates an artifactual kind, it is impossible for a thing to instantiate both an artifactual kind and a natural kind.[38] It follows that a putative compound physical substance of an artifactual kind is not a real thing. This argument is additional evidence that artifacts such as ships, houses, hammers, and so forth, do not really exist.

On the other hand, the property of being a piece of material stuff of a particular sort, for example, copper or quartz, is a natural kind, and some mereological compounds are compositionally homogeneous pieces of material stuff of such a particular sort. However, other mereological compounds are compositionally heterogeneous, and are not pieces of material stuff of a particular sort in this sense. Still, Mereological Compound is itself a natural kind. After all, as we argued earlier, mereological compounds have an internal nature which is in a strong sense a determinant of and a factor limiting their structure and composition over time, and which is a proper object of scientific investigation. In particular, recall that the internal nature, N, of a mereological compound, M, is such that N precludes the logical or metaphysical possibility of M's undergoing mereological change, N strictly determines the range of structural changes that M can undergo (if any), and N is a proper object of investigation in solid-state physics. Thus, Mereological Compound has all of the qualifications necessary for it to count as (a limiting case of) a natural kind. Likewise, an organism is an *organic* living thing, and, as such, belongs to a natural kind (or kinds) which is a proper object of investigation in the biological sciences.[39] Thus, since mereological compounds and organisms instantiate natural substance-kinds, they are not artifacts, and the arguments which tell against the reality of artifacts do not militate against the reality of mereological compounds and organisms.

The second argument undermines the reality of certain artifacts and inanimate natural formations. This argument goes as follows. Natural kinds are proper objects of investigation in natural science. In the case of compound physical things which can undergo mereological change, one of the proper aims of natural science is to investigate the general compositional natures of things of this sort. Thus, a kind of compound physical substance which can undergo mereological change is a natural kind only if, necessarily, all things which instantiate that substance-kind are compositionally alike, and each instance of that substance-kind has its compositional nature essentially.

For example, all organisms in virtue of being *organic* living things are to some extent compositionally similar. In the light of our earlier arguments, we can see that each living organism has a certain compositional nature in virtue of which it is alive, and it has this compositional nature essentially.[40]

In contrast, ships can undergo mereological change, but not all ships are compositionally similar: for example, some are wooden and others are steel. Furthermore, as we have observed, a ship does not have its compositional nature essentially. (If its parts are gradually replaced, a given ship can change from being made of wood to being made of aluminum.) It follows that the kind, being a ship, is not a natural compound substance-kind. Parallel arguments apply to artifacts of many other kinds, for example, houses, chairs, tables, and so on, as well as to inanimate natural formations of many kinds, for example, planets, stars, atmospheres, and so forth, and imply that the corresponding kinds are not natural compound substance-kinds. For instance, even though stars can undergo mereological change, not all stars are compositionally similar, and the compositional nature of a star when it is young may be quite different from its compositional nature when it is old. Thus, our argument implies that the kind, being a star, is not a natural compound substance-kind. Nevertheless, such arguments do not apply to all artifacts and inanimate natural formations. For instance, although a stick of chalk is an artifact which can undergo mereological change, all sticks of chalk are compositionally similar, and each stick of chalk has its compositional nature essentially. Thus, an argument of the sort in question does *not* show that the kind, being a stick of chalk, is not a natural compound substance-kind.[41] Similarly, all quartz crystals are compositionally alike, and each quartz crystal has its compositional nature essentially. Hence, an argument of the sort under discussion also does not show that the kind, being a quartz crystal (as a sort of thing which can undergo mereological change by growing), is not a natural compound substance-kind.[42]

Let us review our reasoning up to this point. As we have argued, a putative compound physical substance, P, is real only if P instantiates a natural compound substance-kind, a compound substance-kind which requires an internal compositional nature of the requisite sort. Thus, if P's being a genuine entity implies its being a physical compound, and if P fails to instantiate a natural compound substance-kind, then P is not a real thing. In particular, since artifacts, for example, ships, tables, and hammers, and typical inanimate natural formations, for example, planets, stars, and atmospheres, do not instantiate natural compound substance-kinds, artifacts and typical inanimate natural formations do not really exist. Finally, since organisms and mereological compounds *do* instantiate natural compound substance-kinds, this line of reasoning does not imply that they do not exist.

In sum, there are a number of plausible arguments against the reality of both artifacts and typical inanimate natural formations, some of the most powerful being the scientific arguments developed in this section employing the notions of intrinsic natures and natural kinds. On the other hand, there is no similarly weighty reason to doubt the reality of mereological compounds or organisms. The following perceptive remark that Wiggins has made about organisms is relevant here.

> Starting off with the idea of a sortal predicate whose sense is such as to involve its extension, and which is the candidate *par excellence* for real definition, we are led to speculate what holds together the extension. So soon as we find that, we also find lawlike norms of starting to exist, existing, and ceasing to exist by reference to which questions of the identity and persistence of individual specimens falling under a definition can be arbitrated. Such norms will be supervenient on basic laws of nature, we have supposed, and represent certain so to say *exploitations* of these laws. But then we have been led by simple conceptual considerations to precisely the kind of account of living substances that biologists can amplify for us *a posteriori*, seeing these as systems open to their surroundings but not in equilibrium with them and so constituted as to be able, by dint of a delicate self-regulating balance of serially linked enzymatic degradative and synthesizing chemical reactions, to renew themselves on the molecular level at the expense of those surroundings – the renewal taking place under a law-determined variety of conditions and always in a species-determined pattern of growth and development towards, and/or persistence, in one particular form.[43]

We conclude that although mereological compounds and organisms are genuine substances, artifacts and typical inanimate natural formations are unreal. Although Wiggins finds the fact that artifacts lack a nature which is a natural kind troubling for the notion that artifacts are real beings, in the final analysis he is inclined to think that artifacts are real things.[44] If our argument in this chapter is sound, then artifacts are unreal, and Wiggins should not have balked at excluding them from his ontology. Since a compound inanimate object is either an artifact, a natural formation, or a mereological compound, the only compound inanimate objects that there might be in addition to mereological compounds are atypical natural formations of a strikingly life-like kind. As we indicated earlier, we remain neutral about whether there are such inanimate natural formations. The only other physical objects whose existence we are prepared to admit are noncompound material objects, i.e., basic particles.

6 THE EXPLOSION OF REALITY: A POPULATION EXPLOSION FOR LIVING THINGS?

Ernest Sosa has argued powerfully that if there are ordinary physical things such as ships, snowballs, mountains, and trees, then we face the prospect of *the explosion of reality*.[45] The nature of this explosion is as follows: for any ordinary physical thing, there are infinitely many physical objects which are in the same place at the same time as that ordinary physical thing. Sosa uses the example of a snowball to help illustrate this ontological population crisis. Sosa assumes that a snowball is essentially a physical object which is constituted by a piece of snow that is approximately spherical. But if there are snowballs, he argues, then there are *snowdiscalls* as well, where a snowdiscall is essentially a physical object that is constituted by a piece of snow that has any shape in the continuum of shapes ranging from an approximate disc to an approximate sphere. Given these accounts of the natures of a snowball and a snowdiscall, whenever there is a snowball, there must be a snowdiscall, other than the snowball, that occupies the same place at the same time as that snowball.[46] Moreover, as Sosa points out, infinitely many other kinds of similar objects can be defined in analogous ways. Thus, it would seem that if there is a snowball, then there are an infinite number of other physical objects in the same place at the same time as that snowball.

Sosa suggests that if a substance realist wants to include non-mereological compounds in his ontology, for example, organic living things, artifacts, or natural formations, then there is no plausible way to prevent the explosion of reality. If, as Sosa seems to think, traditional substance realists must choose between the explosion of reality and the elimination of all organic living things, then this form of realism is faced with choices so unpalatable as to raise a serious doubt about its viability. *We* are traditional substance realists, in the sense of maintaining that there *are* organic living things in addition to basic particles and mereological compounds. So if Sosa's suggestion is correct, then we are stuck with a problematic explosion of reality. In what follows, we respond to Sosa by arguing that our particular scientific realist version of traditional substance realism does *not* lead to the explosion of reality which he forecasts.

To begin with, since our view implies that there are no such things as snowballs, snowdiscalls, and the like, we are not confronted by the specter of an explosion of reality from that quarter. Sosa generates the explosion of reality by using examples such as snow-balls, snowdiscalls, and so forth, and he does not demonstrate that this explosion can be generated by using examples of organisms. Nevertheless, his remarks presuppose that the explosion of reality *can* be produced by utilizing examples of organic living things alone. To produce such an explosion, Sosa would need to construct an example of a kind of organism which parallels his example of a snowdiscall.

The only example of this kind that needs to be considered is the following one. Let us assume that a modern-day horse is essentially an organism of a certain contemporary biological species with which we are familiar.[47] Generalizing from Sosa's argument, one might try to produce a population explosion of spatially coincident organisms by arguing that if there are horses, then there are horsealls too, where a horseall is essentially an organism of any species in the evolutionary history of modern-day horses ranging from the first proto-horse to the modern-day horse. But a putative kind, horseall, is equivalent to a disjunction of different species of horses ranging from that of the first proto-horse to that of the modern-day horse. However, a classification equivalent to a disjunction of different biological species, for example, being a cat or an eagle, is not itself a biological species. That is, a classification equivalent to a disjunction of this kind does not express the internal nature of *any* organism, and therefore such a classification is not a proper object of study in biological science. In other words, a classification of this sort is not a natural organism-kind. A disjunction of different internal natures, or a classification equivalent to such a disjunction, is not itself an internal nature, since *ex hypothesi* it can be exemplified by things with *different* internal natures. Wiggins has argued, in a similar vein, that there are no essentially or irreducibly disjunctive sortal concepts.[48] It follows that the putative kind, horseall, is not a natural kind. Since a compound physical thing which does not exemplify a natural compound substance-kind is unreal, and since a horseall would not exemplify such a natural substance-kind, we conclude that a horseall is not a real thing. Moreover, parallel considerations apply to all of the many other kinds of similar objects that can be defined in analogous ways. Thus, an explosion of reality for organic living things cannot be generated by using examples such as that of the horseall.

As far as we can see at present, no other way of generating an explosion of reality for organic living things is any more plausible than the attempt to do so in terms of the horseall. For example, a cateagle, understood as a creature that is essentially either a cat or an eagle, is subject to the same sort of objection as the horseall, and has the additional drawback of not being coextensive with any coherent range of (biological) forms.[49] In this way, the cateagle is disanalogous to the snowdiscall, which *is* coextensive with a continuous range of (geometric) forms.[50]

For the foregoing reasons, we conclude that even though our version of traditional substance realism implies that there are organic living things in addition to basic particles and mereological compounds, it does *not* lead to an explosion of reality. Although our view implies, contrary to common sense, that artifacts and typical inanimate formations are not real things, this idea is much more plausible than the perplexing notion that organic living things, including humans, are unreal. Indeed, if we are right, it is our scientific and philosophical understanding of the nature of things which explains why basic particles, mereological compounds, and organisms should be considered real individual substances, while artifacts and typical natural formations should not.

7 IS THERE A PRINCIPLE OF COMPOSITION FOR PHYSICAL THINGS?

Few contemporary philosophers have discussed issues about the unity of the parts of nonliving and living individual substances in a systematic way. An important figure who has attempted to deal with these issues in a comprehensive way is Peter Van Inwagen, who should be credited for reviving interest in these fundamental, but neglected, issues.[51]

Van Inwagen is primarily interested in the question of whether the notion of a physical object's *composition* can be analyzed without employing the concept of parthood or any related mereological notion. To do this in the *general* case is to provide a nonmereological analysis of what it is for physical objects P_1 . . . P_n to compose y, where "P_1" . . . "P_n" and "y" are free variables. Van Inwagen finds himself unable to formulate an analysis of this kind. Nevertheless, he thinks that he can provide such an analysis in a *special* case of a certain kind. In particular, Van Inwagen argues that he can analyze what it is for there to exist an x such that physical objects P_1 . . . P_n compose x, where "x" is a bound variable, and "P_1" ... "P_n" are free variables. Furthermore, he believes that unless the notion of composition can be analyzed in non-mereological terms, either in the general case or in the special case (or both), there are no compound physical objects.

We shall refer to such an analysis of the notion of composition for a physical object (or some kind of physical object) as a principle of composition. Notice that Van Inwagen's task of providing a principle of composition for a physical thing is not the same as the task we have set ourselves in providing a principle of unity or organization for the parts of a physical thing of some kind. In other words, analyzing the concept of composition for a physical thing in non-mereological terms is different than analyzing the concept of a causal relation whose instantiation by physical things of some sort is logically necessary and sufficient for them to compose a physical thing of a certain kind. In fact, our analysis of such a causal relation for a mereological compound, i.e., being joined and connected, and the corresponding principle of unity, presuppose a definition employing the concept of proper parthood.[52] Similarly, our analysis of such a causal relation for an organism, i.e., being functionally united, and the corresponding principle of organization, presuppose a series of definitions using the concepts of a part, of a thing's hereditary make-up, and of an organic living thing.[53] Since the aforementioned concepts are mereological or compositional in nature, our conceptions of being joined and connected, and of being functionally united, cannot be used to formulate a principle of composition for physical objects, as the proposed analysis would be viciously circular. On the other hand, because there is no conceptual circularity or triviality involved in analyzing a complex *causal* relation in terms of a mereological one, it seems harmless for a principle of unity or organization to make use of the relation of parthood.

Van Inwagen's principle of composition for physical objects may be stated as follows.

(C1) Necessarily, physical objects P_1 ... P_n compose something [that is, a compound physical substance] if and only if the activity of P_1 ... P_n constitutes a life.[54]

In (C1), Van Inwagen understands a life as a process of a special sort, rather than as a substance of a certain kind. We shall discuss his understanding of this peculiar process in greater detail later. Notice that (C1) implies that the following compositional principle is true of living things.

(C1*) Necessarily, physical objects $P_1 \ldots P_n$ compose a living thing if and only if the activity of $P_1 \ldots P_n$ constitutes a life.

Thus, Van Inwagen's acceptance of (C1) commits him to (C1*).

(C1) implies that *all* compound physical objects are living things. Hence, Van Inwagen believes that there are no compound inanimate objects (nonliving physical substances). According to him, there are inanimate physical objects, but they are elementary particles. Thus, Van Inwagen defends the rather startling proposition that the only individual substances which exist are living things and fundamental particles. This proposition implies, for example, that none of the medium-sized inanimate objects that we seem to perceive with our senses actually exist. Since we find it very plausible that there *are* compound nonliving physical objects, i.e., mereological compounds, it would behoove us to provide an answer to Van Inwagen's argument against their existence.

Van Inwagen's argument against the existence of compound nonliving physical objects is based upon two premises. The first is that if there are compound physical substances of some sort, then there must be a satisfactory compositional principle which applies to entities of that sort. The second is that there is no satisfactory compositional principle which applies to compound nonliving physical objects. These two premises together entail Van Inwagen's conclusion that there are no compound nonliving physical objects.

We shall criticize Van Inwagen's position in three ways. First, we shall dispute Van Inwagen's premise that if there are compound physical substances of some kind, then there must be an adequate compositional principle which applies to entities of that kind. Second, we shall argue that the compositional principle for living things, (C1*), is unsatisfactory in a number of respects. Since (C1*) is entailed by Van Inwagen's compositional principle for physical objects, (C1), such an argument also implies that (C1) is inadequate. Third, we shall try to show that *if* (C1*) were satisfactory, then *would* be a satisfactory principle of composition for physical objects which allows for compound nonliving physical objects.

(1) We think that it is unreasonable for Van Inwagen to demand a nonmereological analysis of composition as the price for an ontology of compound physical things. It is not implausible to suppose that composition, and other mereological notions in terms of which it can be defined, for example, parthood, are concepts which *cannot* be analyzed in nonmereological terms. Indeed, this is suggested by Van

Inwagen's inability to formulate a nonmereological analysis of composition in the general case. If composition has no non-mereological analysis in the general case, then it would not be surprising for it to lack such an analysis in the special case as well. In any event, it is reasonable to suppose that mereological notions, viz., composition, parthood, discreteness, overlap, and so on, form a tightly knit family of logically interrelated concepts: a family whose members can be defined (if at all) only in terms of other concepts belonging to that family. Furthermore, it is *prima facie* plausible to think that compound physical things exist. Hence, it is problematic to assume, as Van Inwagen does, that if composition cannot be analyzed in nonmereological terms (in either the general or the special case), then there are no compound physical things. Thus, the first premise of Van Inwagen's argument against the existence of compound nonliving physical objects is problematic.

(2) Van Inwagen denies that there is a generic notion of parthood applicable to entities belonging to different ontological categories, for example, physical substances, events, properties, places, and times. He thinks that, strictly speaking, mereological notions, for example, composition and parthood, can apply only to physical substances, and that there are analogous notions which are non-mereological and which apply to entities which are not physical substances, viz., the notion of an activity (or an event) being constituted by other activities (or events). Moreover, recall that Van Inwagen conceives of a life as a process, event, or activity of a special kind. In the light of these observations, we can understand why, in his search for an analysis of the composition of physical things, Van Inwagen feels free to employ an unanalyzed notion of the activities of physical things $P_1 \ldots P_n$ constituting a life. Van Inwagen believes that this unanalyzed notion is a nonmereological one, and therefore he thinks that his employing it in his analysis of the composition of physical substances does not render his analysis circular.

In contrast, in defending our analysis of the concept of substance, we argued that there *is* a generic notion of parthood that applies to entities belonging to a wide variety of ontological categories. This argument implies that the notions of an activity being constituted by other activities, a space being constituted by other spaces, a property being constituted by other properties, and so on *are* mereological in character. Hence, by our lights, (C1*) attempts to analyze the composition of a living thing in terms of a *mereological* concept, i.e., the concept of activities $A_1 \ldots A_n$ constituting some activity (a life). If our view that this concept is mereological is correct, then (C1*) is inadmissibly circular, and therefore unsatisfactory.

Furthermore, in order to understand (C1*) we must understand what it is for the activity of physical objects $P_1 \ldots P_n$ to constitute a life. Van Inwagen explains that by a life in this context he means not a living thing, i.e., not a living substance, but rather a highly complex and peculiar kind of self-maintaining metabolic process. Van Inwagen holds that a living thing undergoes a process of this special sort, but he is careful not to define this sort of process in terms of the notion of a living thing.[55]

Unfortunately, Van Inwagen's conception of life as a process is rather obscure. This obscurity is inherited by (C1*). Van Inwagen's notion of a life stands in need of analysis, but he does not provide such an analysis; rather, he speculates that biologists will someday provide a more adequate explanation of the relevant conception of life. Nevertheless, until they do, it is difficult to fathom how our understanding of the concept of composition can be enhanced by appealing to a notion of life that is so incompletely understood. Thus, it seems that (C1*) lacks the explanatory power required for a satisfactory principle of composition.

In addition, (C1*) seems to have unacceptable consequences in possible cases in which an organism's life-processes sustain another organism's life-processes in an intimate way, for example, an adult, A, whose heart pumps blood both for himself and for an infant, i, via some unnatural connection; a human, H, infested with a parasitic tapeworm, W; and a termite, T, which has a symbiotic protozoan, S, living in its intestinal tract.[56] For instance, T's biological activities sustain S, and S's biological activities both help to sustain T and are intimately integrated into T's vital biological processes. Hence, it seems that T's biological activities and S's biological activities constitute a life. Therefore, (C1) appears to imply that some parts of T and some parts of S together compose an organism. Similar arguments of comparable plausibility imply that some parts of A and some parts of i, or some parts of H and some parts of W, would together compose an organism. Yet, it is evident that in these cases the parts in question would not compose an organism. Consequently, it seems that (C1) does not provide a logically sufficient condition for physical objects $P_1 \ldots P_n$ to compose a living thing.

Van Inwagen may want to insist that in cases of this kind the relevant activities do *not* constitute lives (processes of a certain sort).

But what grounds are there for insisting that this is so? As Van Inwagen recognizes, the project of providing a principle of composition for living things precludes the use of the notion of an organism or living substance. So, he cannot justify the claim that the aforementioned activities do not constitute lives by arguing that there are no *organisms* which have these alleged lives. Nor does Van Inwagen offer any other justification for this claim. Thus, there are no grounds for thinking that (C1*) can explain *why* there would not be an organism composed of the parts in question. Surely, though, a satisfactory principle of composition for living things should explain this. Therefore, there is no reason to believe that (C1*) has the requisite explanatory power.

For all of the foregoing reasons, we conclude that (C1*) is not an adequate compositional principle for living substances. Since (C1*) is entailed by (C1), and since (C1*) is unsatisfactory, we conclude that (C1) is unsatisfactory as well.

(3) In any case, we shall now argue that if (C1*) *were* adequate, then there *would be* an adequate principle of composition for physical objects which allows for both compound nonliving things *and* living physical objects. If such an argument is correct, then (C1) is unacceptable.

Van Inwagen's compositional principle for physical objects, (C1), entails that there is a compositional principle for living things, (C1*), formulated in terms of the activity of physical objects constituting a life (an activity of a certain kind). But it seems that if living things have a principle of composition of this kind, then inanimate objects have an analogous principle of composition that can be formulated in terms of the activity or the state of physical objects constituting an activity or a state of being an inanimate object. As far as we can tell, there is no reason to think that this appeal to an activity or a state of being an inanimate object is any less legitimate than Van Inwagen's appeal to an activity of life. Thus, if the principle of composition for living things can be formulated in terms of an activity of life as in (C1*), then there is the following disjunctive principle of composition for physical objects which allows for nonliving as well as living compound physical objects.

(C2) Necessarily, physical objects $P_1 \ldots P_n$ compose something if and only if either (i) the activity of $P_1 \ldots P_n$ constitutes a life or (ii) the activity or the state of $P_1 \ldots P_n$ constitutes an activity or a state of being an inanimate object.

(C2) entails the following principle of composition for inanimate objects which parallels the principle of composition for living things in (C1*):

(C2*) Necessarily, physical objects P_1 ... P_n compose an inanimate object if and only if the activity or the state of P_1 ... P_n constitutes an activity or a state of being an inanimate object.

In explaining his principle of composition for compound physical beings, (C1), Van Inwagen presupposes that there are complex activities which are constituted by other activities. Similarly, in explaining (C2), its proponents may presuppose not only this, but also that there are complex *states* which are constituted by other states. For example, the energy state of the basic particles composing an organism constitute the energy state of the entire organism, the state of some sugar molecules constitutes a state of being crystalline, and the states of certain water molecules constitute states of being solid, liquid, and gaseous, respectively.

Of course, (C2*) seems to have little or no value unless we can elucidate the nature of an activity or a state of being an inanimate object. What is the nature of such an activity or state? An answer can be given to this question that is at least as good as Van Inwagen's answer to the parallel, and equally pressing, question about life, viz., "What is the nature of an activity of life?" According to Van Inwagen, what gives content to the notion of a complex activity of life is the fact that scientists have discovered much about the nature of this activity. But the same is true of an activity or a state of being an inanimate object: scientists have learned much about the nature of this activity or state. For example, in the case of mereological compounds, scientists have found that it is a state characterized by a special kind of *stability* resulting from a balance of opposing forces of certain kinds. More specifically, it is a state that consists of a system of attractive and repulsive states of certain kinds such that each of the former is in equilibrium with one of the latter and vice versa. Furthermore, as we have seen, if there is a compound inanimate object other than a mereological compound, then it is a natural formation having strikingly life-like attributes. In that case, the activity of the parts of this strikingly life-like natural formation constitute a life-like activity which is a proper object of scientific investigation.

For the foregoing reasons, we conclude that (C2*) is at least as plausible a compositional principle as (C1*). Hence, if (C1*) were acceptable, then we should endorse (C2) instead of (C1). But unlike (C1), (C2) does *not* imply Van Inwagen's thesis that there are no compound nonliving physical objects. Furthermore, we have given an argument which implies that the notions of a complex activity (or state) being constituted by other activities (or states) are mereological ones. If we are right, then both (C1*) and (C2*) are inadmissibly circular, and neither of them is a satisfactory compositional principle. If neither (C1*) nor (C2*) is adequate, then both (C1) and (C2) are inadequate compositional principles as well.

In our view, doubts about whether there is a satisfactory principle of composition for inanimate objects or living things do not put the existence of compound inanimate objects or living things in doubt. As we argued earlier, it is unreasonable to demand a nonmereological analysis of composition as the price for an ontology of compound physical things.

Despite our disagreements with Van Inwagen, there are two noteworthy implications of his position with which we find ourselves in agreement. First, like Van Inwagen, we think that the principle of unity for the parts of an organism or living thing *cannot* be identified with a principle of unity for the parts of a compound inanimate object. Van Inwagen accepts this because his view implies that there is *no* principle of unity for the parts of a (compound) inanimate object – and there is, he thinks, therefore, no such object. On the other hand, we have defended the existence of inanimate mereological compounds, but also the view that the principle of unity for their parts differs from the principle of unity for the parts of organisms.

Second, according to both Van Inwagen and ourselves, two humans who are attached by being glued, fastened, or fused to one another are not proper parts of either an animate or an inanimate object. Let us consider, first, why they are not proper parts of an organism. For one, it is intuitively very plausible that two such humans are not proper parts of a third living organism. Moreover, our principle of organization for the parts of an organism implies that two humans of this kind are not proper parts of an organism, since two such humans are not functionally united in the way that our principle of organization requires.

Two attached human beings are also not proper parts of an inanimate object. As we argued earlier, since functioning human beings are composed to a large extent of bodily fluids, two functioning humans who are glued, fastened, or fused together are not proper parts of an inanimate mereological compound composed of things which are joined and connected, as is required by our principle of unity for the parts of a mereological compound. Moreover, as we have also argued, if there is a compound inanimate physical object other than a mereological compound, then it must be a natural formation of a strikingly life-like kind. But two functioning humans who are glued, fastened, or fused together are obviously not proper parts of such a natural formation.

Organisms and natural kinds

The kind, Organism, is the highest genus of all subdivisions of organic living things. It subsumes all more specific biological classifications, for example, animal, vertebrate, mammal, canine, and wolf. Because biology is a natural science, Organism is a natural kind. And since an organism is a compound substance of a certain sort, Organism is a natural compound substance-kind.

As the following line of reasoning implies, for any organism, O, there is at least one other more specific natural compound substance-kind to which O belongs. Organisms of many different kinds exist, for example, horses, elm trees, amoebas, and bacteria. It is evident that in many cases an organism of one of these kinds cannot become an organism of another one of these kinds: for example, a horse cannot become a bacterium. Accordingly, given that Organism is a natural compound substance-kind, it seems that an organism must belong to another *more specific* natural compound substance-kind, that is, to some subdivision of Organism. In the light of the great variety found among organisms, one would expect that there are a large number of subdivisions of this kind. We turn next to the question of what these other subdivisions might be.

In biology, an organism is classified in terms of a hierarchical system of classifications, for example, the species, genus, family, order, class, phylum, and kingdom to which the organism in question belongs. For example, a human belongs to the species *homo sapiens*, the genus *homo*, the family *hominidae*, the order *primates*, the class *mammalia*, the phylum *chordata*, and the kingdom *animalia*. The traditional view is that such biological classifications are paradigm cases of natural kinds.

Although this traditional view continues to influence contemporary biology, it has come under vigorous attack in recent years. For instance, Elliot Sober has written as follows:

> If species have essences, it is surprising that evolutionary biology has not only failed to find them but has also shown scant interest in doing so. A view more in keeping with scientific practice is the idea that species are populations that have organisms as parts, not as members. Two organisms are in the same species in virtue of their genealogical relatedness, not in virtue of their similarity; they are kin, but do not thereby comprise a natural kind.[1]

Sober is a participant in a continuing debate among three schools of thought about the nature of biological classification: pheneticism, cladism, and evolutionary systematics. Pheneticists maintain that organisms (species) belong to the same species (higher-order taxon) wholly in virtue of their similarity; cladists hold that organisms (species) belong to the same species (higher-order taxon) wholly in virtue of their genealogical relatedness; and evolutionary systematists claim that organisms (species) belong to the same species (higher-order taxon) partly in virtue of their similarity and partly in virtue of their genealogical relatedness.[2] Certain versions of pheneticism imply that biological species and higher-order taxa are natural substance-kinds, while cladism and evolutionary systematics imply that they are not. In sum, then, the claim that biological species and higher-order taxa are natural kinds is a matter of controversy among contemporary biologists.

We have doubts of our own about whether species or higher-order taxa are natural compound substance-kinds. Arguably, for any species or higher-order taxon, K, there could be a transitional organism, O, which marginally belongs to K and which could fall outside of K, because O could undergo a mutation.[3] Since a species or higher-order taxon, K, is a natural compound substance-kind only if K must be essential to anything which belongs to K, it can be argued with some plausibility that a species or higher-order taxon is not a natural compound substance-kind.

As an alternative to species, T. E. Wilkerson has proposed that an organism's genotype, a type far more specific than an organism's species, is a natural kind.[4] Unfortunately, though, it appears that for any genotype, G, an organism which has G could lack G through a mutation.[5] Since a natural compound substance-kind must be essential to whatever instantiates it, it seems that an organism's genotype is not a natural compound substance-kind.

Nevertheless, we believe that by using a notion related to that of an organism's genotype, we can identify natural compound substance-kinds which are exemplified by organisms and which are subdivisions of Organism. To begin with, the information implicit in an organism's (O's) genotype at O's first moment of existence corresponds to O's norm of reaction at that time, and to what we have called O's microstructural hereditary blueprint.[6] An organism's (O's) microstructural hereditary blueprint, M, delimits, in virtue of physical necessities alone, the range of M's possible expressions, under varying environmental conditions, consistent with O's continuing to have M. Such a "blueprint," M, is equivalent to a large disjunction of the members of a similarity class of nondisjunctive structural or compositional attributes.

O's having M entails that there is a limited range of structural or compositional natures which O could possess. Yet this entailment does not hold in virtue of physical necessities alone: it is a metaphysical entailment which pertains to the essential nature of a particular organism of a certain kind. For example, even if a tiger could become a nontiger because of a mutation, this nontiger would resemble a tiger in its structural or compositional properties to a considerable degree.[7] In other words, such a nontiger would still be tiger-like. But a tiger could not become an oak tree, a mushroom, or a paramecium, even if, by a succession of continuous changes, we could begin with a tiger and end with an oak tree, or a mushroom, or a paramecium. Nor could a tiger become a machine composed of steel, copper, lucite, and silicon.

Thus, in virtue of its having had a microstructural hereditary blueprint at its inception, an organism, O, exemplifies a natural compound substance-kind which delimits the range of alternative structural or compositional natures possible for O. Such a natural kind is equivalent to a disjunction of the structural or compositional natures which could be had by O. Since organisms of numerous varieties have different ranges of alternative possible structural or compositional natures, there are a large number of natural kinds of this sort. Such a natural compound substance-kind is a subdivision of Organism, which is more general than an organism's genotype or microstructural hereditary blueprint. Such a natural compound substance-kind may also be more general than an organism's species. It should be noted that these natural compound substance-kinds can be expressed in simple everyday terms only if we use language in a somewhat imprecise way. For example, it may be said that a tiger, an organism which belongs to the species, tiger, has the property of being tiger-like, and that this property is a natural compound substance-kind of the sort we have in mind. Parallel remarks apply to any organism, O, and the property of being s-like, where s is the species to which O belongs.

As we have seen, a natural compound substance-kind of the sort in question has physical as well as metaphysical aspects. Such a natural kind includes an organism's microstructural hereditary blueprint, an attribute which plays a role in biological explanations of that organism's characteristics. But it also includes metaphysical limitations upon the range of possible ways in which O's genotype or hereditary-type can be altered. And it seems that these metaphysical limitations are not directly relevant to explanations in biology, for example, explanations in evolutionary or molecular biology. Parallel remarks apply to natural compound substance-kinds which are proper objects of inquiry in other natural sciences. For instance, the kind, Mereological Compound, has physical aspects, for example, the character of the forces which unite the members of a set of parts which compose a mereological compound,[8] as well as metaphysical aspects, for example, a mereological compound's parts being essential to it.[9] These physical aspects figure in physical explanations of the properties of a mereological compound; and in virtue of those aspects, the kind, Mereological Compound, is a proper object of inquiry in physics. In contrast, the metaphysical aspects in question are not directly relevant to physical explanations of the properties of a mereological compound.

In conclusion, since it seems that organisms must belong to natural compound substance-kinds of the special sorts we have identified, and since biology is primarily an inquiry into the nature of organisms, it appears that biology presupposes the existence of such natural compound substance-kinds.

Notes

INTRODUCTION

1 We presuppose a nonreductive account of modality, understood in terms of the standard possible worlds account involving transworld identity. For an argument supporting this standard account, see Gary Rosenkrantz, *Haecceity: An Ontological Essay* (Dordrecht: Kluwer, 1993).

2 The realist doctrine that there are physical objects in this sense has been attacked by idealists, notably George Berkeley, who argued that the existence of houses, mountains, and trees consists in their being perceived. See his *Three Dialogues Between Hylas and Philonous*, and his *Treatise Concerning the Principles of Human Knowledge*. If it is necessarily true that there is an all-perceiving being, as Berkeley believed, then physical objects in the realist sense cannot exist unperceived. Even so, such physical objects, unlike Berkeley's houses, mountains, and trees, do not exist *because* they are perceived.

3 According to Boscovich's single law, *puncta* at a certain distance attract, until upon approaching one another they reach a point at which they repel, and eventually they reach equilibrium. Thus, Boscovich defends a form of dynamism, or the theory that nature is to be understood in terms of force and not mass (where forces are functions of time and distance). By dispensing with extended substance, Boscovich avoided epistemological difficulties facing Locke's natural philosophy and foreshadowed developments in modern physics. Boscovich (1711–1787) is best known for *A Theory of Natural Philosophy Reduced to a Single Law of the Actions Existing in Nature*. For a recent edition see *A Theory of Natural Philosophy* (Cambridge, Mass.: MIT Press, 1966).

4 Cf. René Descartes, *Meditations on First Philosophy*.

5 For a defense of this characterization of a soul, see Joshua Hoffman and Gary Rosenkrantz, *Substance Among Other Categories* (Cambridge: Cambridge University Press, 1994), chap. 5.

6 For a detailed defense of the possibility (though not the existence) of interacting souls and bodies, see *Substance Among Other Categories*, chap. 5.

7 *The Monadology*, in *Leibniz Selections*, ed. Philip Weiner (New York: Charles Scribner's Sons, 1951), 17.

8 David Bohm, "A Suggested Interpretation of the Quantum Theory in Terms of 'Hidden' Variables, I and II," *Physical Review* 85, (1952) pp. 166–193.
9 See David Hume, *A Treatise of Human Nature*, ed. L. A. Selby-Bigge (Oxford: Oxford University Press, 1888), book 1, part 4, secs 5 and 6.

1 THE CONCEPT OF SUBSTANCE IN HISTORY

1 There is much confusion surrounding Aristotle's use of the term primary *ousia*, which is often translated as substance. This translation is somewhat misleading, since one important meaning of "substance" is an individual thing in the ordinary sense, for example, an organism, or an inanimate material object, but this is *not* what Aristotle means by the term primary *ousia*. A more accurate and less misleading translation of this term is primary being (or fundamental entity, or basic entity). This is recognized, for example, in Richard Hope's translation of Aristotle's *Metaphysics* (Ann Arbor: University of Michigan Press, 1968). In the *Categories* Aristotle argued that individual things, for example, inanimate objects and organisms, are the primary beings, and that essences are secondary beings. However, in the later work, the *Metaphysics*, he changed his view about primary beings, and seems to have concluded that forms, and not individual things, are the primary beings. At this point, Aristotle conceived of individual things as, in some sense, combinations of form and matter. Although there may be a technical or philosophical sense of the term "substance" in which it means basic entity, this would be a different meaning than the ordinary sense, that of an individual thing, with which we are concerned in this book.
2 *Categories*, trans. J. Ackrill, in *The Complete Works of Aristotle*, ed. Jonathan Barnes. 2 vols (Princeton: Princeton University Press, 1984), 1:7. Unless otherwise noted, all further references to Aristotle will be to this edition. Contrary properties, such as being round and being square, or being a horse and being a dog, are properties which cannot be possessed by the same object at the same time. Thus, if a single object possesses contrary properties, it must do so at two different times, and it must have changed from the one to the other of those times.
3 *Ibid.*
4 *Ibid.*
5 David Lewis has attempted to define the intrinsic/relational distinction in "Extrinsic Properties," *Philosophical Studies* 44 (1983), pp. 197–200. Lewis admits that his attempt fails. See also Ishtiyaque Haji, "The Unresolved Puzzle about Posthumous Predication," *Grazer Philosophische Studien* 38 (1990), pp. 187–193, and David Hillel-Reuben, "A Puzzle about Posthumous Predication," *Philosophical Review* 97 (1988), pp. 211–236.
6 For example, *Metaphysics*, trans. W. D. Ross, *The Complete Works of Aristotle*, 2:1597.
7 This conclusion is drawn by conjoining (iii) to (i) by P. T. Geach in *Logic Matters* (Berkeley: University of California Press, 1972), pp.

302–318, and by D. H. Mellor in *Real Time* (Cambridge: Cambridge University Press), chaps 7 and 8.

8 The reality of surfaces is affirmed in the following two recent works: Roderick Chisholm, "Boundaries," in *On Metaphysics* (Minneapolis: University of Minnesota Press, 1989), pp. 83–89, and Avrum Stroll, *Surfaces* (Minneapolis: University of Minnesota Press, 1988).

9 *Categories*, trans. J. Ackrill, *The Complete Works of Aristotle*, 1:4.

10 *Ibid.*

11 *Ibid.*, p. 3.

12 This first interpretation of Aristotle is defended by J. L. Ackrill in his translation with notes of Aristotle's *Categories and De Interpretatione* (Oxford: Oxford University Press, 1963), pp. 74–76. Ackrill's interpretation is probably the standard one.

13 *Ibid.*, p. 74.

14 The term "trope" seems to have been coined by D. C. Williams as a name for a concrete "property." See, for example, his *The Principles of Empirical Realism* (Springfield, Ill.: Charles C. Thomas, 1966). Two others who defend the existence of tropes are G. F. Stout, "Are the Characteristics of Particular Things Universal or Particular?," symposium in *Proceedings of the Aristotelian Society*, suppl. vol. 3 (1923), pp. 114–122, and Keith Campbell, *Abstract Particulars* (Oxford: Basil Blackwell, 1990).

15 Montgomery Furth, *Substance, Form, and Psyche: An Aristotelian Metaphysics* (Cambridge: Cambridge University Press, 1988), chap. 1.

16 *Ibid.*, pp. 15–21.

17 With respect to Descartes, see Louis Loeb, *From Descartes to Hume: Continental Metaphysics and the Development of Modern Philosophy* (Ithaca, N.Y.: Cornell University Press, 1981), chap. 2, and R. S. Woolhouse, *Descartes, Spinoza, Leibniz: The Concept of Substance in Seventeenth Century Metaphysics* (New York: Routledge, 1993), chap. 2. For Locke, see D. J. O'Connor, *John Locke* (New York: Dover, 1967), and R. S. Woolhouse, *Locke's Philosophy of Science and Knowledge* (New York: Barnes and Noble, 1971).

18 *An Essay Concerning Human Understanding*, 2 vols, revised ed., ed. John Yolton (New York: Dutton, 1965), vol. 1, chap. 23, p. 245.

19 *The Philosophical Writings of Descartes*, trans. John Cottingham, Robert Stoothoff, and Dugald Murdoch, 2 vols (Cambridge: Cambridge University Press, 1984), 2:114.

20 *Ibid.*, p. 156.

21 M. Wilson, *Descartes* (London: Routledge and Kegan Paul, 1978), suggests this reading.

22 For example, Jonathan Bennett, *Locke, Berkeley, Hume: Central Themes* (Oxford: Oxford University Press, 1971); M. R. Ayers, "The Ideas of Power and Substance in Locke's Philosophy," in *Locke on Human Understanding: Selected Essays*, ed. I. Tipton (Oxford: Oxford University Press, 1977), pp. 77–104; and Martha Bolton, "Substances, Substrata, and Names of Substances in Locke's *Essay*," *Philosophical Review* 85 (1976), pp. 488–513.

23 By a "feature," we mean either a property or a relation. If Descartes

and Locke really are substratum theorists, then they appear to subscribe to ST1. An example of a philosopher who maintains ST2 is Gustav Bergmann, *Realism* (Madison: University of Wisconsin Press, 1967).

24 Some philosophers have suggested that one can grasp or apprehend *oneself* in this way, though not substances other than oneself. See, for example, Bertrand Russell, *The Problems of Philosophy* (London: Oxford University Press, 1950), chap. 5. We find this kind of "direct" awareness of individuals highly implausible.

25 Speaking of a ball, Michael Loux has observed that a theory such as ST2 "drives us to . . . the view that the ordinary way of thinking about the ball is wrong. The ball does not literally possess the properties associated with it; something else does." *Substance and Attribute* (Dordrecht: Reidel, 1978), pp. 109–110. By this "something else," of course, Loux means the substratum. As we have pointed out, however, it is not correct that the substratum literally "possesses" the properties associated with it.

26 *Philosophical Writings of Descartes*, 2:114.

27 *Ibid.*, p. 159.

28 *Ibid.*, p. 210. Compare David Armstrong: "a particular is a substance, logically capable of independent existence. It could exist although nothing else existed." *Nominalism and Realism* (Cambridge: Cambridge University Press, 1978), p. 115.

29 *Philosophical Writings of Descartes*, 2:159.

30 William Mann has defended the coherence of this traditional doctrine of divine simplicity in "Epistemology Supernaturalized." For a critical discussion of this essay, see "Necessity, Contingency, and Mann," by Gary Rosenkrantz. Mann replies in "Reply to Rosenkrantz." All three articles appear in *Faith and Philosophy* 2, no. 4 (1985), pp. 436–467.

31 This point was made by Alfred North Whitehead in *Process and Reality* (Toronto: Collier-Macmillan, 1969), p. 75. As he observes: "The actual entity, in virtue of being *what* it is, is also *where* it is. . . . This is the direct denial of the Cartesian doctrine '. . . an existent thing which requires nothing but itself in order to exist.'"

32 Loeb, *From Descartes to Hume*, chap. 2.

33 A first-order property is a property which can only be instantiated by a concrete individual.

34 Aristotle held that a property exists only if it is instantiated. Thus, his view implies that a first-order property exists only if it is instantiated by a substance. In the following quotation, Descartes appears to subscribe to this view: "It follows that, wherever we find some attributes or qualities, there is necessarily some thing or substance to be found for them to belong to . . ." *The Philosophical Writings of Descartes*, 1:196. Also, "We know them [substances] only by perceiving certain forms or attributes which must inhere in something if they are to exist" (2:156).

35 And in *Substance Among Other Categories* (Cambridge: Cambridge University Press, 1994), chap. 2, we have shown that a substance's being neither said-of nor in a subject does *not* imply that a substance is asymmetrically independent of its properties. Thus, it does not imply

that a property is asymmetrically dependent upon a substance. In the aforementioned chapter, there is a full discussion of whether or not this Aristotelian analysis of substance is an independence theory.

36 Saul Kripke, "Naming and Necessity," in *Semantics of Natural Language*, ed. D. Davidson and G. Harman (Dordrecht: Reidel, 1972), pp. 253–355.

37 Even if Descartes was correct in thinking that a human being could not be a physical object, if his theory of substance requires this assumption, it suffers from another form of lack of ontological neutrality.

38 *The Ethics*, Part I, Definition 3. This quotation is from the Samuel Shirley translation, *The Ethics and Selected Letters*, ed. Seymour Feldman (Indianapolis: Hackett Publishing Company, 1982), p. 31.

39 In the Introduction, section 4.

40 *An Enquiry Concerning Human Understanding* (New York: Liberal Arts Press, 1955), p. 194. Leibniz was critical of views of this kind: "On the contrary, what comes into our mind is the *concretum* conceived as wise, warm, shining, rather than *abstractions* or qualities such as wisdom, warmth, light etc., which are much harder to grasp. (I say 'qualities,' for what the substantial object contains are qualities, not ideas.)" *New Essays on Human Understanding*, trans. Peter Remnant and Jonathan Bennett (Cambridge: Cambridge University Press, 1981), book 2, chap. 23, sec. 1.

41 *A Treatise of Human Nature*, ed. L. A. Selby-Bigge (Oxford: Oxford University Press, 1888), book 1, part 4, sec. 6.

Such an authority of ordinary English usage as *Webster's Third New International Dictionary* (1976) cites this quotation in its article on "Substance," maintaining that in Humean philosophy "substance" means "a collection of qualities regarded as constituting a unity."

42 *The Principles of Human Knowledge*, part 1, paragraph 1. It should be noted that Berkeley did not extend his reductionist view of the nature of *physical* objects to *souls*, which he, unlike Hume, regarded as utterly different from collections of ideas.

43 For an account of the intuitive distinction between concrete and abstract entities see Chapter 2, section 2.

44 H. N. Castañeda seems to imply that a concrete thing is an abstract entity in "Individuation and Non-Identity: A New Look," *American Philosophical Quarterly* 12 (1975), pp. 131–140. Also Bertrand Russell in *Human Knowledge: Its Scope and Limits* (New York: Simon and Schuster, 1948), p. 83.

45 The term "mereological," derives from the Greek μέρος, meaning "part." Thus, mereology is the theory of parts, or more specifically, Lesniewski's formal theory of parts. See Stanislaw Lesniewski, *Collected Works* (Dordrecht: Kluwer, 1991).

Typically, a mereological theory employs terms such as the following: proper part, improper part, overlapping (having a part in common), disjoint (not overlapping), mereological product (the "intersection" of overlapping objects), mereological sum (a collection of parts), mereological difference, the universal sum, mereological complement, and atom (that which has no proper parts). Formal mereologies are axiomatic systems. Lesniewski's Mereology and Nelson Goodman's formal mereology (which he calls the "Calculus of Individuals") are intended to be compatible with nominalism, i.e., the intention is that no reference be made to sets, properties, or other abstract entities. Lesniewski hoped that his Mereology, with its many parallels to set theory, would provide an alternative to set theory as a foundation for mathematics. For Goodman's formal mereology see his *The Structure of Appearance*, 2nd ed. (Indianapolis, Ind.: Bobbs-Merrill, 1966). For an authoritative discussion of the principles of formal mereological systems, see Peter Simons, *Parts: A Study in Ontology* (Oxford: Oxford University Press, 1987). For a defense of the claim that Set and Collection are exclusive categories see *Substance Among Other Categories*, p. 186.

46 For example, see G. F. Stout, "The Nature of Universals and Propositions," *Proceedings of the British Academy* 10 (1921–1923), pp. 157–172; and D. C. Williams, "The Elements of Being," I and II, *Review of Metaphysics* 6 (1953), pp. 3–18 and 171–193.

47 Of course, necessarily, for any x, if x is a soul, then x does not have parts. On the other hand, necessarily, for any x, and for any y, if x is a nonmaterial physical substance, and y is part of x, then y is either a physical substance or a portion of physical stuff.

48 Of course, such strictures apply to an attempt to reject any of the intuitive data for being a substance.

49 Just as plausibly, sets have their elements essentially. For a defense of this claim, see James Van Cleve, "Why a Set Contains its Members Essentially," *Nous* 19 (1986), pp. 585–602.

50 See section 2 of the Introduction for a possible example of this kind.

51 Russell, *Human Knowledge: Its Scope and Limits*, chaps 7–8; H. N. Castañeda, "Thinking and the Structure of the World," *Critica* 6, no. 18 (1972), pp. 43–81, and "Perception, Belief, and the Structure of Physical Objects and Consciousness," *Synthese* 35 (1977), pp. 285–351.

52 Castañeda's substantial collections or sets contain not tropes but what he calls "ontological guises." Guises themselves are said by Castañeda to be concrete entities constructed out of abstract properties (thus, for Castañeda, substances are "bundles of bundles"). Similarly, Russell's collections or "complexes" contain universals. Nevertheless, the basic strategy of Castañeda and Russell for unifying guises or universals into substances can be adapted by a trope collectionist.

53 In "Perception, Belief, and the Structure of Physical Objects and Consciousness," Castañeda offers a set of axioms for the consubstantiation relation (the "Law of Communion," the "Law of Conditional Reflexivity," etc.). However, these axioms do not explicitly *define* consubstantiation, since that notion occurs within them. Nor do we accept the idea that they provide a so-called implicit definition of consubstantiation, since more than one relation could satisfy the axioms. In our view, without an intended interpretation, axioms are mere uninterpreted schemata. For a defense of this view, see Gary Rosenkrantz, "The Nature of Geometry," *American Philosophical Quarterly* 18 (1981), pp. 101–110.

54 *Human Knowledge: Its Scope and Limits*, p. 329.

55 For detailed criticisms of other collectionist proposals using strategies (Pi)–(Piv), see *Substance Among Other Categories*, chap. 3.

56 For cogent criticisms of a variant of the view we have just rejected, see James Van Cleve, "Three Versions of the Bundle Theory," *Philosophical Studies* 47 (1985), pp. 95–107. According to this variant, a substance is identical with a set of world-indexed dated properties, with the world-indexing having the aim of avoiding just the problem about change which we raised in the text. We remind the reader that we reject all views which identify substances with sets of abstract properties on the grounds that such sets, unlike substances, are abstract.

57 It might be thought that a temporal sequence is merely a collection *over time* – a four-dimensional collection – and hence that the category of being a temporal sequence is a subspecies of the category of being a collection. However, the following line of reasoning shows that this idea is mistaken. First of all, it is presumably *possible* for three-dimensional space and one-dimensional time to exist, and it is therefore *not necessary*, if there is a temporal sequence, for four-dimensional space-time to exist. However, necessarily, if there exists a collection (in time, as opposed to in space-time), then that collection could not continue to exist *after* one of its parts ceased to exist, but possibly, there is a temporal sequence (in time, not in space-time) which continues to exist after one of its parts ceases to exist (if there is a part in the sequence which succeeds the part that has ceased to exist). It follows that it is possible for there to be a temporal sequence (one which is in time, as opposed to in space-time) which is not identical with a collection. Hence, the category of being a temporal sequence is *not* a subspecies of (is not subsumed by) the category of being a collection.

58 Bertrand Russell, "Philosophy of the Twentieth Century," in *Twentieth Century Philosophy*, ed. Dagobert D. Runes (New York: Philosophical Library, 1943), p. 247. Russell's is a sequentialism of events rather than of collections of tropes. Russell offers a fuller development of this theory in *Human Knowledge: Its Scope and Limits*. In that work, Russell makes clear that according to him, events are themselves collections of "compresent" qualities (p. 83). Thus, his developed view is that a substance is a sequence of collections of such qualities: "A complex of compresence which does not recur takes the place traditionally occupied by 'particulars'; a single such complex, or a string of such complexes causally connected in a certain way, is the ᶬd of object to which it is conventionally appropriate to give a proper name" (p. 307). Hence, if his theory is a reductionist and not an eliminationist one with respect to substances and events, then Russell identifies a substance with an event or string of events. The view that a substance is an event is one we criticized earlier as a category mistake, while the view that it is a string of events is subject to criticisms parallel to those we make later of other forms of sequentialism. As for Russell's identification of events with collections of qualities, we have already criticized the idea that a *concretum* can be identified with a cluster of *abstracta*. It was for that

reason that we found versions of collectionism which identify substances with collections of tropes to be superior to the sort of theory Russell embraces.

59 See the first section of this chapter.
60 See *Substance Among Other Categories*, chap. 5.
61 For an argument to this effect see *ibid.*, chap. 5.
62 "Thinking and the Structure of the World," pp. 67–68.

2 AN INDEPENDENCE THEORY OF SUBSTANCE

1 Saul Kripke, "Naming and Necessity," in *Semantics of Natural Language*, ed. D. Davidson and G. Harman (Dordrecht: Reidel, 1972), pp. 253–355.
2 See Hume's *Treatise of Human Nature*, ed. L. A. Selby-Bigge (Oxford: Oxford University Press, 1888), book 1, part 4, sec. 5, p. 233.
3 To say that time (or space) is *absolute* is to say that it can exist unoccupied; and to say that time (or space) is *relational* is to say that it cannot exist unless it has at least two temporally (or spatially) related occupants.
4 The notion of an ontological category's being at level C can be analyzed wholly in terms of logical relationships that such a category bears to the categories on L. An *instantiable* ontic category is one which is possibly instantiated. We make the background assumption that there are at least two such categories of *concreta* at level C (at least one of which is on L), and likewise for categories of *abstracta*. The notion of an ontic category's being at level C can be analyzed as follows. A category on L is at level C just when it is instantiable; and an ontic category not on L is at level C just when (i) it neither subsumes, nor is subsumed by, an instantiable category on L, and (ii) it is not subsumed by an ontic category not on L which satisfies (i). (To say that a category $C1$ *subsumes* a category $C2$ is to say that necessarily, whatever instantiates $C2$ instantiates $C1$, and possibly, something instantiates $C1$ without instantiating $C2$.) See *Substance Among Other Categories* (Cambridge: Cambridge University Press, 1994), chap. 1, sec. II.
5 Note that the relation of parthood is transitive: necessarily, if x is part of y, and y is part of z, then x is part of z. In contrast, the set-theoretical relation of elementhood is intransitive: for instance, a is an element of $\{a\}$, $\{a\}$ is an element of $\{\{a\}\}$, but a is not an element of $\{\{a\}\}$. Thus, parthood and elementhood are different relations.
6 For a defense of this analysis of the concrete/abstract distinction, and criticisms of other attempts to analyze this distinction, see *Substance Among Other Categories*, appendix 1.
7 The intelligibility of the view that God is atemporal has recently been defended by Norman Kretzmann and Eleonore Stump, "Eternity," *Journal of Philosophy* 78 (1981), pp. 429–458.
8 Thus, our argument here is compatible with the following two possibilities: first, that an extended nonatomic substance is dependent upon other substances which are its parts; and, second, that a substance, for

instance, a human being, is dependent upon certain other earlier substances which played a role in its production, for example, a certain sperm and egg.

9 D. M. Armstrong, *Nominalism and Realism* (Cambridge: Cambridge University Press, 1978).

10 The notion of a higher-order property can be understood along the following lines. A first-order property is a property that could only be exemplified by a concrete individual. A second-order property is a property of a first-order property that could only be exemplified by a first-order property. Higher-order properties can then be defined in a fashion parallel to the way in which a second-order property was defined, for example, a third-order property is a property of a second-order property which could only be exemplified by a second-order property.

11 The notion of a higher-order trope can be understood as follows. A first-order trope is one that could only be possessed by or belong to a concrete individual other than a trope. A second-order trope is one that could only be possessed by or belong to a first-order trope. Higher-order tropes can then be defined in a fashion parallel to the way in which a second-order trope was defined.

12 Obviously, if a place or time is not atomic, then it will have parts which are places or times, and there will not be just one place or time.

13 Note that two spatial entities of this kind may be proper parts of a third spatial entity, and that two occurrences of this kind may be proper parts of a third occurrence.

14 See *Substance Among Other Categories*, chap. 4, sec. V.

15 The paradoxical nature of the conclusion that extended minimal places and times do not have boundaries does not surprise us; as we argued in *Substance Among Other Categories*, chap. 4, sec. V, entities of this kind are impossible.

16 Note that this state of affairs is compatible with the existence of one or more gaps in space or time that are surrounded by continuous subregions of space or time.

17 This implies that a two-dimensional physical substance would not have a surface (a two-dimensional limit). Nor would it have a subsurface. Also note that there could be a place that is not a limit. For instance, there could be a three-dimensional Euclidean space which is not a limit of a four-dimensional entity.

18 For instance, Mark Heller, *The Ontology of Physical Objects: Four Dimensional Hunks of Matter* (Cambridge: Cambridge University Press, 1990). Other four-dimensionalists include McTaggart, Russell, Carnap, Quine, and Smart.

19 Peter Simons, *Parts: A Study in Ontology* (Oxford: Oxford University Press, 1987), pp. 121–127. We take no side in this dispute in this book.

20 The letters "*F*" and "*G*" are schematic, and are to be replaced with an appropriate predicate expression.

21 These remarks do not purport to provide principles of identity or individuation for categories. Rather, they are only intended to introduce a simplifying verbal stipulation and to define a useful technical sense of categorial equivalence.

22 For example, Alfred North Whitehead, *Process and Reality* (Toronto: Collier-Macmillan, 1969).
23 The categorial status of being a concrete proper part was discussed in the third section of this chapter.
24 See section 1 of the Introduction, where we argued that a substance cannot be identified with either a property, an event, a privation, a limit, a place, or a time; and Chapter 1, section 4, where we argued that cluster theories of substance are incorrect.
25 This is an intuitive datum for the ordinary notion of a physical substance.
26 For a defense of a slightly modified version of (D3) which does not require the assumption that it is possible for there to be a substance that has no other substance as a part see *Substance Among Other Categories*, chap. 4.

3 ON THE UNITY OF THE PARTS OF MEREOLOGICAL COMPOUNDS

1 In Chapter 5, we shall argue that there cannot be a mereological compound that is alive, and that while mereological compounds and organisms are real things, artifacts and typical inanimate natural formations are not.
2 This rather droll figure was employed by Roderick Chisholm in an undergraduate metaphysics class at Brown University, *circa* 1973.
3 *Ontology, Modality, and the Fallacy of Reference* (Cambridge: Cambridge University Press, 1992), p. 2.
4 *Ibid.*, p. 5.
5 Leibniz defends monadism in his *Monadology*, though it is likely that his version of monadism is a form of idealism.
6 Collectivism is defended by Stanislaw Lesniewski, *Collected Works* (Dordrecht: Kluwer, 1991), and Nelson Goodman, *The Structure of Appearance*, 2nd ed. (Indianapolis, Ind.: Bobbs-Merrill, 1966). A more recent defender of collectivism is Michael Jubien. Jubien's argument for collectivism is based upon his claim that thinghood is not an objective property. We criticized this claim in the preceding section. Thus, these criticisms militate against Jubien's argument for collectivism as well.
7 Monism is defended by Parmenides in *The Way of Truth*. Among the followers of Parmenides are Zeno of Elea and Melissus. Monism is also defended by Spinoza in the *Ethics*.
8 Jonathan Lowe, in his *Kinds of Being* (Oxford: Basil Blackwell, 1989), p. 89, has pointed out that such a notion of connectedness is germane to characterizing the principle of unity for the parts of a physical substance.
9 Quoted in *Greek and Roman Philosophy after Aristotle*, ed. J. Saunders (New York: The Free Press, 1966), p. 86.
10 To say that two entities are discrete is to say that they have no part (proper or improper) in common.
11 The metaphor of "love" and "hate" is inspired by the doctrine of the presocratic philosopher Empedocles, who believed that all natural processes are due to the operation of these two opposing influences. See

Jonathan Barnes, *Early Greek Philosophy* (London: Penguin Books, 1987), pp. 161–201.

12 Compare David Tabor, *Gases, Liquids, and Solids* (Cambridge: Cambridge University Press, 1991), p. 23.

13 For an account of Seeber's ideas see Rodney Cotterill, *The Cambridge Guide to the Material World* (Cambridge: Cambridge University Press, 1985), p. 23.

14 *Ibid.*, p. 25.

15 A caveat is necessary here. In recent years, physicists have proposed theories that recognize fewer than the four fundamental forces we have mentioned, attempting to reduce some of them to others or to some new force such as the "electroweak" force. These theories remain controversial.

16 For a good general discussion of the nature of these forces see Tabor, *Gases, Liquids, and Solids*.

17 See Cotterill, *The Cambridge Guide to the Material World*, pp. 43–45, and 87–89.

4 ON THE UNITY OF THE PARTS OF ORGANISMS

1 For a discussion of the difficulties in defining life, see Fred Feldman's entry on life in *A Companion to Metaphysics*, ed. Jaegwon Kim and Ernest Sosa (Oxford: Basil Blackwell, 1995), pp. 272–74.

2 On the other hand, an eminent biologist has offered the following two criteria for something's being alive: (i) that it have a metabolism; and (ii) that its parts have natural functions. See John Maynard Smith, *The Problems of Biology* (Oxford: Oxford University Press, 1986), p. 1. We are inclined to agree with condition (i), but as we shall argue later, condition (ii) faces a serious difficulty.

3 Cf. N. W. Pirie, "The Meaninglessness of the Terms Life and Living," in *Perspectives in Biochemistry*, ed. J. Needham and D. Green (Cambridge: University of Cambridge Press, 1937).

4 For example, see John Kendrew, *The Thread of Life* (Cambridge, Mass.: Harvard University Press, 1966), p. 91. Concerning the debate over whether viruses are alive, Kendrew remarks that "These arguments are only important if one supposes that there is a fundamental distinction between living things and nonliving things, some kind of boundary on one side or the other of which everything must be placed. Personally I do not think there is any evidence of such a boundary, or any difference in essence between the living and the nonliving, and I think most molecular biologists would share this view."

5 It should be noted that there are many quite serviceable (and indispensable) concepts employed in the sciences which lack the sort of precise definition demanded by those sceptical about the concept of life, for example, the concepts of a theory, a cause, and a law of nature.

6 This leaves open the possibility that there are organic living entities which are neither organisms nor parts of organisms. It can be argued

that a malignant cell, a living heart which is detached from an organism, or cells kept alive in a tissue culture are such organic living entities.

7   All references to Aristotle in this chapter are to *The Complete Works of Aristotle*, 2 vols (Princeton: Princeton University Press, 1984), edited by Jonathan Barnes. We shall refer to the following biological works of Aristotle: *Parts of Animals*, trans. W. Ogle; *Generation of Animals*, trans. A. Platt; and *Progression of Animals*, trans. A. S. L. Farquharson.

8   *The Life and Letters of Charles Darwin*, ed. Francis Darwin (New York and London: D. Appelton, 1919), 2:427.

9   *Parts of Animals*, 1:1021. Aristotle overstates the case by the use of "alone" in the passage quoted, but he is correct to emphasize the vital importance of functional explanation in biology. Compare Maynard Smith, *The Problems of Biology*, chap. 1.

10 *Progression of Animals*, 1:1097.

11 *Parts of Animals*, 1:1005.

12 An example of a contemporary figure who is in agreement with Aristotle on this point is Larry Wright, *Teleological Explanations* (Berkeley: University of California Press, 1976).

13 *Parts of Animals*, 1:998.

14 *Ibid.*, p. 1004.

15 *Ibid.*, pp. 1025–1026.

16 *Ibid.*, p. 1031.

17 That is, in terms of an efficient cause which is roughly contemporaneous with its effect. As we shall see, an object's having a natural function implies that there is an historical process of causation which extends well into the past.

18 It should also be noted that modern science implies that Aristotle was wrong in believing that the motions of falling objects are *natural* as opposed to *forced* motions.

19 *Generation of Animals*, 1:1204.

20 *Parts of Animals*, 1:998.

21 *Ibid.*, p. 1004.

22 *Ibid.*, p. 1006.

23 This sort of account is defended by Andrew Woodfield in *Teleology* (Cambridge: Cambridge University Press, 1976).

24 For a representative example see Larry Wright, "Functions," *Philosophical Review* 82 (1973), pp. 139–168, and *Teleological Explanations* (1976).

25 *Parts of Animals*, 1:996.

26 *Ibid.*, p. 1005.

27 *Ibid.*, p. 1038.

28 *Ibid.*, pp. 1004–1005, and 1038.

29 *Ibid.*, pp. 1013–1014, and 1039.

30 *Ibid.*, pp. 1005–1006; and *Generation of Animals*, 1:1111.

31 *Parts of Animals*, 1:1057.

32 *Ibid.*, p. 1044.

33 *Generation of Animals*, 1:1187–1196.

34 Here we use the term "natural function" in such a way that it covers

only biological functions. In particular, we do not claim to provide a reduction of psychological functions.

35 Charles Darwin, the founder of modern evolutionary thought in biology, took the units of natural selection to be individual organisms. Unlike Darwin, most contemporary evolutionary biologists take these units to be species, populations, or genes. Thus, these biologists would understand survival or reproductive value just in terms of one or more of the latter three units.

36 Compare Wright, *Teleological Explanations*, pp. 84–87.

37 The pattern of historical explanation in question can be understood as follows. Suppose that there is an organic living thing, O, for example, a human, having a part, x, for instance, a heart, of a biological kind, K, for example, being a human heart, where x has the function, f, of performing an activity, A, for example, pumping blood, where x possesses the capacity, C, to perform A, and where x's having some structural property, S, for instance, being a compressible sac of muscular tissue of a certain kind, explains (nonhistorically) x's having C. (It should be noted that such a structural property, S, is equivalent to a large range or disjunction of structures.) In that case, x's having S is explained (historically) by x's having f (or x's having C) in the sense that (i) it is a natural law that whatever has $(f \& K)$ has S [or whatever has $(C \& K)$ has S], and (ii) x has $(f \& K)$ [or x has $(C \& K)$] because exemplifying the trait, T, of having a part with C had survival or reproductive value for one or more of O's ancestors, and x is produced by a process that either naturally selects T for O, or naturally selected T for one or more ancestors of O, by copying parts of kind K from one generation to the next, so that O inherits having T.

38 Note that this does not imply that if an organic entity, O, has a part with a natural function, then O is either an organic living thing or a part of one. Viruses are organic entities that are not parts of other living things, and arguably, viruses are nonliving things that possess parts that have natural functions, for example, DNA molecules for replicating the virus. Even so, a virus is an essentially "parasitic" entity that cannot exist in the absence of organic life.

39 The term "protobiont" first appears in Ann Synge's translation of Aleksandr Ivanovich Oparin's *The Chemical Origin of Life* (Springfield, Ill.: C. C. Thomas, 1964). In literature on the origin of life, this term has been used to refer either to a precursor, x, of a first organic living thing, where x was on the verge of organic life, or to a first organic living thing. As we use the term "protobiont," it refers only to a first organic living thing, that is, to an organism which is a member of a species of living thing that was not preceded by any species.

40 See *Life: Its Nature, Origin, and Development* (New York: Academic Press, 1966), p. 87.

41 See Fox's "Simulated Natural Experiments in Spontaneous Organization of Morphological Units from Proteinoid," in *The Origins of Prebiological Systems*, ed. Sidney Fox (New York: Academic Press, 1965), pp. 361–373, and Fox's *The Emergence of Life* (New York: Basic Books, 1988).

42 See Kripke's "Naming and Necessity," in *Semantics of Natural Language*, ed. D. Davidson and G. Harman (Dordrecht: Reidel, 1972), pp. 253–355. Cf. Hilary Putnam, "The Meaning of 'Meaning'," in *Minnesota Studies in the Philosophy of Science VII: Language, Mind, and Knowledge*, ed. K. Gunderson (Minneapolis: University of Minnesota Press, 1975).

43 George Bealer, "The Philosophical Limits of Scientific Essentialism," in *Philosophical Perspectives, 1, Metaphysics* (Atascadero, Calif.: Ridgeview, 1987), pp. 289–365.

44 *The Problems of Biology*, p. 7.

45 *Ibid.*, p. 114.

46 It should be noted that although variation is necessary for biological evolution to occur, it will not be included in *S*. But we do not consider variation to be a *biological activity* of a living thing. Rather, it is the upshot of either random variability in protobionts, random errors in copying or replication, or environmental causes.

47 Cf. Oparin, *Life: Its Nature, Origin, and Development*, pp. 72–75, and Maynard Smith, *The Problems of Biology*, pp. 1–2.

48 *Teleology*, pp. 132–133.

49 Nor would it be correct to say that the atoms which compose a hammer have a function, even though the hammer has a function.

50 A similar suggestion is made by Larry Wright in *Teleological Explanations*, p. 111.

51 This is consistent with the position taken by Larry Wright, *ibid.*, pp. 98–100. Compare T. Dobzhansky, "On Cartesian and Darwinian Aspects of Biology," in *Philosophy, Science, and Method*, ed. S. Morgenbesser, P. Suppes, and M. White (London: Macmillan, 1969), pp. 172–173, and Philip Kitcher in "Function and Design," *Midwest Studies in Philosophy* 18 (1993), pp. 379–397. Kitcher's views are critically examined by Peter Godfrey-Smith in "Functions: Consensus Without Unity," *Pacific Philosophical Quarterly* 74 (1993), pp. 196–208.

52 Compare Kitcher, "Function and Design."

53 Peter Godfrey-Smith, "A Modern History Theory of Functions," *Nous* 28 (1994), pp. 344–362.

54 For a discussion of the concept of a norm of reaction, see Gilbert Gottlieb, *Individual Development and Evolution: The Genesis of Novel Behavior* (Oxford: Oxford University Press, 1992).

55 By means of existentially quantifying over times, both (D4) and (D5) allow the length of time from *t* until *t'* to vary from one case of a vital part to another. This is a desirable feature: although in typical cases the heart and the liver are both vital organs, the loss of heart-function ordinarily results in death much more quickly than the loss of liver-function.

56 This concept of entailment is discussed further in section 13, where we provide additional support for our claim that certain parts of an organism are vital as in (D5).

57 As is well known, the difficulties involved in providing a philosophical analysis of such an ordinary or intuitive causal concept are formidable.

This should not and does not prevent scientists and philosophers from usefully employing such ordinary causal concepts.

58 This argument implies that a part of an organism may be vital at one time and nonvital at another. For instance, typically, when a creature has two kidneys, neither of them is vital, but if one of them is lost, then the remaining kidney becomes vital. And if the creature subsequently receives a kidney to replace the one it lost, then both of its kidneys are nonvital.

59 Our definitions are silent on the question of whether it is correct to say that an *organism* is a system composed of some set of parts which have a joint natural function. (D6) implies that if it is correct to say that an organism is such a system, then an organism has a natural function. Although the claim that an organism has a natural function is controversial, we are unaware of any good *a priori* reason to deny the intelligibility of this claim. For example, it might be argued that an organism is *for* maintaining, sustaining, regulating, and reproducing itself in a particular way over time.

60 *Parts of Animals*, 1:1016, 1022, and 1037–1039.

61 *Generation of Animals*, 1:1193.

62 *Ibid.*, p. 1196.

63 Whenever we say that an object, x, regulates, controls, causally contributes to, or sustains, processes or activities of an object, y, this is shorthand for saying that processes or activities of x regulate, control, causally contribute to, or sustain, processes or activities of y.

64 Of course, the nervous system as a whole, a system consisting of the central nervous system together with the peripheral nerves which branch out from it, may also be said to regulate these life-functions.

65 x *indirectly* regulates $y \Leftrightarrow x$ regulates y by regulating some z, other than x and y, which regulates y. x *directly* regulates $y \Leftrightarrow x$ regulates y, but not indirectly. For example, by directly regulating the peripheral nervous system, the central nervous system indirectly regulates motions of the arms and legs.

66 Of course, it would be a good thing to have an analysis of the ordinary or scientific causal concepts employed in our account. In particular, if we were to possess analyses of the concepts of a sustaining cause and a regulating cause, then it would deepen our understanding of the principle of organization for the parts of an organism. But an inquiry into the nature of these causal concepts falls outside the scope of this study. Although the application of these causal concepts to particular cases may be imprecise to some degree, their application is sufficiently precise for our purposes.

67 In a case where y is a master-part, x is *ultimately* under the control or regulation of y. However, this is compatible with x's being under the control of another part of O which is not a master-part. For example, consider a functional part, p, of a heart cell, c, which is a part of an organism O. While p may be regulated in part by the nucleus of c, p *ultimately* will also be regulated by a master-part of O. Thus, there may be a hierarchy of control or regulation over a given part of an organism. The relation defined in (D7) is one which *all* of the organic living or

functional parts of an organism bear to a controlling or regulating "master-part."

68 It should be noted that a function may consist of a conjunction of other functions.

69 In Chapter 5 we further discuss and defend the idea that an organism is an entity of a natural kind of the sort we have described.

70 Thus, an organism has functionally interrelated levels of composition. As we noted earlier, Aristotle also thought that organisms have such levels of composition. But the levels of composition we allow are not the same as those allowed by Aristotle. To cite one difference, Aristotle denies the existence of fundamental particles, and we do not.

71 See Chapter 3 for an explication of what it is to be joined in this sense.

72 See Chapter 3.

73 We presuppose the biological notion that a part of an organism encodes hereditary information which is expressed in a particular way under certain environmental conditions. Although this notion stands in need of further analysis, it is clear enough for present purposes.

74 (D7) allows this length to vary from the case of one basic biotic part to another.

75 Note that the entire nervous system of a human being, i.e., the central nervous system together with the peripheral nervous system, also appears to qualify as a master-part.

76 For a nonlinguistic characterization of the notion of a *de re* essential property in terms of *de dicto* metaphysical necessity see Gary Rosen-krantz, *Haecceity: An Ontological Essay* (Dordrecht: Kluwer, 1993), pp. 166–167.

77 We would argue that if P_y is replaced with a nonliving machine, rather than with an organic living transplant, then the resulting complex system is not an organism, but merely some of the *remains* of a deceased organism being kept alive on artificial life-support, or perhaps (in some remotely possible case) an entity of a new kind, for example, a cyborg. However, the line of reasoning that we shall advance in the text does not depend upon such an argument.

78 For parallel reasons, the possibility of S's surviving the replacement of one of its vital parts with a proxy is compatible with our claim that P_y is a vital part of S as in (D5), i.e., that so long as the degree of naturalness of S's life-processes remains constant, S's life continuing much longer entails that S's life is sustained by P_y's functional activities. Parallel considerations apply to any organism (existing in any possible world), and to any vital part of that organism (in the possible world in question). See the ninth section of this chapter.

79 See the twelfth section in this chapter.

80 See Chapter 3.

81 See section 11 in this chapter.

82 See sections 11 and 12 in this chapter.

83 See Leslie Brainerd Arey, *Developmental Anatomy: A Textbook and Laboratory Manual of Embryology*, revised 7th ed. (Philadelphia: W. B. Saunders, 1974), pp. 174–198.

5   WHAT KINDS OF PHYSICAL SUBSTANCES ARE THERE?

1 See Joshua Hoffman and Gary Rosenkrantz, *Substance Among Other Categories* (Cambridge: Cambridge University Press, 1994), pp. 100–113 and pp. 188–193.
2 We discussed Democritean atoms in Chapter 2, section 3.
3 E. J. Lowe, "Primitive Substances," *Philosophy and Phenomenological Research* 54 (1994), pp. 531–552.
4 See Chapter 1.
5 Mereological compounds are not to be confused with *mereological sums*. Entities of the latter sort are collections, not substances, while mereological compounds are substances, not collections. As we argued in Chapter 3, the parts of a mereological sum, unlike the parts of a mereological compound, need not be joined and connected.
6 A case like this is discussed below in the form of the problem of the ship of Theseus.
7 We assume that all of the parts which composed the mereological compound that originally constituted the statue have not been re-assembled. Then it follows that not all of the parts of this mereological compound are joined and connected once the statue has undergone mereological change.
8 Eli Hirsch, *The Persistence of Objects* (Philadelphia: University City Science Center, 1976), pp. 51–55.
9 Roderick Chisholm, *Person and Object* (La Salle, Ill.: Open Court, 1976), pp. 145–158.
10 *Ibid.*, pp. 157–158.
11 This is to say that if *x* is an organism, then *x* could not exist unless *x* were an organism. In other words, being an organism is an essential attribute of an organism. A parallel claim about certain other attributes of organisms is false. For instance, a green organism, *x*, is not essentially green, since *x* could survive a change in its color from green to yellow. Thus, being green is an accidental attribute of the organism in question.
12 At least one prominent biologist, Maynard Smith, takes the position that a freeze-dried insect which can become a functioning organism at a later time "is not alive: it was alive, and may be alive again in the future." *The Problems of Biology* (Oxford: Oxford University Press, 1986), p. 2.
13 Of course, a freeze-dried insect which can be revived later retains a potentiality for engaging in life-processes. If we are right, then the possession of such a potentiality is insufficient for an object's counting as a living thing.
14 *An Essay Concerning Human Understanding*, ed. John Yolton (London: Dent, 1974), book 2, chap. 27, "Of Identity and Diversity."
15 For an argument which supports our view, see Joshua Hoffman, "Locke on Whether a Thing Can Have Two Beginnings of Existence," *Ratio* 22 (1980), pp. 106–111.
16 See David Wiggins, *Sameness and Substance* (Cambridge, Mass.: Harvard University Press, 1980), pp. 90–91. Cf. E. J. Lowe, "On the Identity of Artifacts," *Journal of Philosophy* 80 (1983), pp. 222–223.

17 See *Sameness and Substance*, pp. 95–96.

18 Some of these questions will be discussed in the fifth section of this chapter and in an appendix.

19 *The Lives of the Noble Grecians and Romans* (Chicago: Great Books, Encyclopedia Britannica, 1952), p. 8.

20 The problem of the ship of Theseus may also be presented in the form of a paradox, as done by Thomas Hobbes in the following passage: "Two bodies existing both at once would be one and the same numerical body. For if, for example, that ship of Theseus, concerning the difference whereof made by continued reparation in taking out the old planks and putting in new, the sophisters of Athens were wont to dispute, were after all the planks were changed, the same numerical ship it was at the beginning; and if some man had kept the old planks as they were taken out, and by putting them afterwards together in the same order, had again made a ship of them, this, without doubt, had also been the same numerical ship with that which was at the beginning; and so there would have been two ships numerically the same, which is absurd." *De Corpore*, trans. W. Molesworth, in *English Works* (Aalen, Ger.: Scientia-Verlag, 1966), II, 11.

21 Cf. Aristotle, *Physics*, trans. R. P. Hardie and R. K. Gaye, in *The Complete Works of Aristotle*, ed. Jonathan Barnes, 2 vols. (Princeton: Princeton University Press, 1984), 1:329: "By nature the animals and their parts exist, and the plants and the simple bodies. . . . All of the things mentioned plainly differ from things which are *not* constituted by nature. For each of them has within itself a principle of motion and of stationariness (in respect of place, or of growth and decrease, or by way of alteration). . . . Nature is a principle or cause of being moved and of being at rest in that to which it belongs primarily, in virtue of itself and not accidentally."

22 Intuitively speaking, the only structural modifications that a mereological compound could undergo (if any) would be due to stretching or compression. Theoretically speaking, however, it seems that a mereological compound could also undergo structural modifications as a result of relativistic effects predicted by Einstein's theory of special relativity: for example, a mereological compound could undergo an increase in mass and a decrease in length as its velocity approaches that of light. Nevertheless, the nature of a mereological compound at rest is a causal determinant (in a strong sense) of these relativistic effects and their range. For example, when at rest a mereological compound has its least mass and its greatest length, and relativistic increases or decreases in mass or length are proportional to a mereological compound's mass or length at rest.

23 On the other hand, it should be noted that organic living things have an internal principle that can control and regulate their *decrease* of parts under appropriate dietary conditions.

24 Cf. Aristotle, *Physics*, in *The Complete Works of Aristotle*, 1:329–330: "A bed and a coat and anything else of that sort, *qua* receiving these designations – i.e., in so far as they are products of art – have no innate

impulse to change. But in so far as they happen to be composed of stone or earth . . . they do have such an impulse, and just to that extent. . . . If you planted a bed and the rotting wood acquired the power of sending up a shoot, it would not be a bed that would come up, but *wood* which shows that the arrangement in accordance with the rules of the art is merely an accidental attribute, whereas the substance is the other, which, further, persists continuously through the process. . . . Man is born from man, but not bed from bed."

25 Note that in one important way this distinguishes a snowball from a ship: the snowball must be made of snow, but the ship can be made at one time of cedar and at another time of oak or even aluminum.

26 Note, though, that a crystal must be constituted by a crystalline mereological compound, but that a glacier, lake, or planet need not be constituted by a mereological compound.

27 See William J. Broad, "The Core of the Earth May Be a Gigantic Crystal Made of Iron," *The New York Times*, April 4, 1995, p. B7.

28 See Saul Kripke, "Naming and Necessity," Hilary Putnam, "The Meaning of 'Meaning'," and Nelson Goodman, *Fact, Fiction, and Forecast* (Indianapolis, Ind.: Bobbs-Merrill, 1965). Compare W. V. Quine, "Natural Kinds," in *Ontological Relativity and Other Essays* (New York: Columbia University Press, 1969), pp. 114–138. Also see Stephen Schwartz's collection *Naming, Necessity, and Natural Kinds* (Ithaca, N.Y.: Cornell University Press, 1977), including Schwartz's introduction, pp. 13–41.

29 See *Sameness and Substance*, chap. 3.

30 *Ibid.*, p. 83.

31 Compare Leibniz's observations in the preface to his *Nouveaux Essais*: "Substances cannot be conceived in their bare essence without any activity; that activity belongs to the essence of substance in general. . . . Before all else it is necessary to consider that the modifications which may belong naturally or without miracle to a subject, must come to it from the limitations or variations of a real genus, or of a constant and absolute original nature. . . . And every time that we find some quality in a subject, we must believe that if we understood the nature of this subject and of this quality, we should conceive how this quality can result therefrom. Thus, in the order of nature, it is not optional with God to give to substances indifferently such or such qualities, and he will never give them any but those which are natural to them; that is, which can be derived from their nature as explicable modifications. . . . That which is natural, must be able to become distinctly conceivable if we were admitted into the secrets of things." *Leibniz Selections*, ed. Philip Weiner (New York: Charles Scribner's Sons, 1951), pp. 390–391.

32 "Natural Kinds," *Philosophy* 63 (1988), pp. 29–30.

33 *Sameness and Substance*, p. 89.

34 *Ibid.*, p. 84.

35 Cf. Wilkerson, "Natural Kinds," pp. 29–42. We further discuss some of the issues pertaining to biological natural kinds in the Appendix.

36 Apparent examples of natural kinds which are neither substance-kinds,

nor kinds of stuff, include *event*-kinds, for example, rays of light, electric currents, courses of stellar development, processes of glaciation, crystallization, and so forth. These event-kinds are plausibly regarded as natural kinds for reasons that parallel those cited in our discussion of natural substance-kinds.

37 Cf. Wiggins, *Sameness and Substance*, p. 175, n. 30.

38 It might be thought that a statue does not instantiate an artifactual kind essentially. For example, it might be thought that what at one time instantiates the artifactual kind, being a (copper) statue, could at another time instantiate the natural kind, being a piece of (statue-shaped) copper. But this is a mistake, for the identity-conditions of a piece of copper are not the same as the identity-conditions of a statue. In particular, a piece of copper has all of its parts essentially, while a statue does not. Thus, no entity which instantiates being a (copper) statue could instantiate being a piece of (statue-shaped) copper.

39 In the Appendix, we shall briefly explore the question whether biological species, or the higher taxa, are natural kinds. We note, however, that a living organism's falling under a natural kind does not require that the familiar biological classifications of species, families, orders, and so forth be genuine natural kinds in our sense. All that is required is that *being a living organism* be such a natural kind.

40 Of course, not all mereological compounds are compositionally alike. But this is irrelevant to the argument, since a mereological compound cannot undergo mereological change. It follows that a mereological compound has its compositional nature essentially. And as we have argued, Mereological Compound is a natural substance-kind.

41 Nonetheless, as we have argued, this kind is not a natural compound substance-kind, since it is an artifact-kind.

42 Nevertheless, our earlier argument that crystals of this kind are not real things implies that being such a crystal is not a natural compound substance-kind.

43 *Sameness and Substance*, pp. 85–86.

44 *Ibid.*, pp. 88ff.

45 Ernest Sosa, "Subjects Among Other Things," in *Philosophical Perspectives*, 1, *Metaphysics* (Atascadero, Calif.: Ridgeview, 1987), pp. 155–187.

46 In Sosa's view, the snowdiscall is other than the snowball, because given his definitions of these things, the snowball could be destroyed, by reshaping the snow of which it is made into a disc-shaped mass, without destroying the snowdiscall.

47 Sosa appears to assume that an organism's species is essential to it, for example, that a tiger is essentially a tiger. It is extremely doubtful that he can apply his strategy for generating an explosion of reality to organisms without either this assumption or the related assumption that if an organism, *O*, belongs to a species, *s*, then *O* is essentially *s*-like, for example, that a tiger is essentially tiger-like. Thus, in answering Sosa, we shall suppose that one or the other of these assumptions is correct. However, for the sake of brevity, we shall state our argument

in terms of the former assumption, on the understanding that a parallel argument applies given the latter assumption.

48 *Sameness and Substance*, pp. 71–72.

49 By a *coherent* range of forms we mean either a range of forms that are part of a single history of evolutionary development or a range of forms which is continuous.

50 It should be noted that there are also dissimilarities between horsealls and snowdiscalls, ones which weaken the analogy between them and impede the attempt to use horsealls in generating a population explosion of living things paralleling Sosa's explosion of reality. For example, it is not clear that it is possible for a horse to be destroyed without annihilating the accompanying horseall, but this possibility is needed to establish the diversity of a horse and a horseall, since it is not possible for a horseall to be destroyed without annihilating the accompanying horse. It is at best a (remote) logical possibility that a horse could be destroyed without annihilating its accompanying horseall, viz., by gradually replacing a horse's parts in such a way that a member of a species of an appropriate evolutionary precursor is thereby created. Unlike the case of the snowball and its accompanying snowdiscall, where simply compacting the relevant snow into a disc-like shape results in the snowball's being destroyed while the snowdiscall survives, it is no mean feat, if it is possible at all, to destroy a horse without annihilating its accompanying horseall.

Another disanalogy between a horseall and a snowdiscall is that the former is equivalent merely to a *finite* disjunction of forms, in this case biological species, whereas the latter is equivalent to an *infinite* disjunction of forms, in this instance, shapes. Thus, strictly speaking, an argument based just upon putative kinds such as the horseall does not entail that there are *infinitely* many material objects in the same place at the same time. Thus, such an argument does not lead to the bizarre ontological exuberance of Sosa's explosion of reality, though, in our view, the more modest population explosion that it might be thought to entail would still be troublesome.

51 See Van Inwagen's *Material Beings* (Ithaca: Cornell University Press, 1990).

52 See the definiens of (D3) in Chapter 3.

53 For example, see the definiens of (D2), of (D3), and of (D7) in Chapter 4.

54 Following Van Inwagen, we state (C1) in a slightly simplified form. Consistency with Van Inwagen's strict formulation of (C1) requires the addition of the disjunct "or there is only one of $P_1 \ldots P_n$" to (C1)'s definiens. Van Inwagen adds this disjunct "to secure the reflexivity of parthood." See *Material Beings*, p. 82, n. 29. In the text, we ignore this minor complication in the case of (C1) and other similar principles.

55 Van Inwagen argues that since the latter notion is a notion of a certain kind of *compound* physical object, it cannot be used to analyze the notion of *composition* for living things, on pain of vicious circularity.

56 See Chapter 4, section 13 for more detailed descriptions of these possible cases.

APPENDIX: ORGANISMS AND NATURAL KINDS

1 This quotation is from Sober's entry on natural kinds in *A Companion to Metaphysics*, ed. Jaegwon Kim and Ernest Sosa (Oxford: Basil Blackwell, 1995), p. 346. For a full presentation of Sober's reasons for rejecting the idea that biological species and higher-order taxa are natural kinds see his *Philosophy of Biology* (Boulder, Colo.: Westview, 1993).

2 Sober's chapter on systematics in *Philosophy of Biology* provides a useful discussion of these three schools of thought, pp. 143–183.

3 Chapter 5, section 3.

4 "Species, Essences, and the Names of Natural Kinds," *Philosophical Quarterly* 43 (1993), pp. 1–19.

5 Cf. Chapter 5, section 3.

6 A qualification is needed here. If some of O's hereditary information is encoded in molecular structures other than O's genes, then a norm of reaction or a microstructural hereditary blueprint can reflect this information even though it is not implicit in O's genotype. For a discussion of the notions of a microstructural hereditary blueprint and a norm of reaction see the eighth section of Chapter 4.

7 Cf. Chapter 5, section 3.

8 In Chapter 3, we discuss the character of these forces.

9 See Chapter 5 for a discussion of this feature of a mereological compound.

Index

abstract entities 27–8, 47–9, 54
Ackrill, John 14–16
Anaxagoras 11
Anaximander 47
Anaximenes 47
Aristotle ix, 1, 9–16, 20–1, 24, 29,
    42, 44, 65, 69, 94–8, 100–1,
    119, 123, 125, 151, 161, 170
Armstrong, David M. 53
artifacts 73, 95, 118; unreality of
    154–79
artifactual substance-kinds 172–6
atoms: Democritean 13, 73, 150–2;
    parts of not substances 51–5
Audi, Robert x

Bealer, George 108
Berkeley, George ix, 26, 28–9
Bohm, David 8
Boscovich, Roger Joseph x, 5
Broad, C. D. 62

Castañeda, Hector-Neri 36, 41
categories: Aristotle's theory of
    13–16, 64; equivalent 63;
    instantiability of 50; at level C
    48 – , 70, 199n4; levels of
    generality among 47–8;
    ontological 1, 46–50; vs.
    properties 46–7
category mistake 2, 77
causes: regulating or controlling
    126–7; sustaining 122–3
change: intrinsic 10–13; relational
    10–13

Chisholm, Roderick 62, 152–3
Clinton, William Jefferson 3
Collection: category of 47, 69
collections: as distinguished from
    substances 60
collectivism 77–9, 89–90
commonsense ontology 1, 7, 25,
    29
composition: principle of 179–80
compound physical substances 72;
    unity of the parts of 72
compresence relation 36
concrete/abstract distinction 49–50
concrete entities 27–9, 47–9, 54
constituting relation 155–7
consubstantiation relation 36, 41
Crane, Tim x
Cuvier, Georges 94

Darwin, Charles 94
Democritus 13
Descartes, René ix, 5, 17, 20–4,
    28, 42, 44, 151
dynamic equilibrium: relation of
    82–4, 88

essentialism: Aristotelian 161;
    mereological 152–65; problem
    of excessive 31, 34, 37–42;
    species 161–2
Event: category of 47, 60–2
events: as distinguished from
    substances 60–2; impossibility
    of change in 12–13;
    instantaneous 60–1

explosion of reality argument
177–9

Feldman, Fred x
Fox, Sydney 106–111
Frege, Gottlob 171
functions 95; Aristotelian 93–9;
    artificial 95, 118; emergence of
    113–15; joint natural 123–5;
    natural 94–6, 98–9, 105–18;
    reduction of 98–105, 115–18
Furth, Montgomery 15

Geach, Peter 62
Godfrey-Smith, Peter 117–18
Goodman, Nelson 170

heredity 110, 119–20
Hirsch, Eli 152
Hume, David ix, 26, 28–9, 45

identity: of physical objects 153,
    163–70
inanimate natural formations 73,
    168, 170, 174
increase: problem of 154–63
independence: as asymmetrical
    relation 24; different senses of
    22; throughout interval of time
    61; within one's kind 50
intermittent existence 159–60

Jubien, Michael 76

Kant, Immanuel ix, 9
Kim, Jaegwon x
King, John x
Kirchoff, Bruce x
Kripke, Saul 24–5, 108, 170

Leibniz, Gottfried ix, 6,
    150
Limit: category of 47
limits: as distinct from substances
    59–60
Linnaeus, Karl 94
Locke, John ix, 17, 28,
    159
Lowe, Jonathan x, 151

macromolecules 105–6, 111
material objects: metaphysical
    natures of 4; vs. nonmaterial
    physical objects 5
mereological compounds 73–90,
    150–87; connectedness of the
    parts of 86–90; joining of the
    parts of 84–90; nature of 166,
    174, 209n22; unity of the parts
    of 73–90
mereology 196–7n45
modalities 191n1; de dicto 3, 108;
    de re 3, 108, 136
monadism 77–9, 89–90
monism 77–9

natural kinds 170–3; see also
    organisms, and natural kinds
natural selection and evolution 97,
    99, 102–5, 111, 115–8
naturalness: degrees of 118–21
Nemesius 8
norm of reaction 120
Number, category of 47

Ockham, William of 114
O'Hara, Robert x
ontological neutrality 13, 16, 43–4,
    51, 65
ontological parsimony 27, 155,
    158, 165
Oparin, Aleksandr 106, 109, 111
ordinary physical objects 151–87;
    not natural substance-kinds
    170–6
organic life: definition of 91–3
organisms: Aristotle's theory of
    the unity of 100–2; and basic
    biotic entities 131–2; and biotic
    entities 128–9; and functional
    connectedness 130; and
    functional subordination 126–8;
    and functional unity 130, 134–9,
    fundamental activities of
    108–12; master parts of 127–8;
    and natural kinds 188–9; natures
    of 166–7, 174; and nonbasic
    biotic entities 132; and nonbasic
    biotic parts 141–5; not parts of

other organisms 93; parts of not joined and connected 99–100, 157–60; regulation of 126; unity of the parts of 80, 91–149; vital parts of 101, 121–5

parasitism 139–40
parts: different kinds of 49; of times 49
persistence of substances 41
Phalereus, Demetrius 164
Place: category of 47
places: as distinguished from substances 55–8
Plato 11, 37–9, 49
Plutarch 163
point-particles 5
point-positions 60
point-times 59
possible worlds 3, 192n1
Prior, Arthur 62
Privation: category of 47, 63–9
privations: analysis of 66; as distinguished from substances 63–9; parts of 66–9
Proper Part: category of 52; category of Abstract 52, 66; category of Concrete 52, 66
properties: accidental 2, 15; causal theories of 53–5; as distinguished from substances 53–5; essential 2, 15; first-order 200n10; higher order 200n10; intrinsic 2, 10–11; parts of 50; platonistic theories of 53–5; relational 2, 11
Property: category of 47, 53–5
Proposition: category of 47, 54
Protagoras 11 protenoid microspheres 106–12; 169
protobionts 105–15, 138–9, 204n39
Putnam, Hilary 170–1

Raabe, Jenny x
Relation: category of 54
Russell, Bertrand 36, 38, 197
Ryle, Gilbert 2

Seeber, Ludwig 83

Sense-Datum: category of 70
Set: category of 54
sets: theory of 27–8, 38
Simons, Peter 62
singularity 58
Smith, John Maynard 109–10
Sober, Elliot 189
Socrates 2, 11, 15
Sosa, Ernest x, 177
souls 5–7; existence of 6–7; philosophical arguments against 6; possibility of 6
space: atomic 56–7; dense continuum of 55–6; discontinuous 56–7; and possibility of motion 57–8
space-time 7, 62
Space-Time: category of 71–2
Spinoza, Baruch ix, 20, 25, 51
substance: Aristotle's theories of 9–16, 193n1; cluster theories of 26–42; collectionist theories of 28–42; commonsense concept of 1; Descartes's theories of 17, 21–5; eliminative theories of 26; independence theories of 20–6, 43–72; inherence theories of 20; Locke's theory of 17; metaphysical features of 2; and modern physics 7–8, 25–6; parts of 68–9; and persistence through qualitative change 2, 9–13; philosophical analysis of 8, 43; reductionist theories of 26–7; sequentialist theories of 38–41; Spinoza's theory of 25–6, 51; substratum theories of 17–20; temporal parts of 62; two senses of 74
Substance: category of 46–53
symbiosis 140, 146–7

Thales 47
Theseus 163–4, 169; ship of 163–5, 209n20
time: absolute 45; atomic 56–7; dense continuum of 55; discontinuous 56–7; as distinguished from substances

58, 60; and possibility of change 57–8; relational 54
Time: category of 47
Trope: category of 47
tropes 15, 200n11; collections of 29–42; as distinguished from substances 54–5; not parts of substances 30–1

unity of qualities problem 31–7, 40

Van Inwagen, Peter 179–86
viruses 105–6
Wiggins, David 159–60; 170–2, 176, 178
Wilkerson, T. E. 171, 189
Woodfield, Andrew 114

Zeno 11
zero-dimensional entities 5, 60